IMAGES
of America

WEST PLAINS
1880–1930

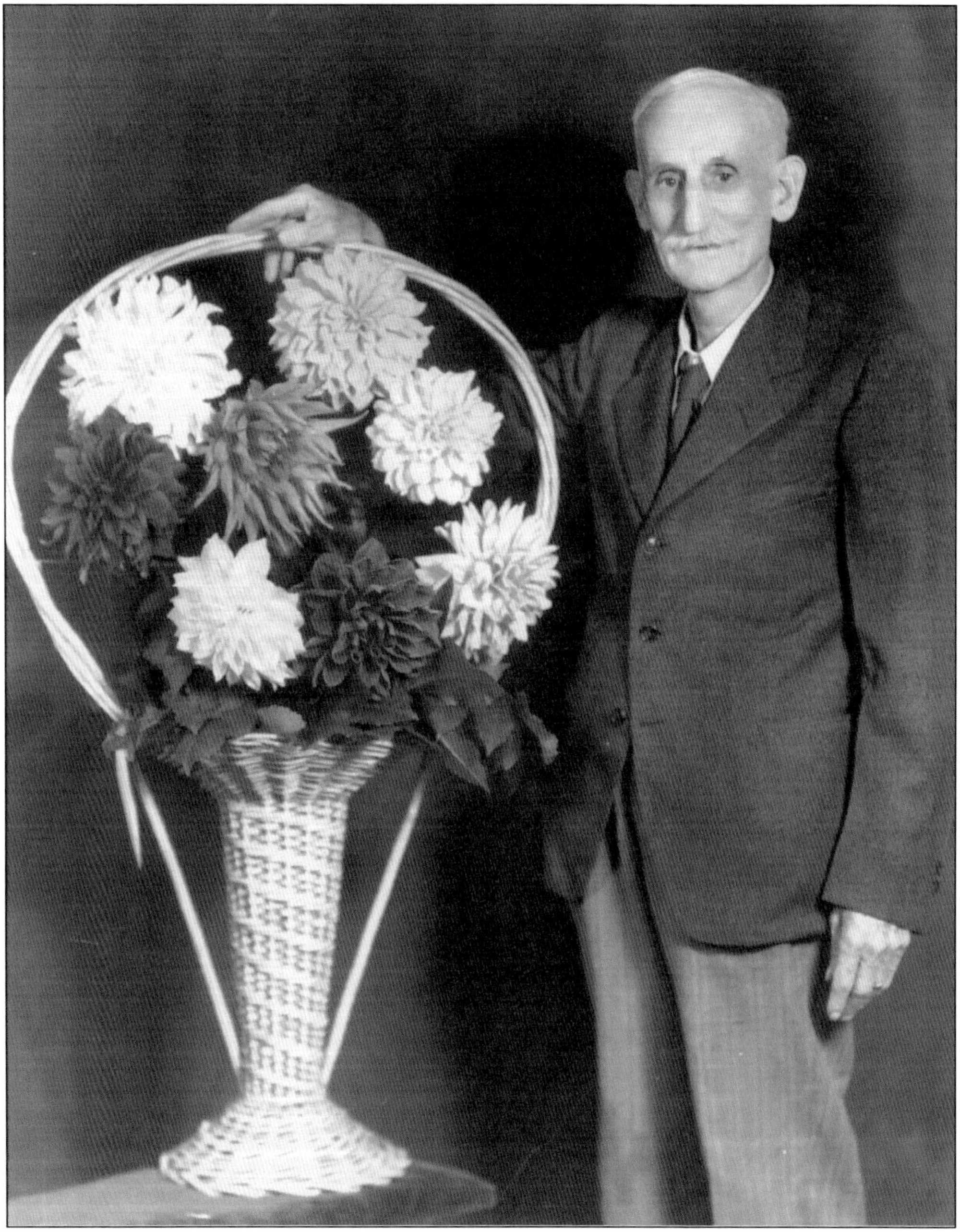

This book is dedicated to my great-grandfather Charles Theodore Aid. He is shown here with a bouquet of prize Zinnias, his favorite flower. He loved to travel the roads around West Plains and see them growing. To promote their propagation he annually gave away thousands of packages of Zinnia seeds. My first job at Aid Hardware was scooping these seeds into small packages and stamping them: "Aid's Prize Zinnias."

IMAGES
of America

WEST PLAINS
1880–1930

Toney Aid

ARCADIA
PUBLISHING

ISBN 978-0-7385-3159-5

Published by Arcadia Publishing
Charleston, South Carolina

Printed in the United States of America

Library of Congress Catalog Card Number: 2003107531

For all general information contact Arcadia Publishing at:
Telephone 843-853-2070
Fax 843-853-0044
E-mail sales@arcadiapublishing.com
For customer service and orders:
Toll-Free 1-888-313-2665

Visit us on the Internet at www.arcadiapublishing.com

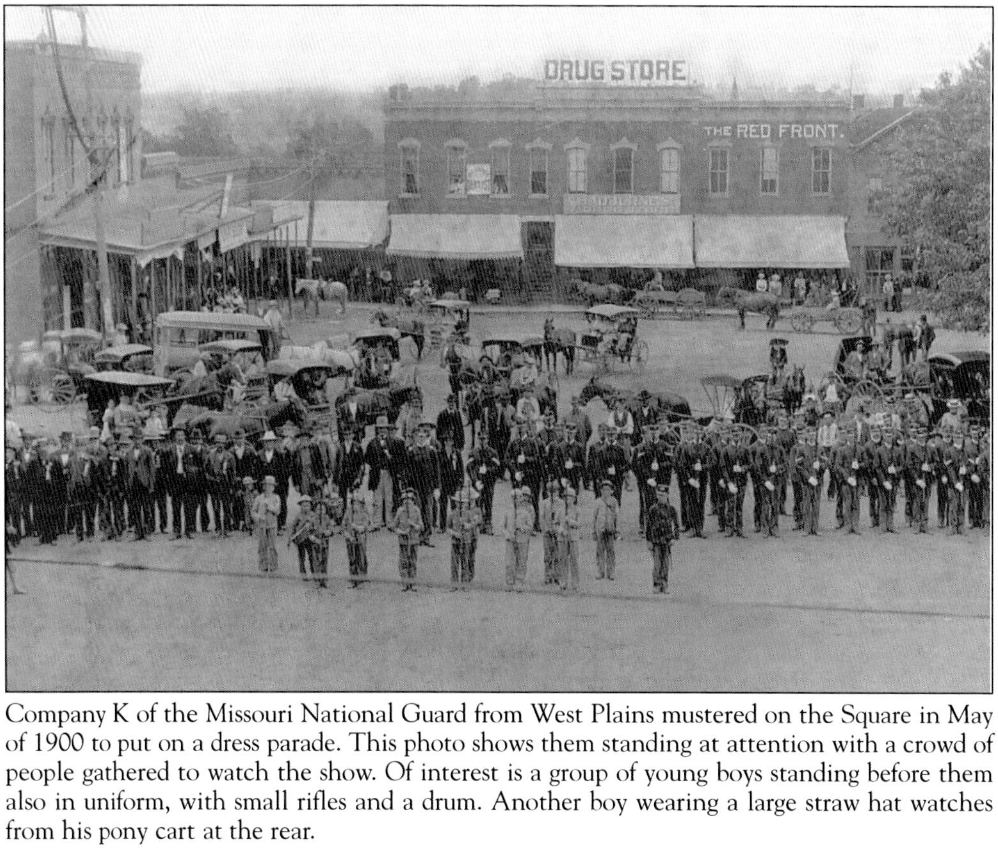

Company K of the Missouri National Guard from West Plains mustered on the Square in May of 1900 to put on a dress parade. This photo shows them standing at attention with a crowd of people gathered to watch the show. Of interest is a group of young boys standing before them also in uniform, with small rifles and a drum. Another boy wearing a large straw hat watches from his pony cart at the rear.

Contents

ACKNOWLEDGMENTS

When acknowledging historians of West Plains, you must begin with Colonel William Monks. The *West Plains Journal* published Monks' book, *A History of Southern Missouri and Northern Arkansas*, in 1907. In it he records the history of West Plains from its beginning through the conflicts that followed the Civil War. It is an invaluable primary resource. Sam and Alice Cary Risley wrote another early history. Sam was a partner in founding the *Journal* newspaper in 1870. He published a brief history of West Plains in his newspaper for the United States Centennial in 1876. Alice Cary, Sam's wife, expanded on his history for a presentation to the Farmers' Institute at a local meeting in 1896. That history has been reprinted in several publications, including *The 100th Anniversary of West Plains, Missouri*, a centennial history published in 1952.

In recent years, four people have devoted a great amount of time to recording the history of West Plains. Dorotha Reavis has been preserving Howell County history all of her life. In articles, programs, and storytelling she is the first lady of Howell County history. Russ Cochran, in the 30 volumes of the *West Plains Gazette* published from 1978 to 1987, has done more to put the town's photos and history into print than any other person. The volume and the quality of this work are unsurpassed. Gerald and Charlotte Groves compiled a huge amount of basic source material from court and newspaper records in their five-volume history, *Howell County, Missouri, Post Offices, Postmasters and Their Communities*. Volume Five on West Plains has over 300 pages of the town's history. Best of all, it has an accurate index of all personal names. And finally, the publication of *West Plains as I Knew It* by Robert Neathery, as told to Marideth Sisco, gives us a reminiscent history of a life spanning two-thirds of the entire history of West Plains. Bob makes you feel you were present when the events in his book occurred.

I also wish to thank Becky Snider, Ph.D. and Historic Preservation Consultant, of Columbia, Mo. Becky gave me access to records she compiled during the nomination of the Historic District in Downtown West Plains for inclusion on the National Register of Historic Places.

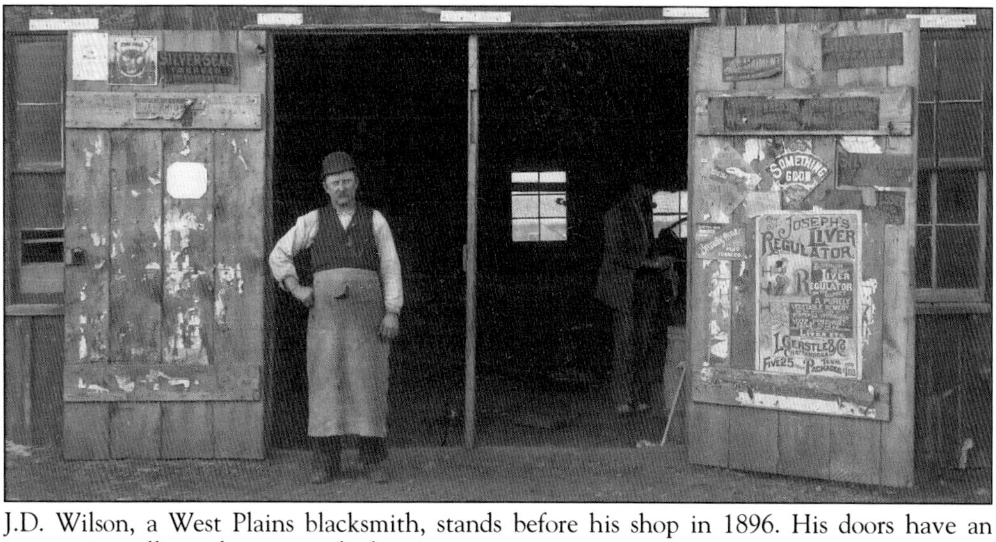

J.D. Wilson, a West Plains blacksmith, stands before his shop in 1896. His doors have an interesting collage of posters and advertisements.

INTRODUCTION

If you were assigned to record what life is like in West Plains today, you would probably make a documentary movie. Passing from business to church to school, your tape would show people working, playing, and going about their daily lives. You would search out human interest stories and include little known facts. It would contain stories of disasters, interesting people, and might even discuss problems like crime. When you were through, the tape would give a comprehensive "walking, talking" presentation about the town.

This history seeks to make a "documentary" of life in West Plains between 1880 and 1930 using photographs. The earliest surviving photos of West Plains were taken around 1882, 25 years after the town's creation. Once photographers began to take pictures, the detail and clarity of the images they produced were remarkable. At the same time, the written record of the town's history gained new clarity with the introduction of newspapers. The first West Plains newspaper, *The Type of the Times*, was published in 1868. It was short-lived but was followed by the *South Missouri Journal* (1870), the *Daily Gazette* (1889), the *Howell County News* (1895), and the *Quill* (1903). Additional written accounts, like court records and the reminiscences of early settlers, add more detail to the story.

So pick up this book and wax nostalgic, while we turn back the clock. Turn it back to a time when the town's businessmen set aside a week every year to go fishing together; a time when a trip into town was an uncommon and exciting event; a time when a single airplane flying overhead could empty every home and business in town; a time when the circus arrived on five trains and 10,000 people filled the town to see it; a time when the nation listened in tears to a ballad about a dancehall explosion in a small Ozarks town; a time when everything was different and yet, still the same.

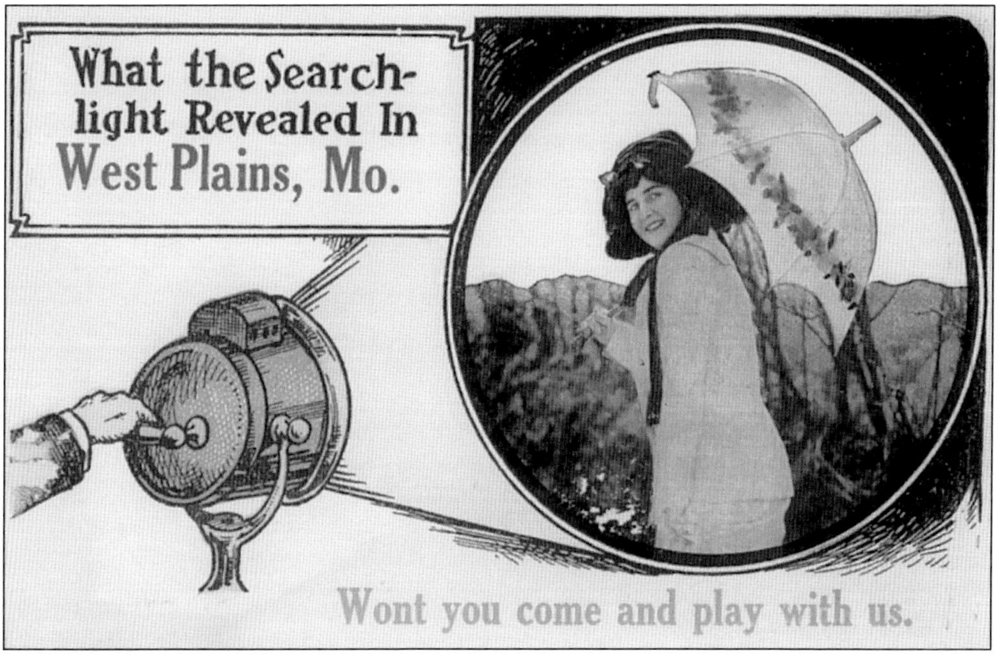

Prelude

1839–1879

The first white settler within the current limits of West Plains was a hunter named Adams. In the summer of 1839 he settled beside a spring one block east of the current Square. The area surrounding the spring had been an Indian campground for centuries, and quickly became a gathering place for new settlers. By fall, Adams had sold his improvement to the Howell family from Tennessee. Josiah Howell, the head of the clan, arrived in what was then Oregon County, Missouri, with his wife Sarah, four of their children, their families, and a small group of slaves.

Josiah's second son, Josephus M. Howell, became the first postmaster of West Plains December 7, 1848. The new post office was in his home, a log cabin, east of the current high school football field. Judge John R. Woodside who lived at Thomasville, the county seat, is said to have named the new post office. He picked West Plains because Howell's home was west of Thomasville across the plains. Early land surveyor records and letters of settlers confirm that the rolling hills between Thomasville and West Plains were indeed clear of trees and covered with tall prairie grass.

Thomas Jefferson Howell, Josiah's oldest son, settled where Adams had lived by the spring and became the first State Representative from Oregon County. When Howell County was created on March 2, 1857, it was named in honor of him. That same year a committee appointed by the state selected West Plains to be the new county seat. In January of 1858, South Street, North Street, and Main, passing through the Square from east to west, had been surveyed and marked out. The first business on the Square was a tan yard located at its northwest corner. Next came a small general store owned by Frank Durham and Dick Campbell. Lots began to sell, homes were built, and the population grew to 150. The village was barely on its feet when the Civil War broke out in 1861. The Ozarks suffered from deadly guerrilla warfare for four years. Howell County was depopulated, West Plains burned to the ground, and many lives were lost.

Reconstruction was slow, but by 1870 West Plains was growing again. There were 250 residents, a newspaper, a courthouse, one church and four merchants, one whiskey dealer, a tavern, two wagon makers, a blacksmith, a brick mason, one schoolteacher, and three physicians. The brick mason must have been a busy chimney builder, because it would be ten years before a brick building was constructed in town. In the next decade business and population continued to increase at a slow pace. Then, on December 25th, 1882, the first locomotive of the Kansas City, Fort Scott and Memphis Railroad chugged into town. The railroad's Christmas present to West Plains was an instant economic boom! In ten years the population multiplied from 300 to 2,000, and 40 new brick buildings were built. West Plains never stopped to look back from that first big boost.

The new era that arrived with the railroad was one of great agricultural production and created a new class of merchant "princes." It lasted for 40 years until the Great Depression. During that period, the downtown area took on the appearance it has today: a system of schools was built; water lines, sewers, and electrical power came to town; churches proliferated; and the town moved from a small county seat to a regional hub of business and activity. Throughout this growth West Plains retained a "country" spirit. It was a small town grown up, but that soon changed.

Most significantly, World War I took away the town's country spirit. Young men went away to war, returning as a generation transformed. More young people left for college, Sears Roebuck and Montgomery Ward brought national competition to local retailers, and paved roads and automobiles drastically changed the economy. As its centennial approached, West Plains headed for a new economy to be fired by industry, health care, and retail businesses owned by regional and national corporations. There this chronicle ends, hopefully to be picked up by another later.

One

Railroad Boomtown

West Plains experienced its biggest period of growth when the Kansas City, Fort Scott and Memphis Railroad arrived in December of 1882. Before then freight was shipped to town by wagon or ox cart from the railroad at Rolla or the steamboat landing in Batesville, Arkansas, both one hundred miles distant. Excitement began to build as soon as news of the railroad's route was known. Less desirable land that was still available for homesteading began to disappear. The price of commercial lots in town escalated as prospective business owners arrived in anticipation of the coming boom. Few were disappointed. In ten years, the population multiplied over six times, and West Plains became the regional center of commerce its founders had dreamed about.

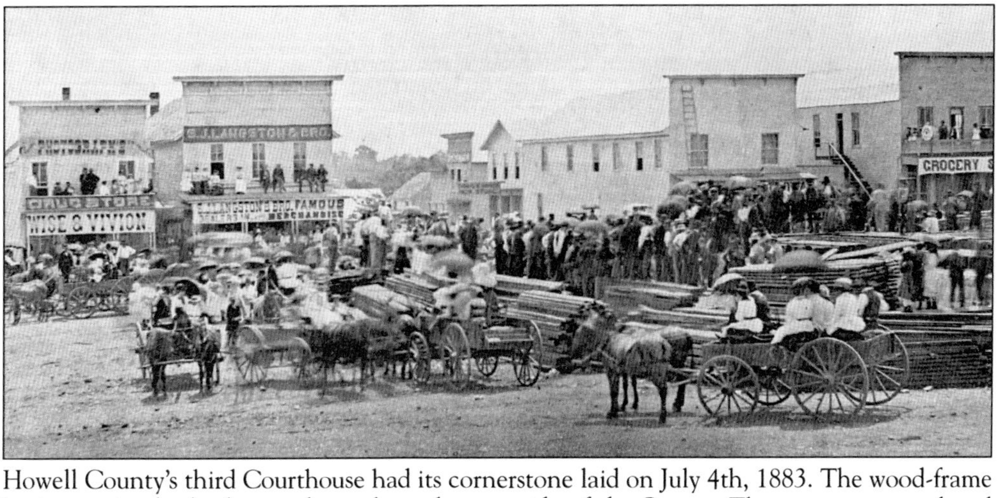

Howell County's third Courthouse had its cornerstone laid on July 4th, 1883. The wood-frame businesses in the background are along the east side of the Square. They were soon replaced by larger brick structures during the building boom created by the railroad's arrival. Note the photographer's sign on the building to the left. He probably took this photo and the one at the top of the next page.

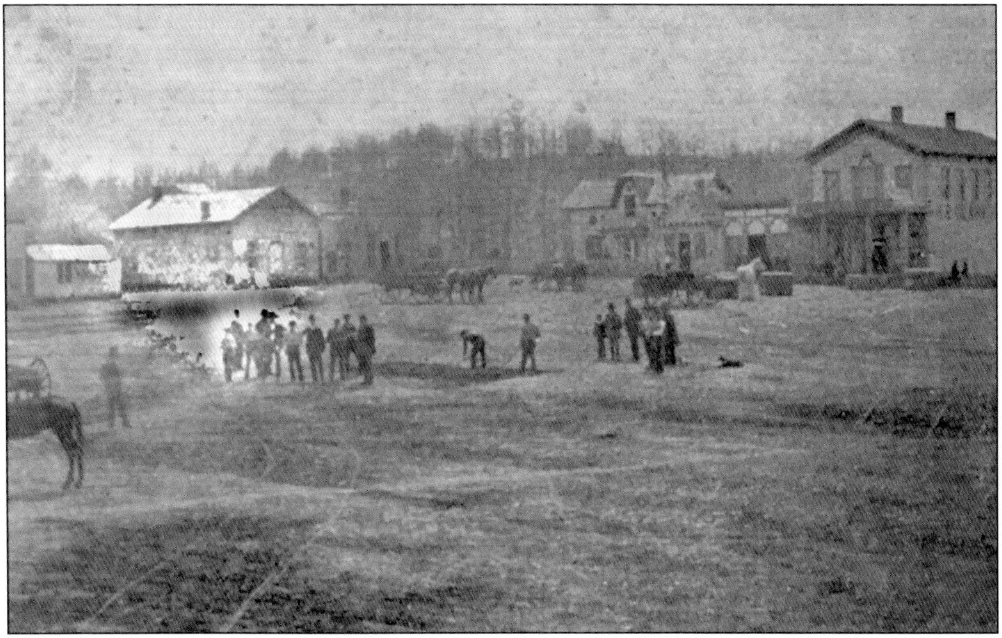

These men are breaking ground for the new Courthouse during the summer of 1883. This photo is important for its rare view of the "pre-railroad" Public Square in West Plains. One of the two buildings highlighted at the left rear, along the south side of the Square, is the previous Courthouse. It was built in 1866 after the first Courthouse was burned during the Civil War.

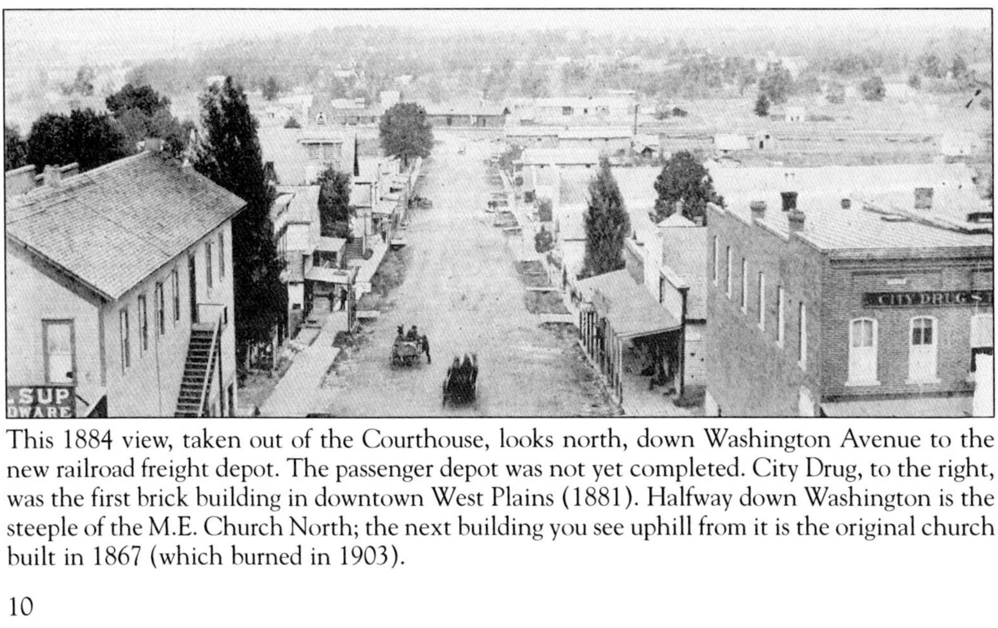

This 1884 view, taken out of the Courthouse, looks north, down Washington Avenue to the new railroad freight depot. The passenger depot was not yet completed. City Drug, to the right, was the first brick building in downtown West Plains (1881). Halfway down Washington is the steeple of the M.E. Church North; the next building you see uphill from it is the original church built in 1867 (which burned in 1903).

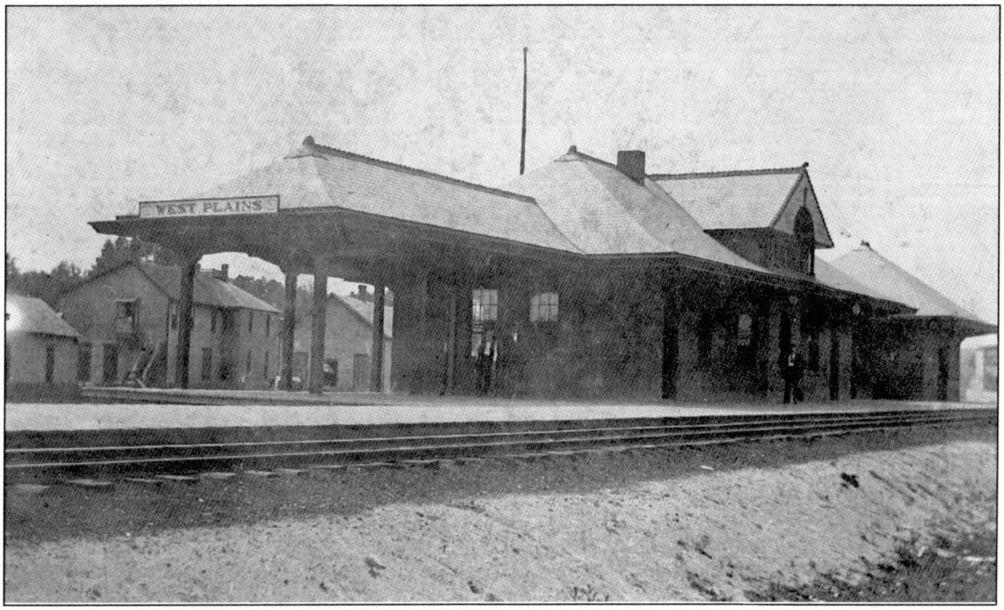

The depot of the Kansas City, Fort Scott and Memphis Railroad was the first thing most people saw as they arrived in West Plains in the 1890s. It was a busy place with its docks full of passengers and luggage. All the town's mail arrived and left from its platform. The water tank stood across the tracks to the north. Many people came to sit on its benches and watch the trains arrive.

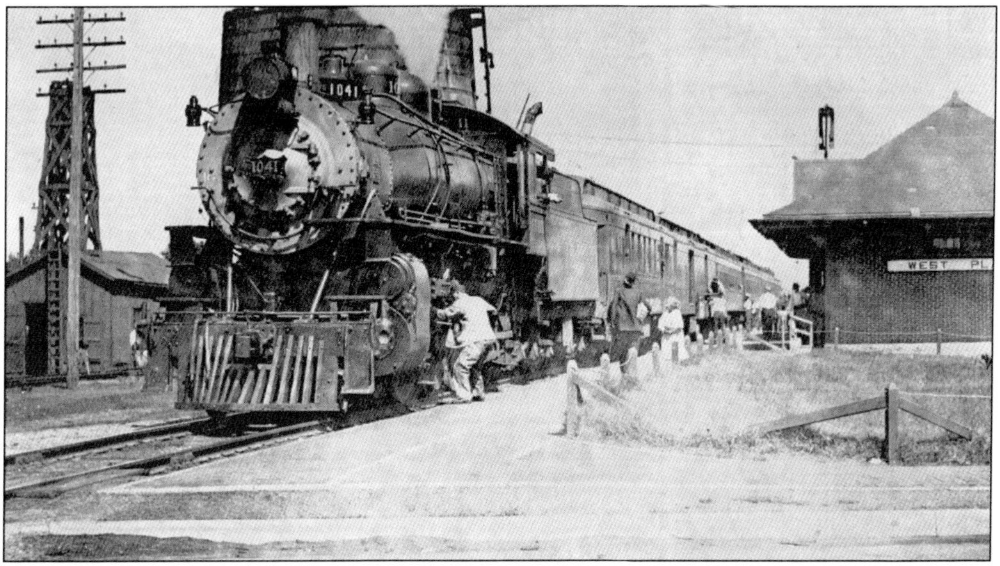

Imagine you have just arrived in West Plains on this train. The following photos illustrate a walk you might have taken in the 1890s through the town's business district. From the depot you head south, uphill on Washington Avenue, drawn by the sight of the new Courthouse five blocks ahead at the top of the hill.

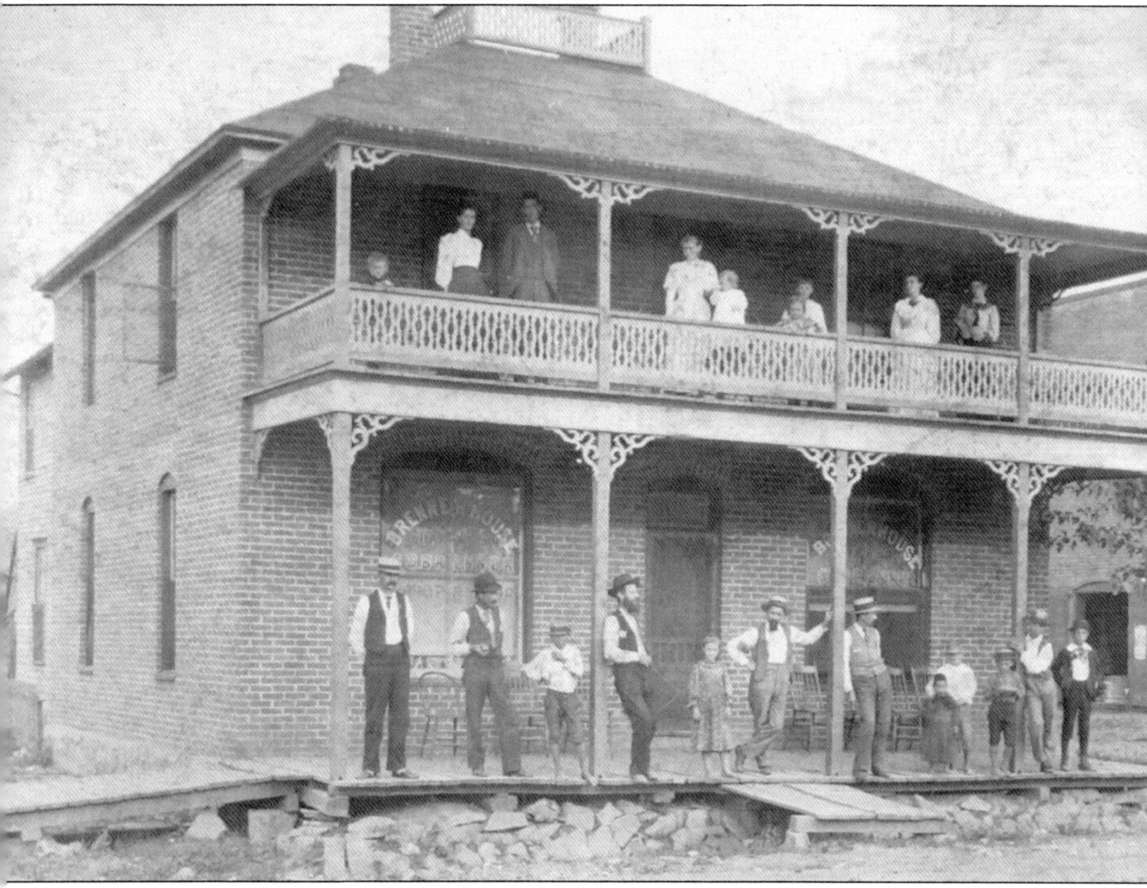

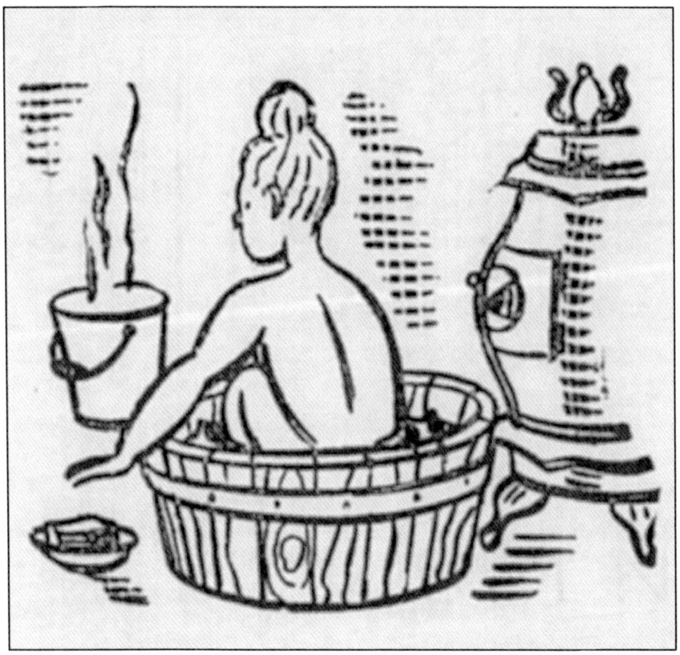

The Brenner Hotel, on the northeast corner of Washington and Michigan (later Broadway), is one of the first buildings we pass. It is a "first-class $1.00 a night hotel" catering to railroad passengers and traveling salesmen. After this photo was taken Galloway and Powles Saloon was built on its north side. Both buildings burned in February of 1896. The West Plains Lumber Planing Mill is in the background.

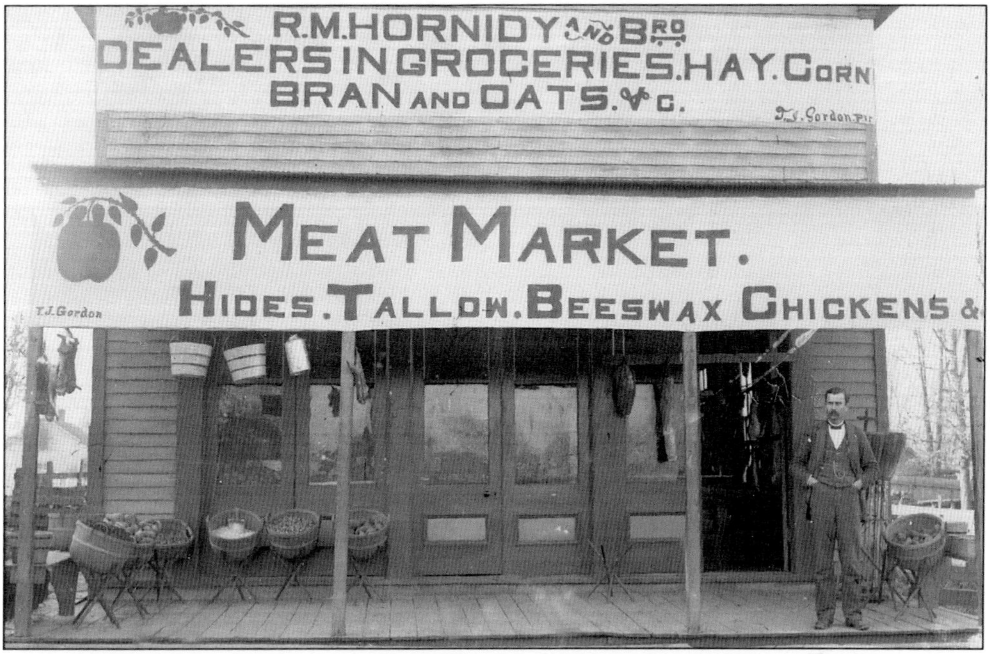

R.M. Hornidy's Meat Market is across Washington Avenue from the Brenner House Hotel. R.M. and his brother J.P. opened this business in May of 1896. Visible is local fare, from rabbit and squirrel to sweet potatoes and nuts. Hornidy, at right, had served as County School Commissioner in 1891. Later he ran his own hotel and restaurant near this location.

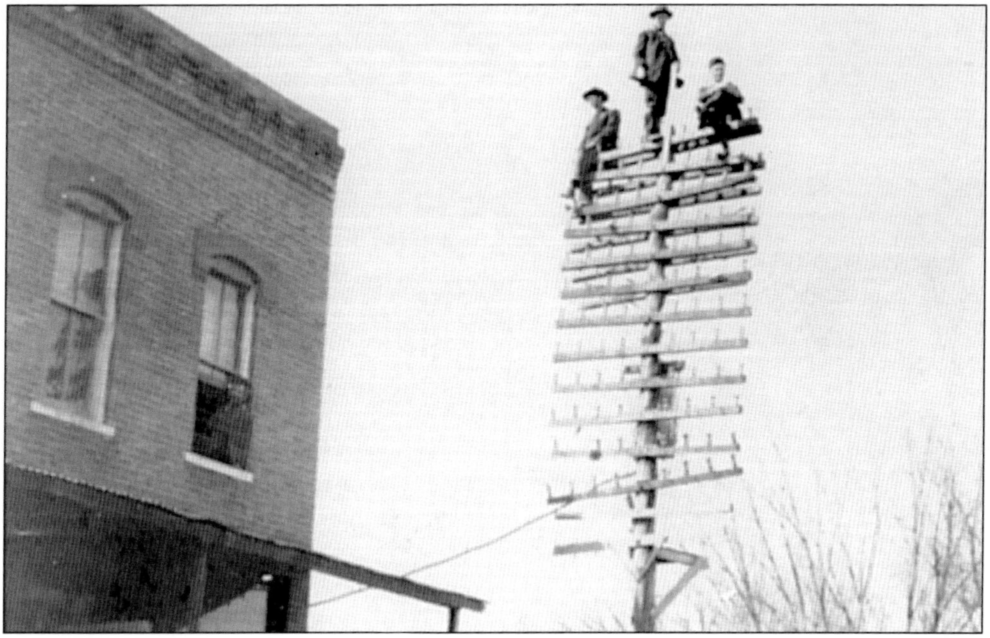

The Zorn family built this building in 1892. It still stands at 313 Washington Avenue. Joe Pumphrey had a store here in 1893. Charles Gale obtained the first franchise for the West Plains Telephone Company in July of 1896. It is believed that the first switchboard was on the second floor of this building. This picture shows the telephone lines running into the building.

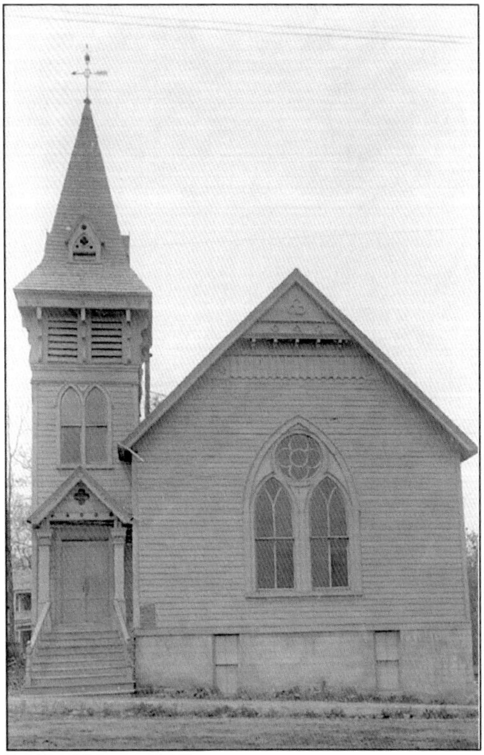

One block further uphill, on the west side, we see the new M.E. Church North, built in 1883. Past it is a small boarding house and then the old church built in 1867. The first church was home to several denominations and had the Masonic Lodge upstairs. When the new church was built, the Masons moved to the top floor of the Courthouse, and the old church was sold for use as a business building. It burned in 1903.

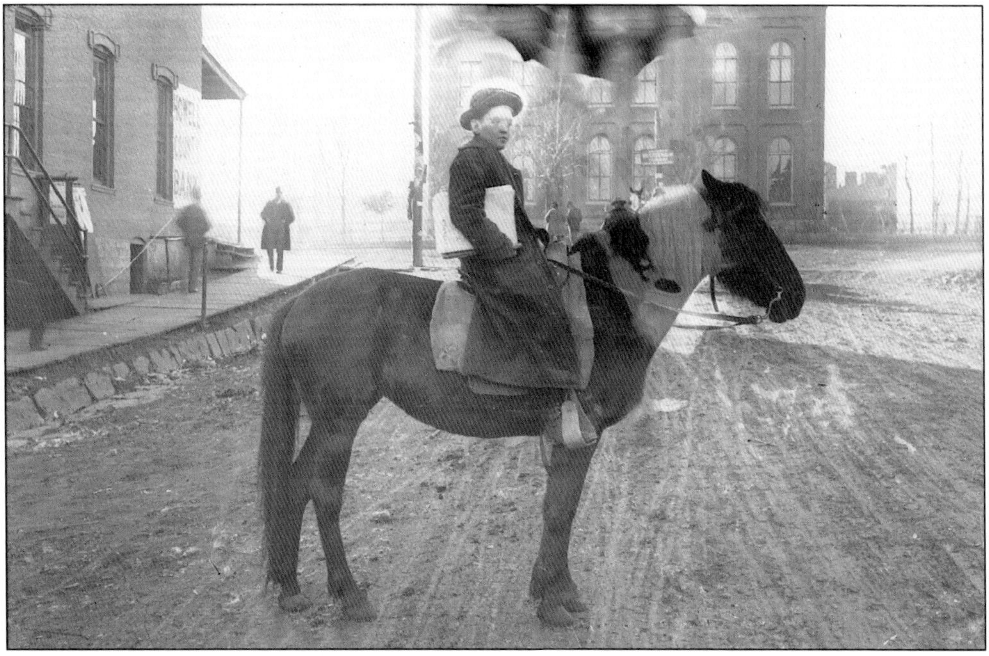

Climbing toward the Square we meet a paperboy delivering his papers on horseback. Taken from an early 1896 glass slide, this photo is damaged, but shows an interesting view. The Howell County bank, established in 1890, is on the left. Straight ahead is the Courthouse and just to its right is the silhouette of the Truex building being rebuilt after the fire of September 1895.

Further up Washington, we pass Noe and Jones Saloon. This building was built by the West Plains Bank in 1883 and was the home of the first bank in town. The bank occupied this site until 1889 when they sold it and moved to a new building on the east side of the Square. This building still stands at 107 Washington and is on the National Register of Historic Places.

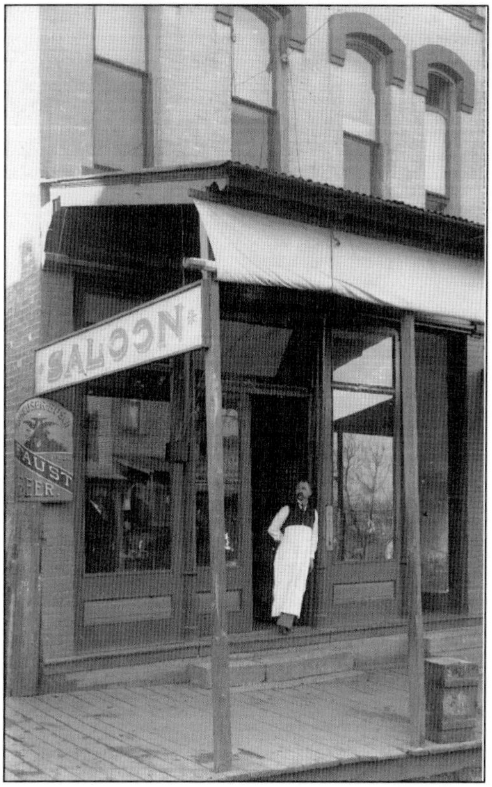

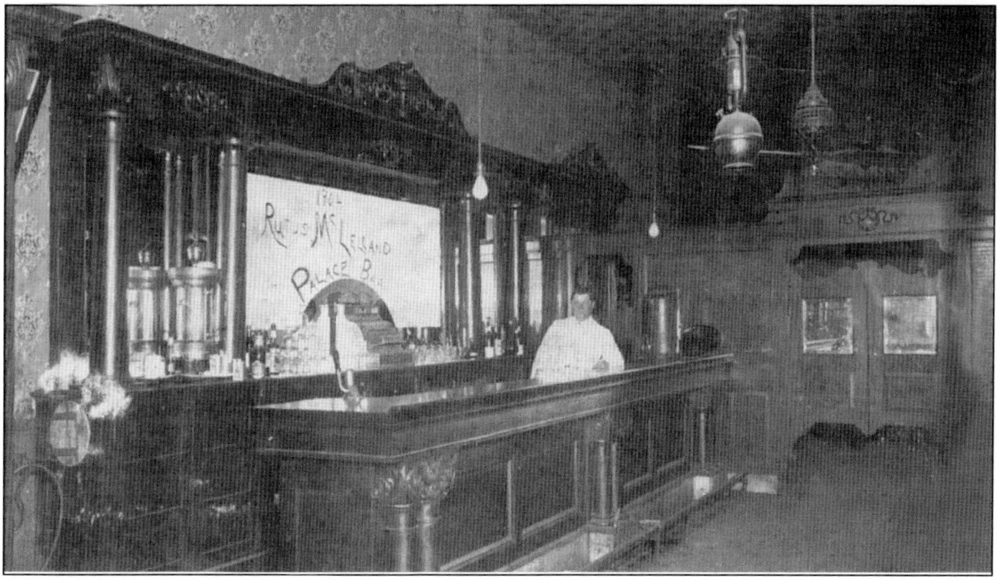

This photo shows the interior of another saloon from the same time period. It is the Palace Bar, owned by Rufus McLelland. West Plains beat the nation to prohibition by passing a local option banning liquor sales on January 31, 1907. The law was fought for two years, but in 1909 the last saloon in town sold it fixtures, its bar going to a lunchroom in Koshkonong, Missouri.

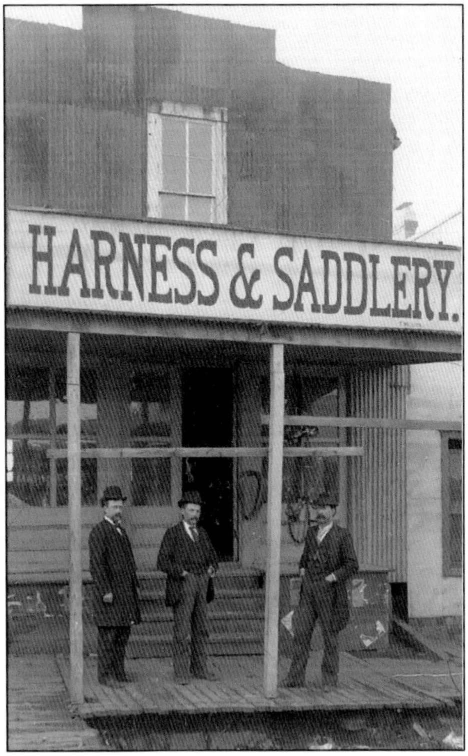

Proceeding up the west side of Washington this Harness and Saddlery is the last building we pass before reaching the Square. Today it is the site of a parking lot at 105 Washington Avenue. Clad with corrugated iron siding it must have been hot working inside during the Ozarks summer.

The 1883 Courthouse greets us as we arrive at the Square. We enter from Washington Avenue at the far right in the background next to the Carter Hardware with the hipped roof. Henry Hoenschild of Rolla, Missouri, a 19-year-old architect, designed this courthouse. The county paid for it with $16,600 in bonds. The building contractor was George Goodlander. The tiny building on the lawn of the Courthouse is a newspaper stand.

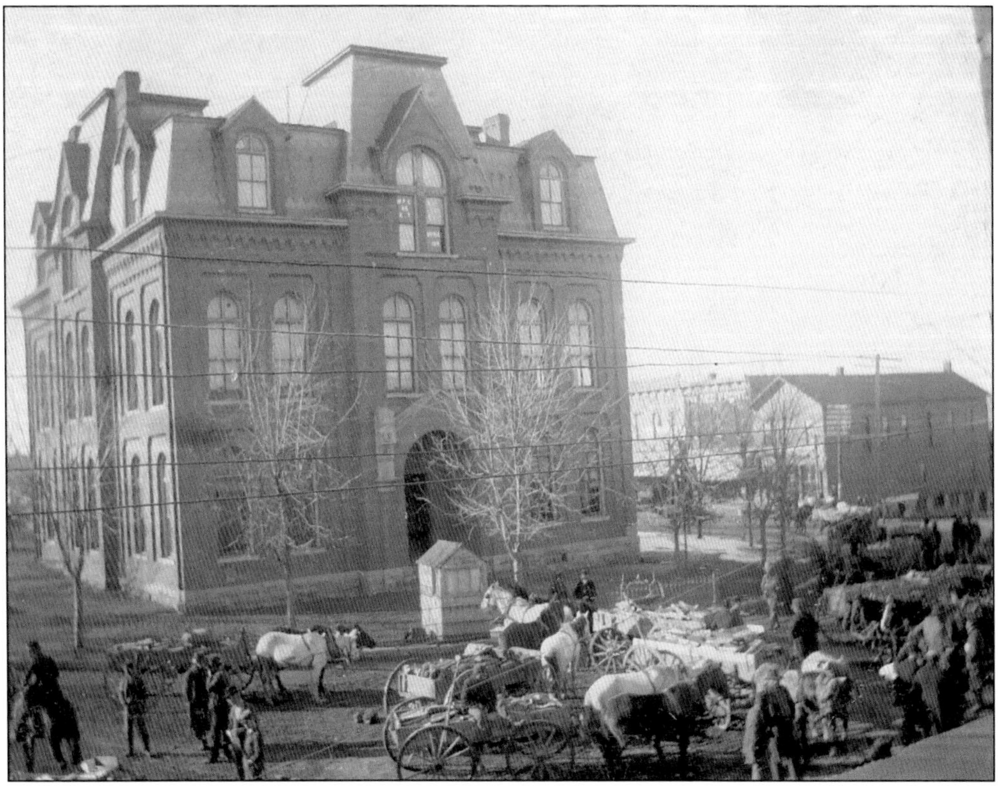

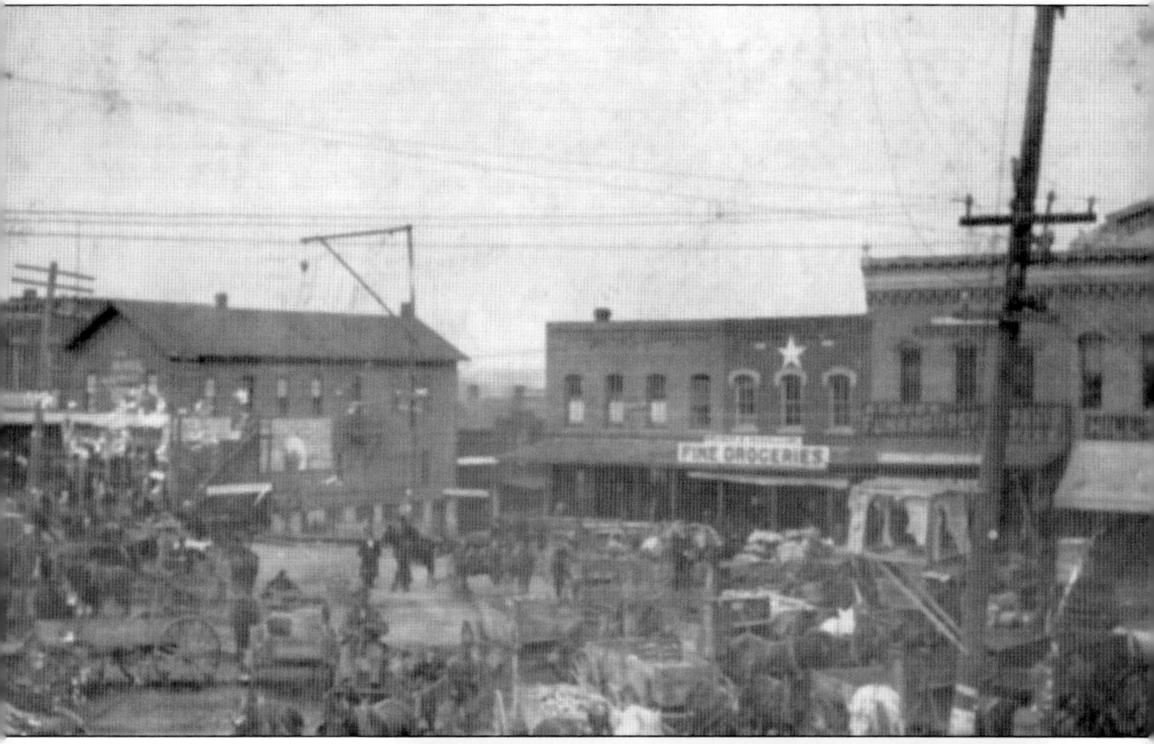

This busy scene on the Square in the 1890s illustrates that parking has always been a problem in downtown West Plains. The north side of the Square is shown here with Washington Avenue in the middle. Vehicle pollution had a completely different meaning in the late 1800s. A city ordinance passed at the time asked visitors to park their teams off the Square on lots provided by the city to keep manure cleanup to a minimum.

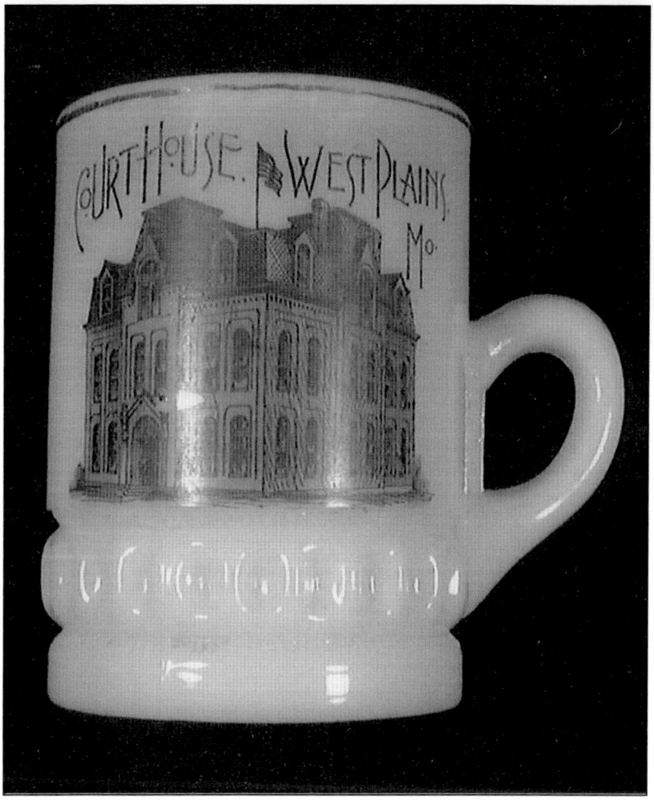

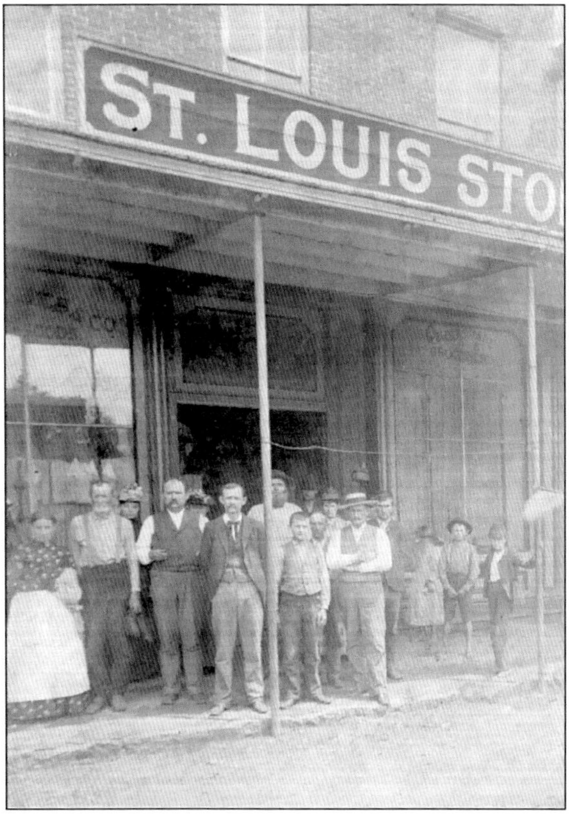

From Carter's Hardware (1867) we circle the Square counterclockwise. The first business we pass is the St. Louis Store (later the "Red Front") at 24 Court Square. Its specialty was queensware and dry goods. This store occupied the east section of a business "block," one large segmented commercial building, built in 1888. Three different owners, the Alsup, Risley, and Skillman families, built the block's three sections.

This view of the middle section of the Alsup, Risley, and Skillman block shows the original cast-iron columns brought in on the railroad from St. Louis for its construction. Curry, Shadburne, and Bohrer Drug Stores all did business at this location. Most of the brick in the buildings around the Square were made in West Plains. The Martin and the Brown Companies were the largest of these brick makers.

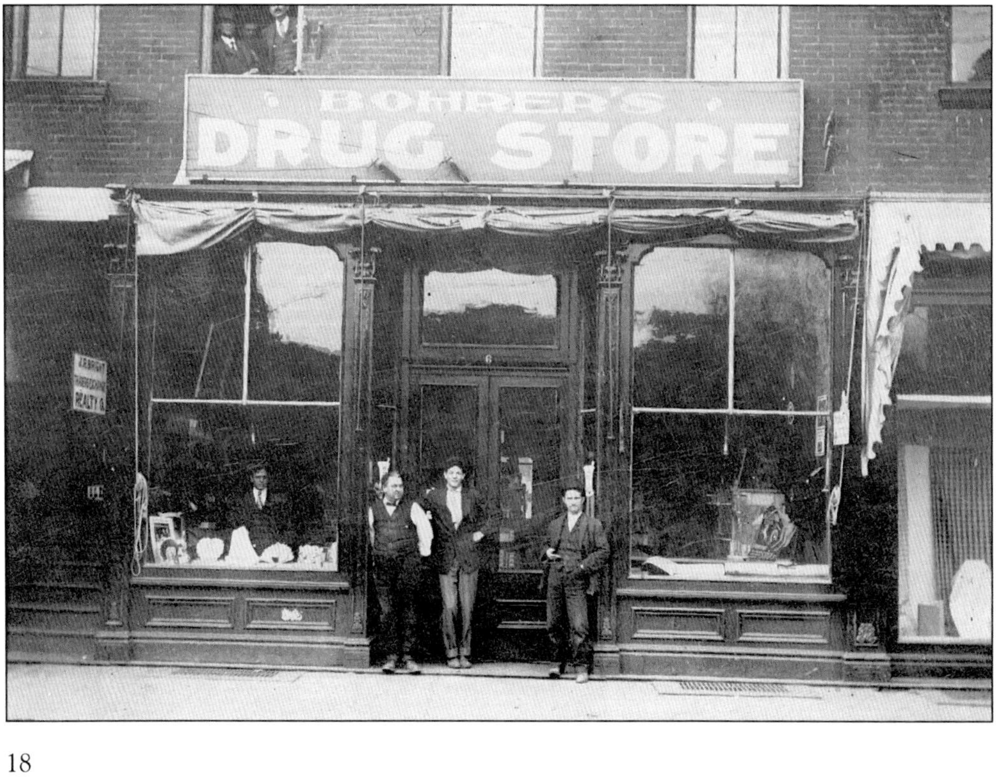

This is the final section on the west end of the Alsup, Risley, and Skillman block. This view is from 1888, right after the building was completed. Pieces of brick from the building's construction litter the street, and the Famous Grocery, built next door in 1889, has not been started. Note the large pocket watch-shaped sign over the right side of the door and a line strung with pocket watches across the right window.

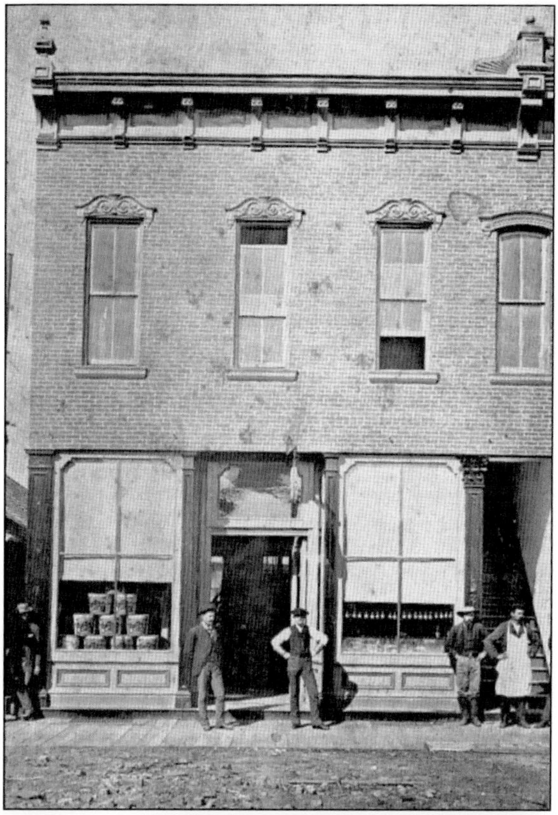

At the northwest corner of the Square we come to the first grocery in West Plains, the Famous, built by J.L. Elledge in 1889. The herringbone-patterned wood ceiling still exists in this building at 28 Court Square. It was placed on the National Register of Historic Places in 2001. Grocery stores selling pre-packed goods and exotic bananas were another business made possible by the railroad.

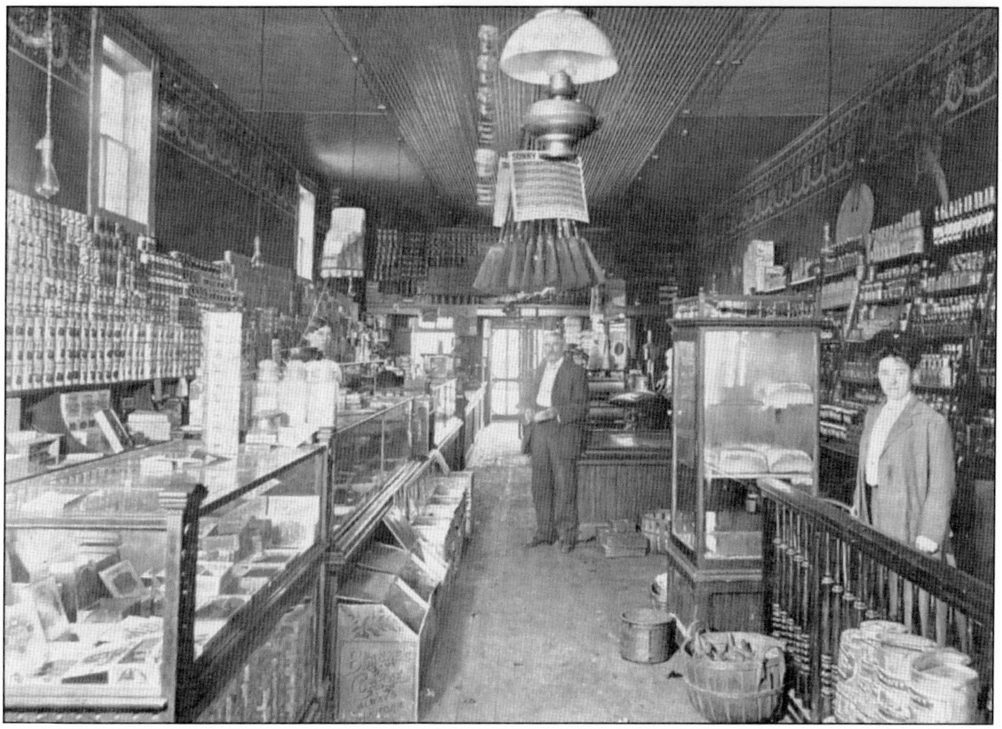

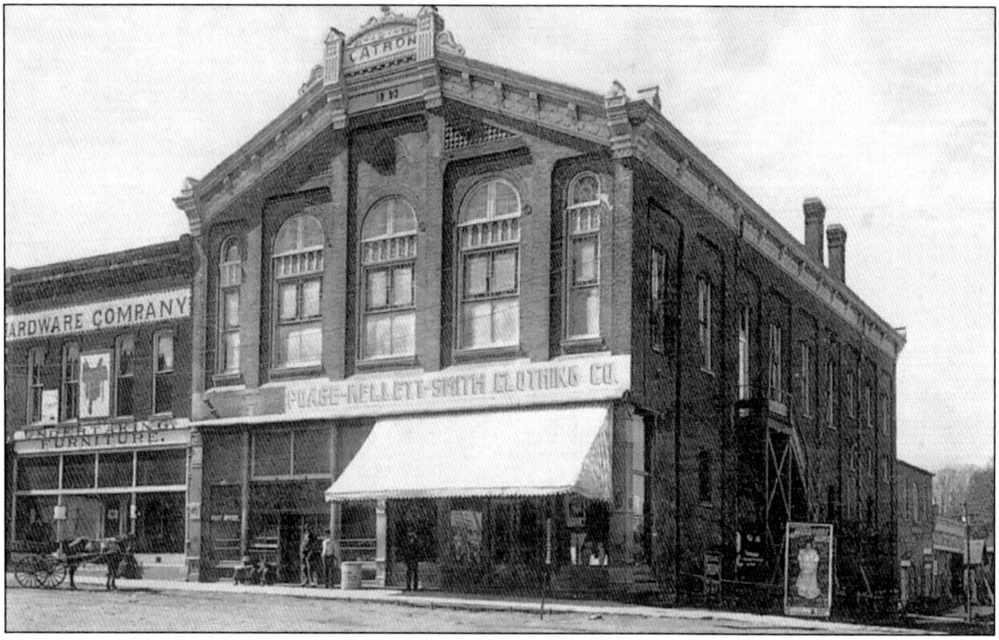

Traveling a block south around the Court Square we cross West Main Street and come to the Johnson Opera House, built in 1892–1893 by Thomas Johnson and Oliver Hazard Perry Catron. It featured retail stores on the first floor and had an "Opera House" or theater on the second floor with a stage, orchestra pit, and balcony. Catron soon bought out Johnson's share and renamed it the Catron Opera House.

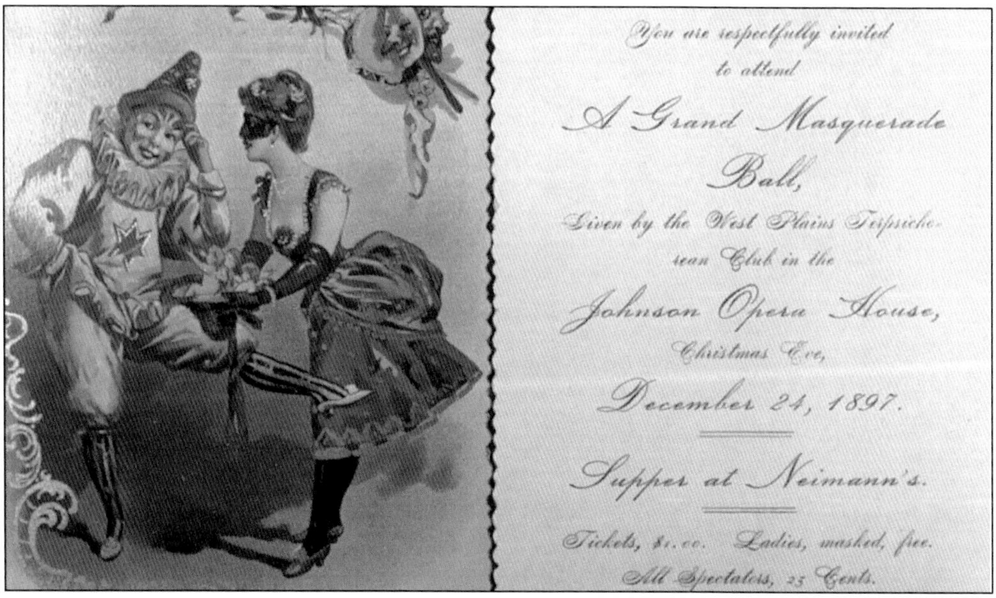

This program is for a "Grand Masquerade Ball, Given by the West Plains Terpsichorean Club in the Johnson Opera House, Christmas Eve, 1897." The card says that tickets will be $1, masked ladies will be admitted free of charge, and that spectators in the balcony will be charged 25¢. Such events featured a grand march and lavish suppers including roast quail, fresh oysters, pheasant, and other gourmet dishes.

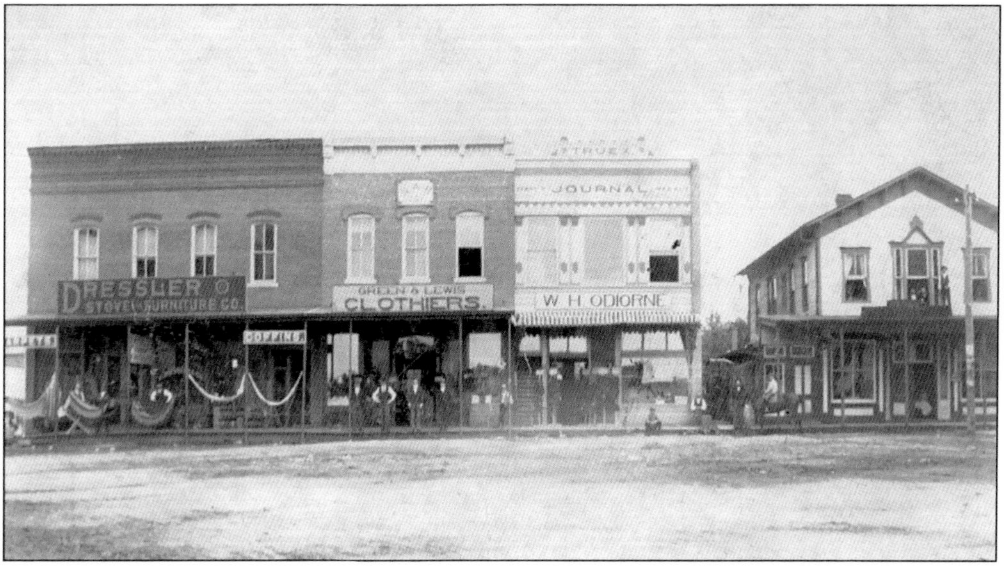

On the south side of the Square we pass a wood building with a millinery store and a restaurant on its first floor. Next is the Truex building built by Judson A. Truex to house the *Journal* newspaper. The second floor of the clothiers next door holds the meeting hall of the Grand Army of the Republic. Finally, we pass Dressler Furniture before reaching South Street. These buildings all burned in September of 1895.

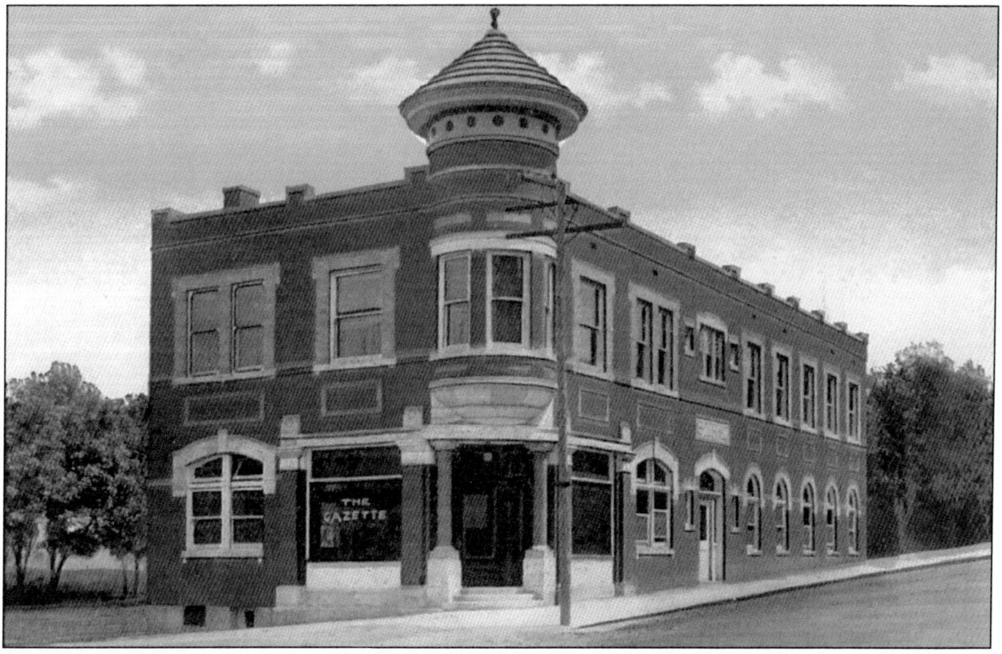

Crossing South Street, we see the *Howell County Gazette* building a block south. Will Zorn built it in 1911–1912. The newspaper offices for the *Gazette* were on the first floor and Zorn's living quarters on the second. He was active in Democratic politics and served as postmaster from 1915 until 1922. In 1892 Zorn operated a woolen mill in town and later was the manager of the Catron Opera House.

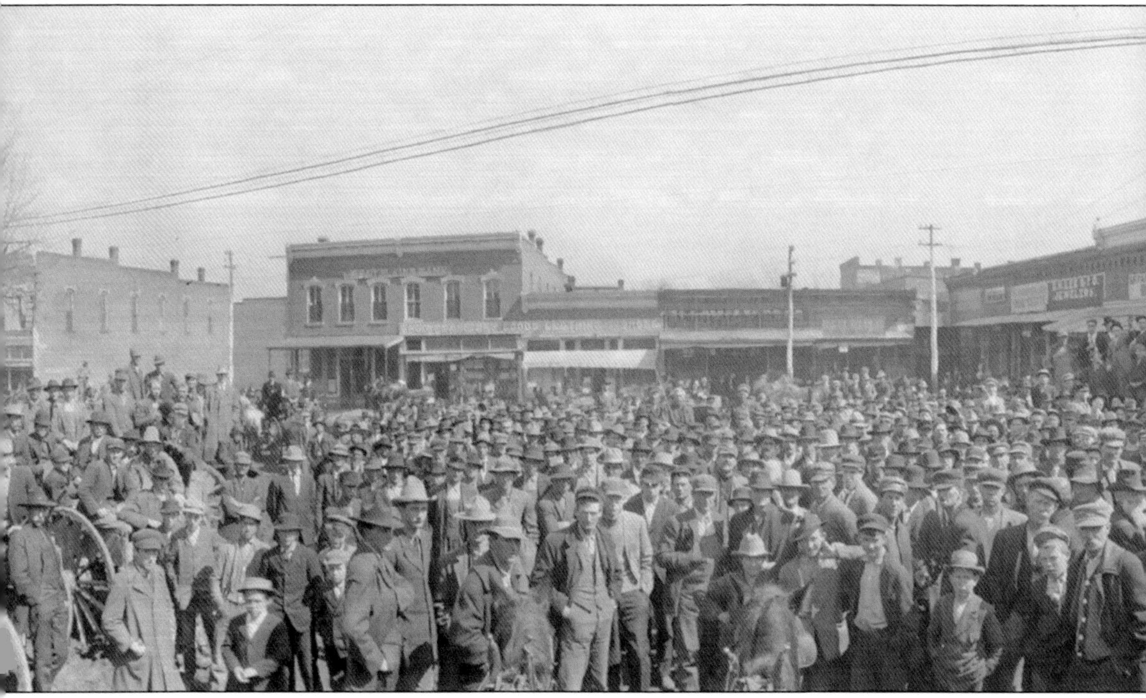

Crossing South Street we reach Aid Hardware. Although this photo was taken in 1912, all the buildings visible on the Square were built before 1900. The occasion is Aid Hardware's Oliver Plow Day Sale, held in March of each year (see Chapter Four). At the right is Aid Hardware's first building built in 1885. On the left, at the corner of East Main, is the second West Plains Bank, built in 1889. Examination of this photo with a magnifying glass reveals less than 10

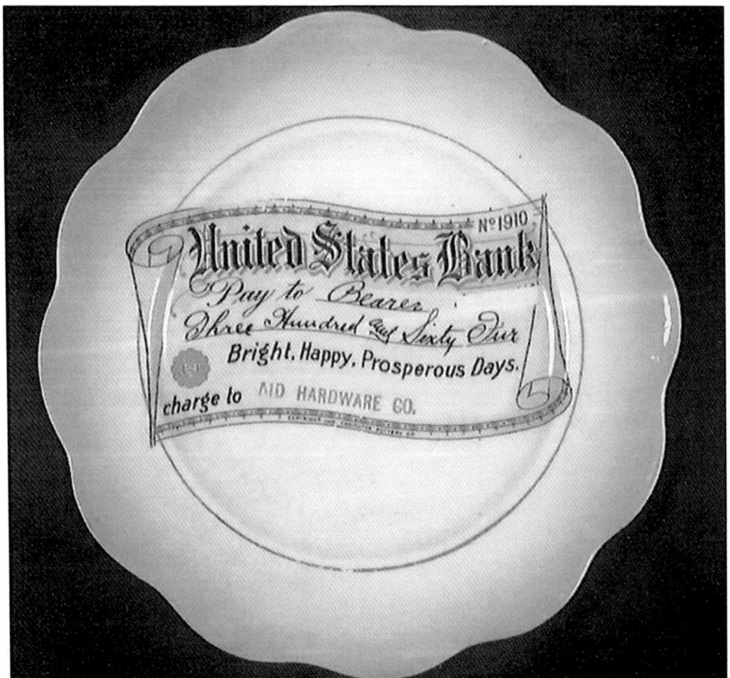

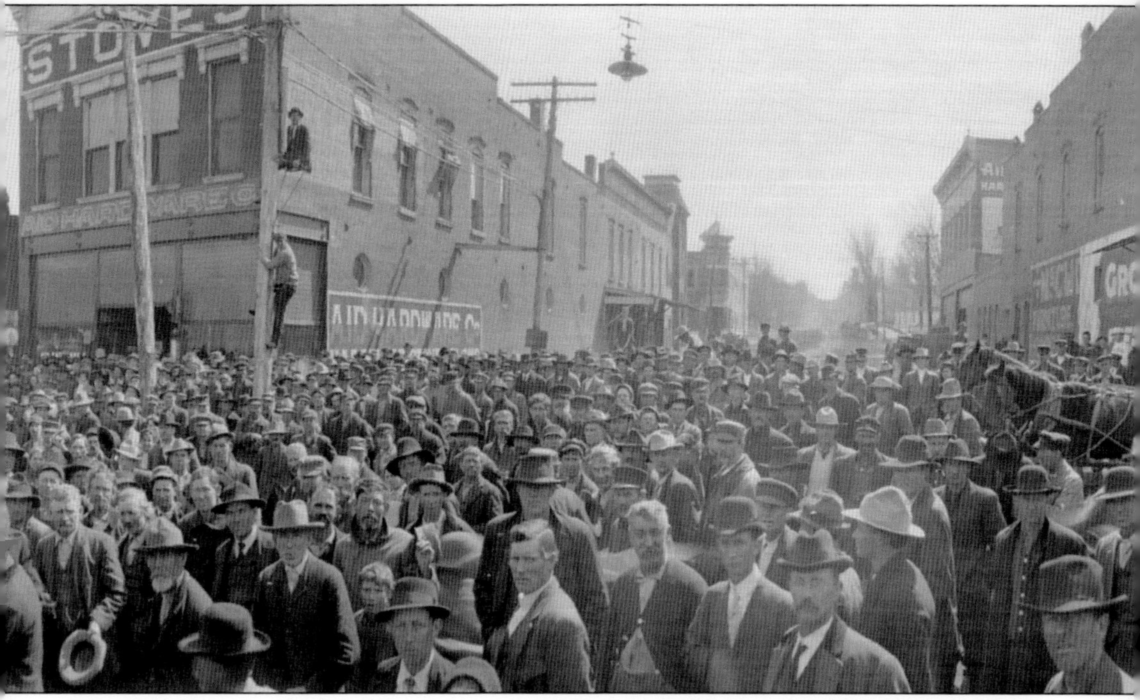

women in the entire crowd. Perhaps they are inside shopping. T.J. Howell, a local photographer, took this scene with his panoramic camera. His studio was upstairs at 108 East Main, one of the buildings destroyed in the dance hall explosion of 1928 (Chapter Six).

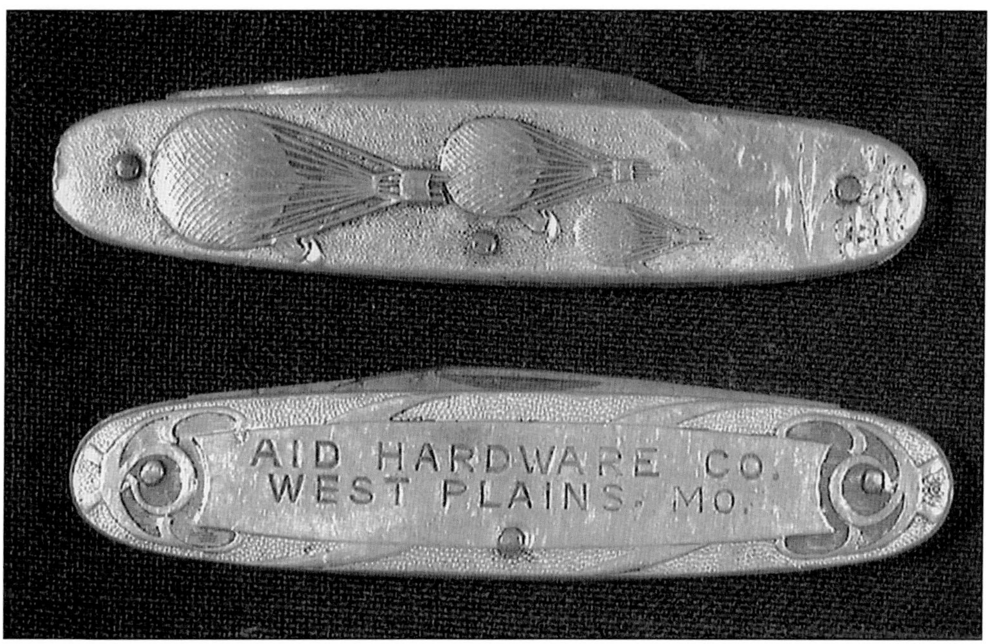

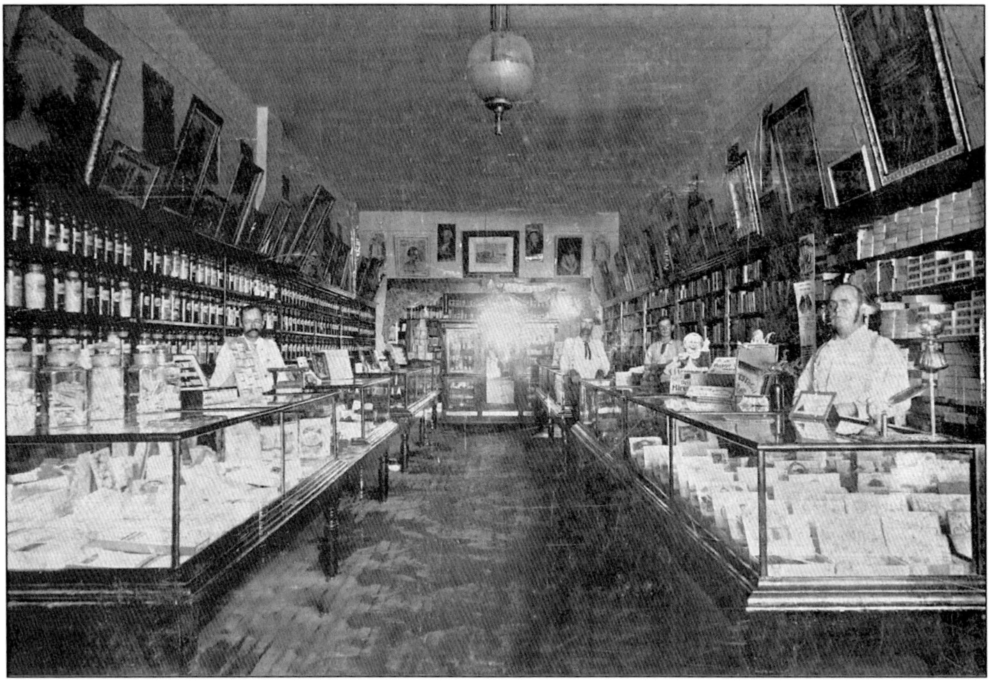

This is the interior of the Red Apple Drug Store shortly after it opened in 1894. It occupied the same building on the southeast corner of the Square for over 100 years. Dr. John W. Martin and his nephew, Thomas D. Martin, were its first owners. After Dr. Martin died in March of 1905, Thomas ran it until 1916, when he sold it to C.E. "Earl" Armstrong.

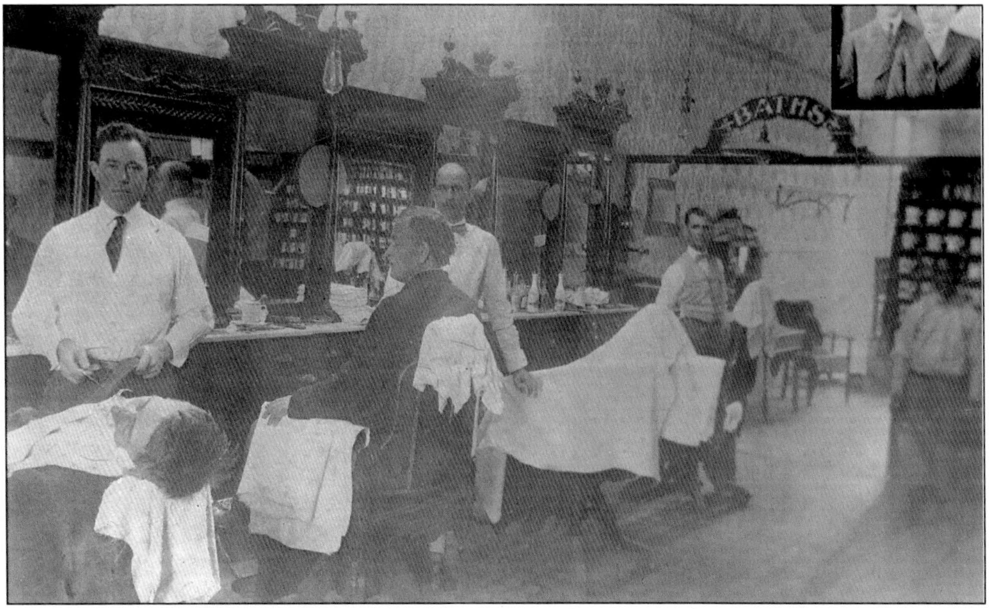

Past the Red Apple at the entrance to Evans Arcade we can glance inside the A.P. Clark Barbershop. Clark is the barber at left. Pony Thomas, the black shoeshine man is at the back right, in front of a cabinet holding regular customer's shaving mugs. Baths were available in the rear. The Evans Arcade was open from the Square through to Walnut Street.

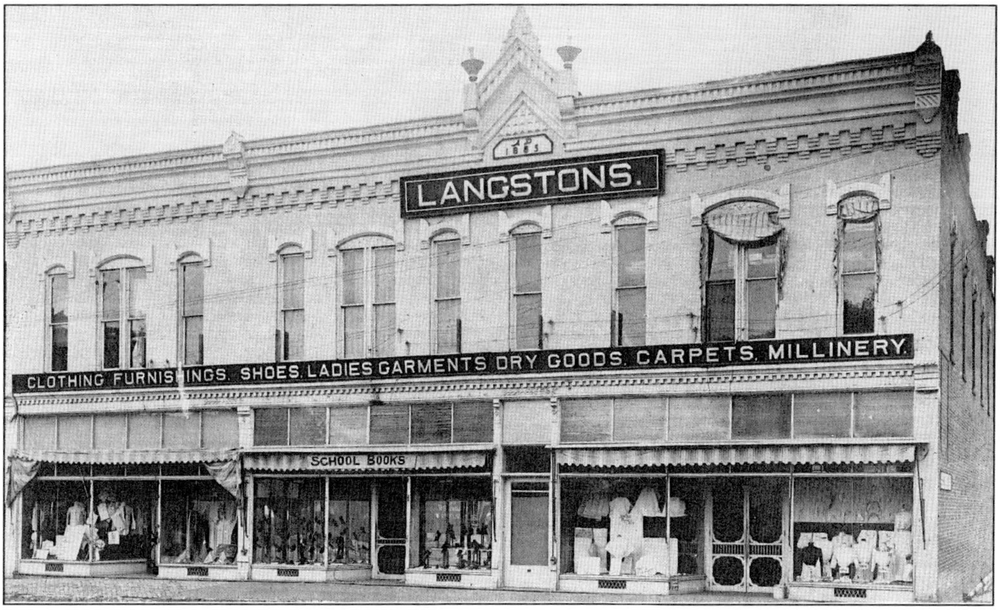

Across East Main is Langston's General Mercantile. In 1876, Samuel Jackson Langston and his brother Thomas Jefferson Langston bought Blackburn Thomas's store on this same spot and opened for business. You can see that building in the first photograph in this chapter. It was a wood frame building that burned in 1885. The impressive "business block" before us was built to replace it.

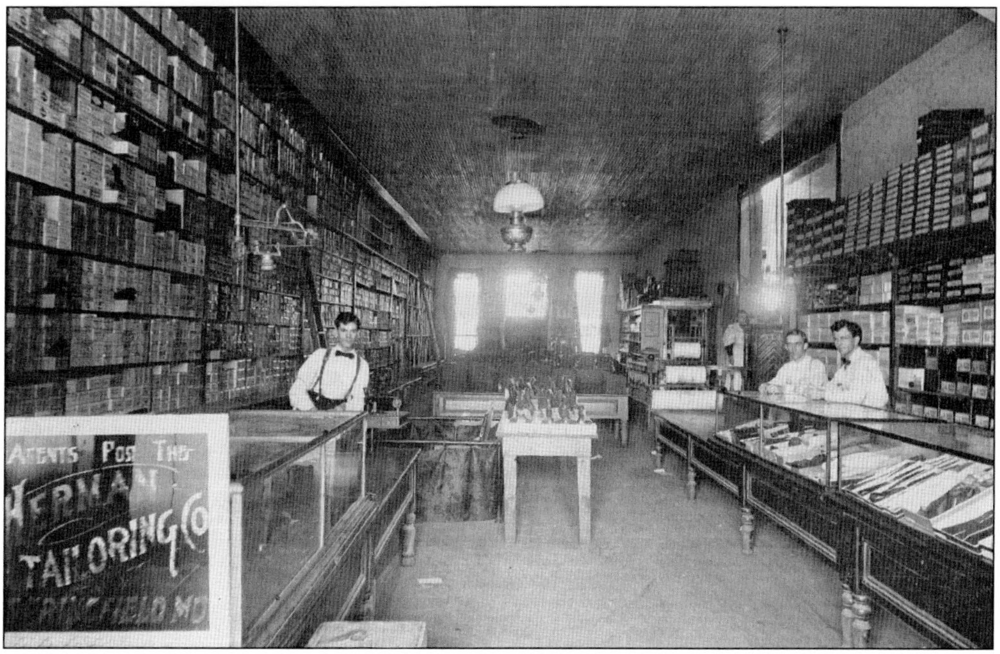

Let's step inside the center section of the Langston Block to visit their shoe department. There to greet us, left to right, are the following: Ben McGinty, Anna Martin, Wayne Langston, and Brid Smith. A large fire destroyed this building in 1915. Other catastrophic fires of that same era burned the Aid Hardware buildings in 1914 and the Dixon Block in 1919.

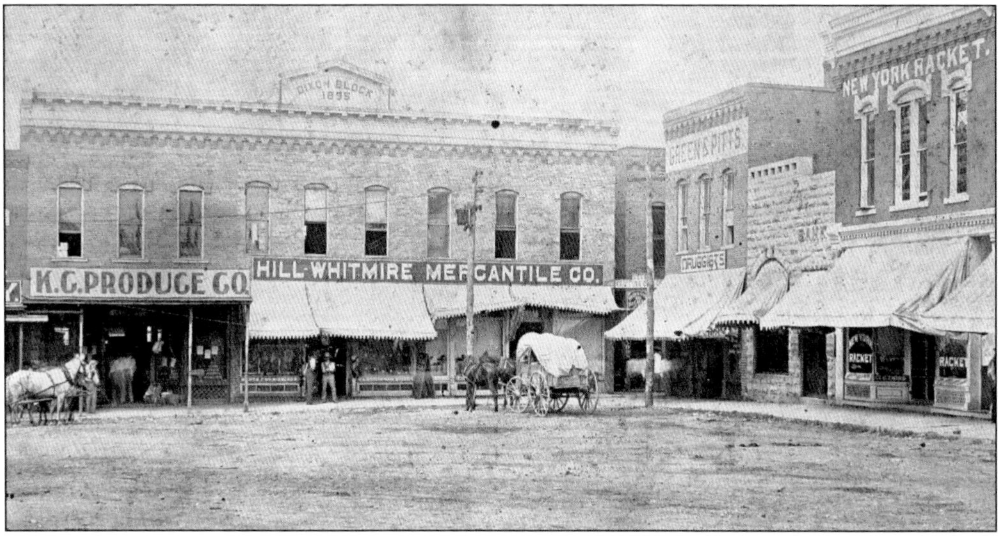

Continuing our walk, we pass the new Farmers and Merchants Bank (1893–1896) built of stone quarried on the Porter Farm north of town. Next is the Green and Pitts Drugstore. At the northeast corner of the Square is the Dixon Block. Dr. J.C.B. Dixon built it in 1895. Dr. Dixon was one of the largest property owners in town. He owned more than 50 business houses and residences.

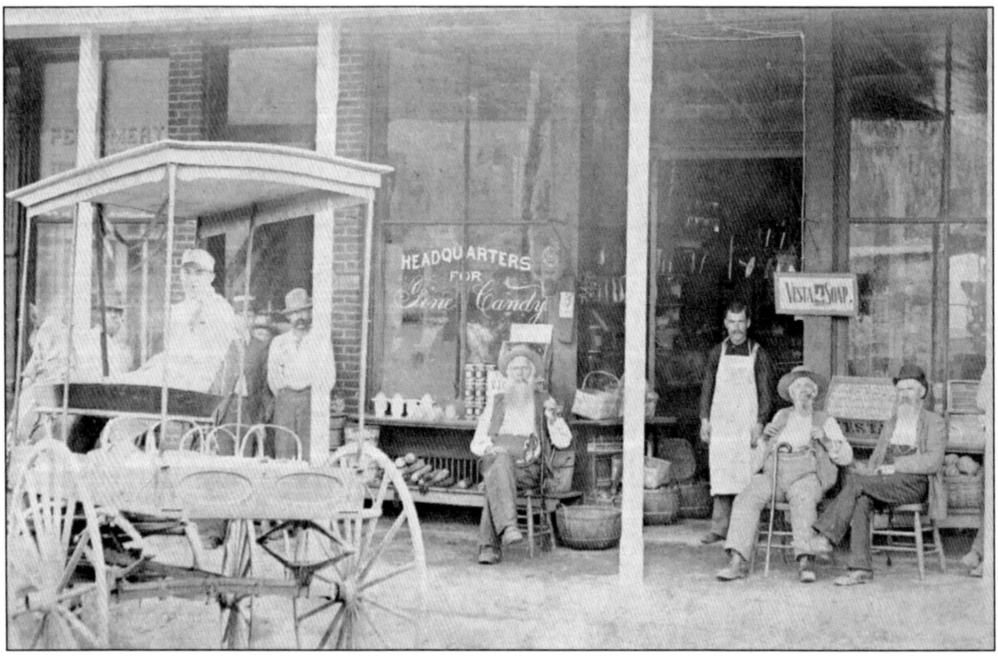

Past the Dixon Block is the Star Grocery (c. 1890), owned by D.H. Bement and Son. The building just past it, out of sight to the left, is one we saw earlier in an 1883 photo as the City Drug Company. In 1890, the Howell County Bank bought it for their offices. A new façade was put on the building in 1910. It had terracotta finish brick with a marble column guarding its corner entrance.

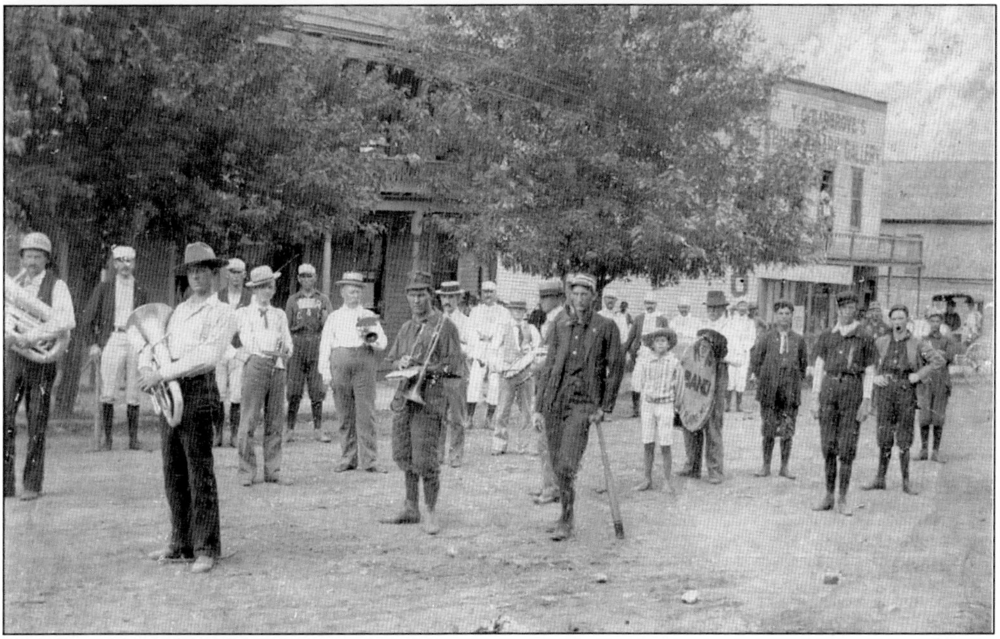

Returning to East Main, we meet a parade of two baseball teams lead by the Knights Pythias brass band. They are out drumming up a crowd for a game at Sportsman Park on St. Louis Street at the railroad tracks. In the left background is the Commercial Hotel. Beyond it is a two-story commercial building with "T.G. Hargrove's Photography Studio" painted on its front.

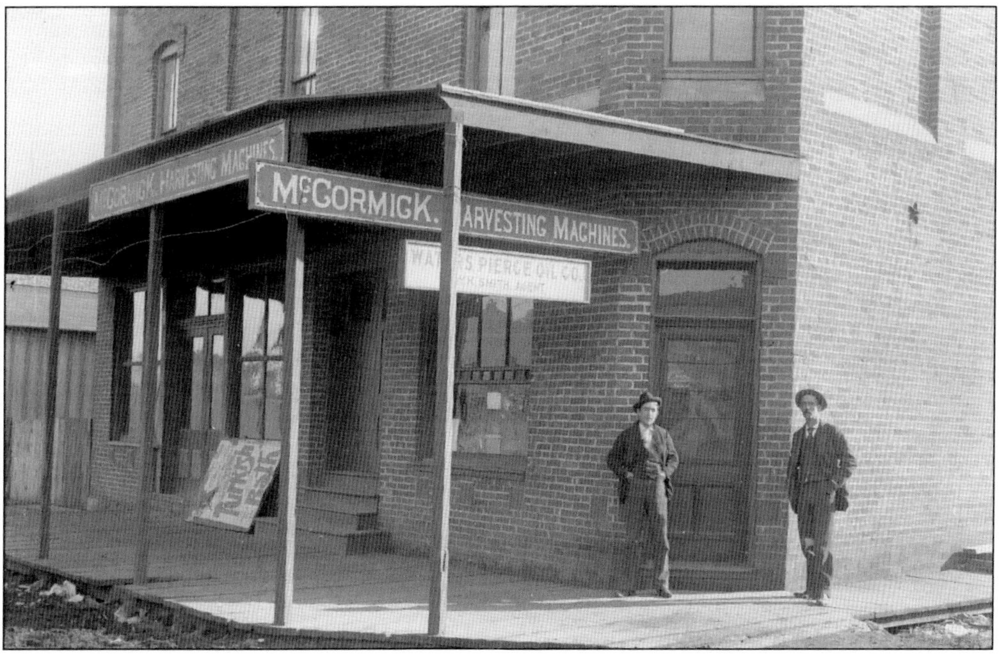

The first building past Spring Park on the south side of East Main is the Grand Opera House. It faces the Commercial Hotel. Much smaller than the Catron Opera House, the Grand has a machinery shop on its ground floor and a theater upstairs. The theater must not have been popular, as Ed Coker converted this building into a mule barn in 1905.

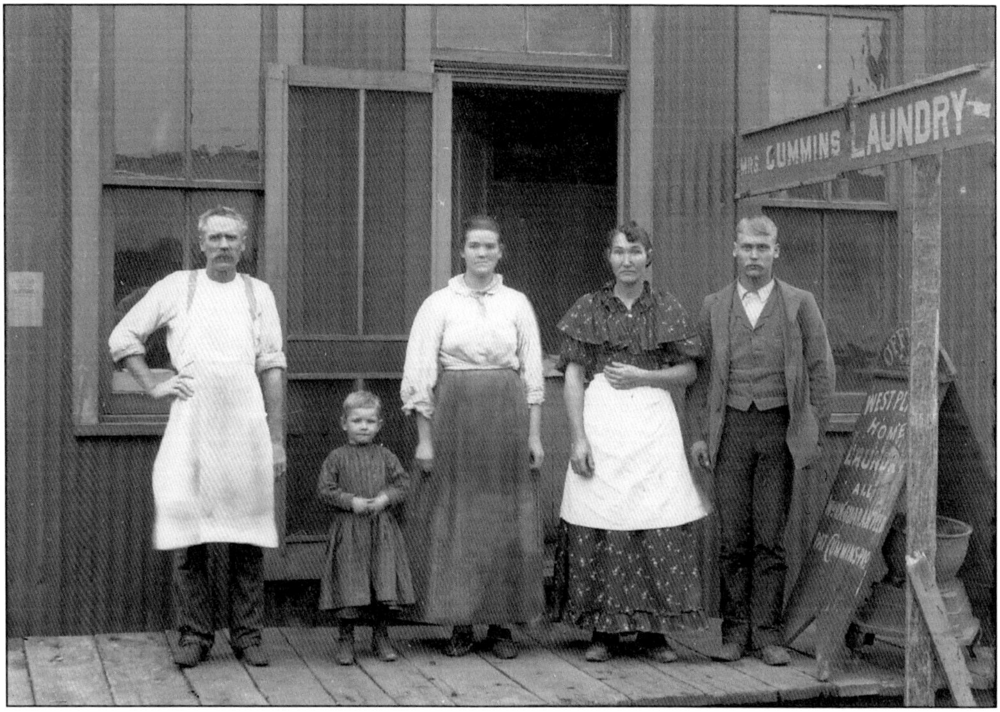

At the next street we turn north on St. Louis Street, back toward the depot. There we pass Pat Cummins' Laundry. She is one of the few businesswomen in West Plains at this time. The small boy shown wearing a dress was not an unusual sight in the 1890s. Boys often wore dresses then until they were three or four years old.

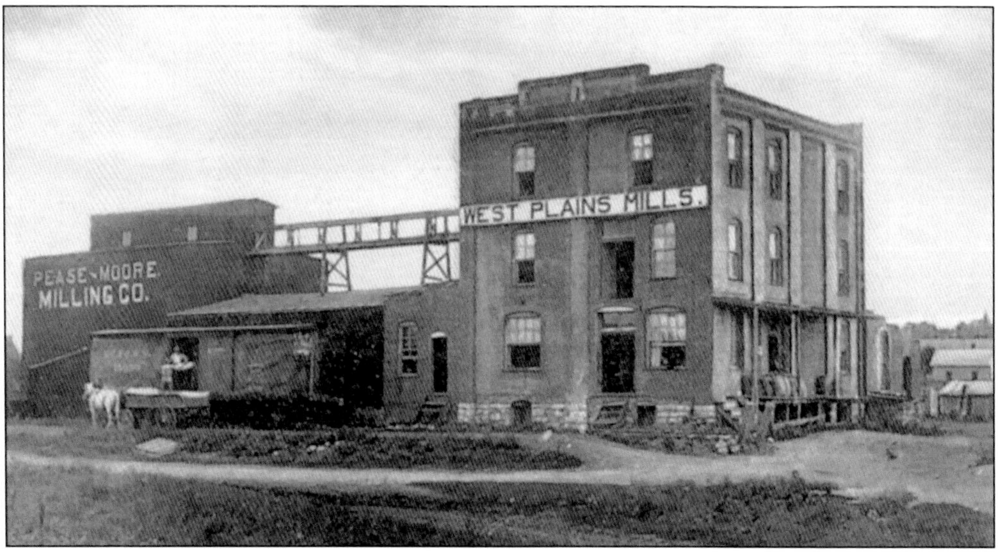

As we reach the railroad tracks we pass Sportsman Park on our right and come to Pease-Moore Milling Company on the left. They make "Raven" brand flour for sale in the markets at Memphis. C.M. Pease is the president. The mill can produce 175 barrels of flour a day. His company also owns the Enterprise Mills three blocks west on the railroad at Lincoln Avenue. Beyond the mill we complete our tour at the depot.

Two

West Plains at Work

The railroad may have started the growth boom in West Plains, but the citizens of the town kept it going with a strong work ethic. The railroad provided the first opportunity to develop the natural assets of the area. Small farms were the backbone of the economy, but other opportunities soon became apparent. Howell County became known as the land of the "Big Red Apple" as companies organized to plant large tracts of land in orchards. Mining companies were created to take advantage of local deposits of iron and zinc. Merchants built large "trade houses" around the Square to supply the farmer with everything from yard goods to plows. The newspapers were full of the ads of all types of tradesmen, from blacksmiths and carpenters to hotelkeepers, ready to serve the area's needs.

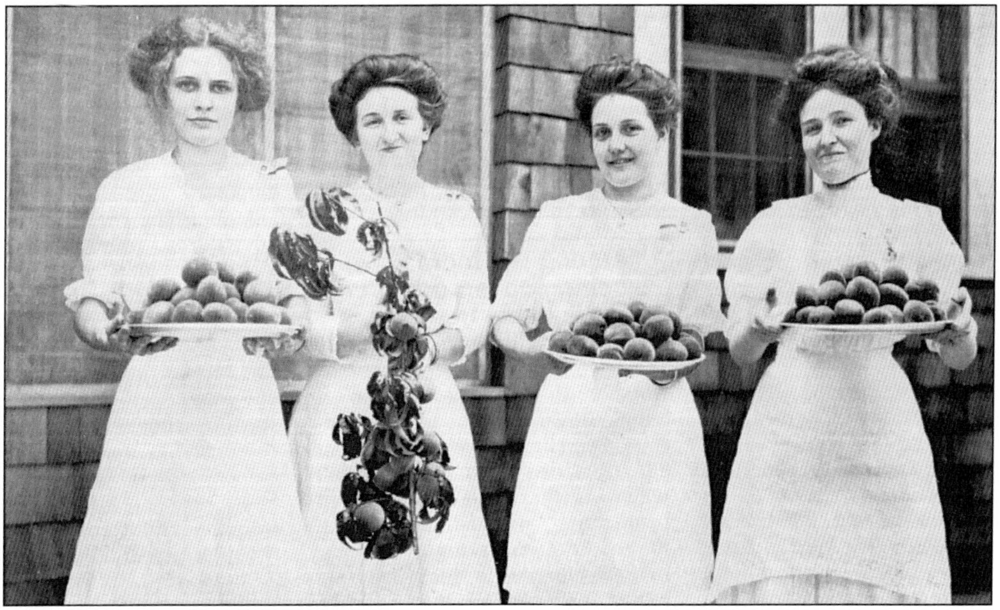

The arrival of the railroad in 1883 had a greater influence on agriculture than any other industry in the area. Peaches and apples were shipped out of Howell County by the train carload. These lovely belles at Col. Torrey's Peach Carnival in 1912 were pictured on the cover of Collier's Magazine. The area around West Plains became known as the land of "The Big Red Apple."

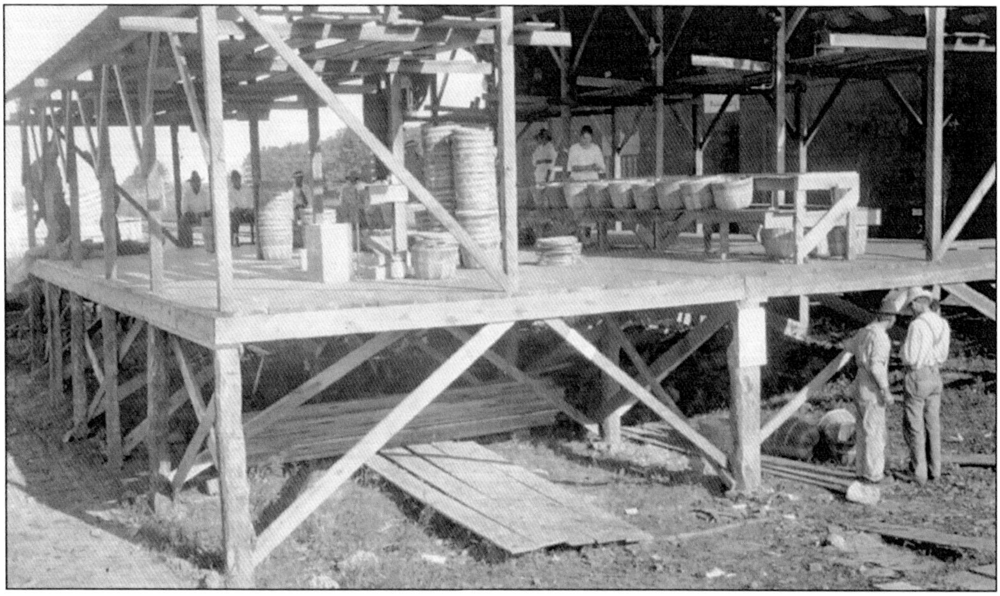

These photos show the packing shed at Chapin, on the railroad five miles southeast of West Plains. Apples and peaches right off the trees were brought to sheds like this one beside railroad spurs. There they were unloaded from farm wagons, repacked, and loaded onto railroad cars for immediate shipment to Memphis and Kansas City.

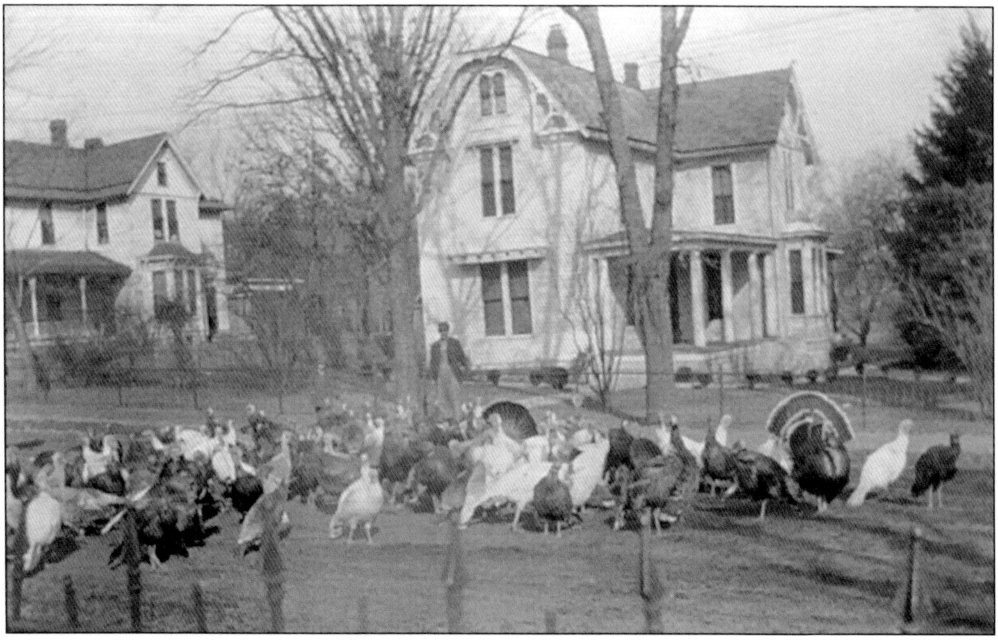

Herding turkeys was a common sight around 1900. This flock is headed down West Main toward the Square. Granvil Vaughn once told about helping his father drive a flock to town from Moody when he was seven years old. As they approached the Square, the "huge" Courthouse came into view. No words could explain the excitement he felt, driving those turkeys around the Square among those tall and imposing buildings.

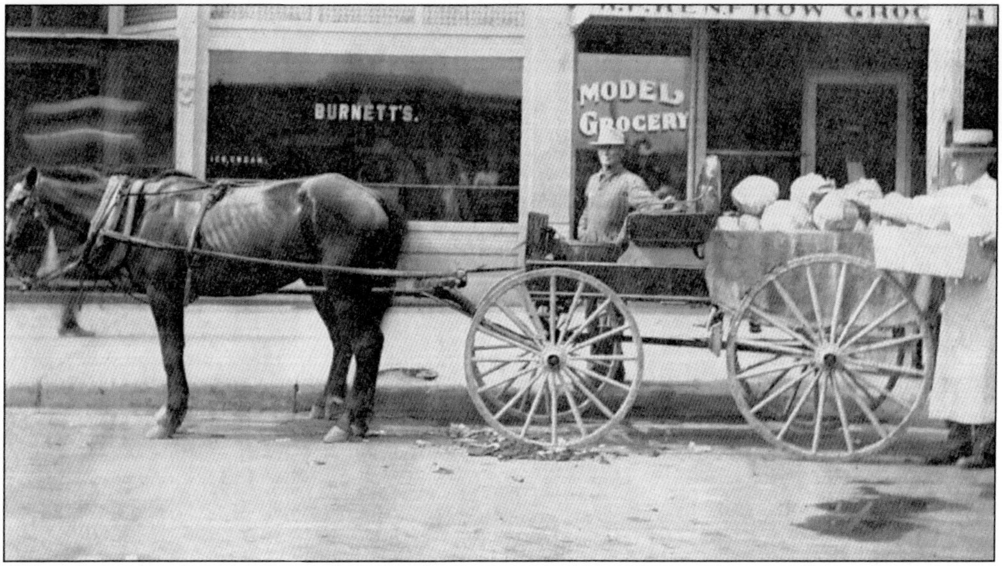

S.M. Mock of Bakersfield Route sold W.P. Renfrow 100 cabbages in 1919. The load of produce earned Mock $14.06. When Renfrow moved here in 1905 from Harrison, Arkansas, he bought this building with its grocery at 41 Court Square from W.A. Albright. Burnett's Ice Cream Parlor is to the left. Note that the Square had been paved in 1917; gone are the muddy streets.

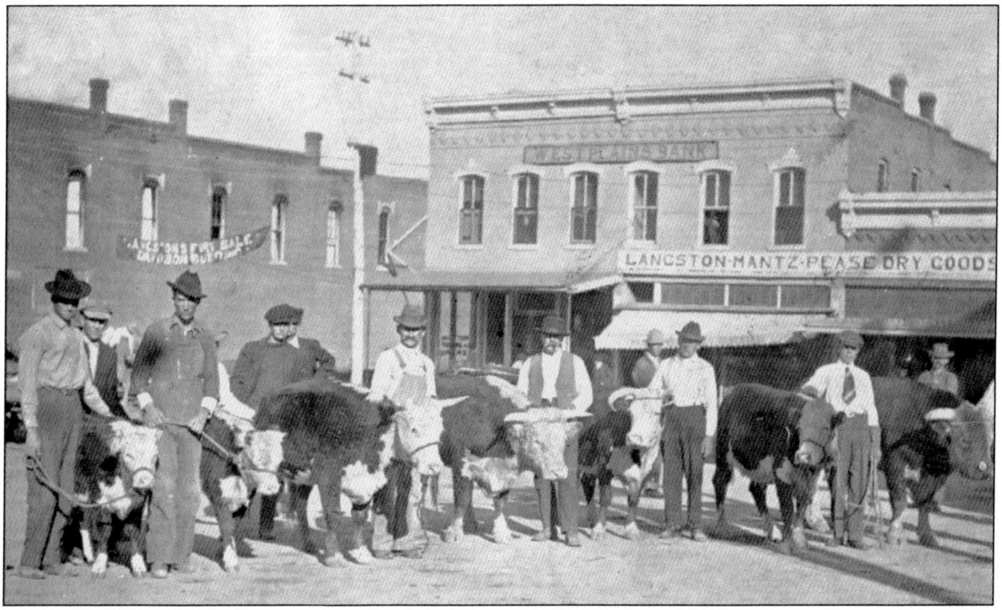

Cattle, unlike cotton or fruit, were moneymakers farmers learned to stick with. Today they are the number one agricultural product in the area. This scene from 1915 is probably related to an early county fair. County fairs were held at Davidson Park, now named Peoples Park. The county bought 10 acres from Joe and Henry Davidson for this park in 1906. Davidson Park replaced the old city park at the town spring.

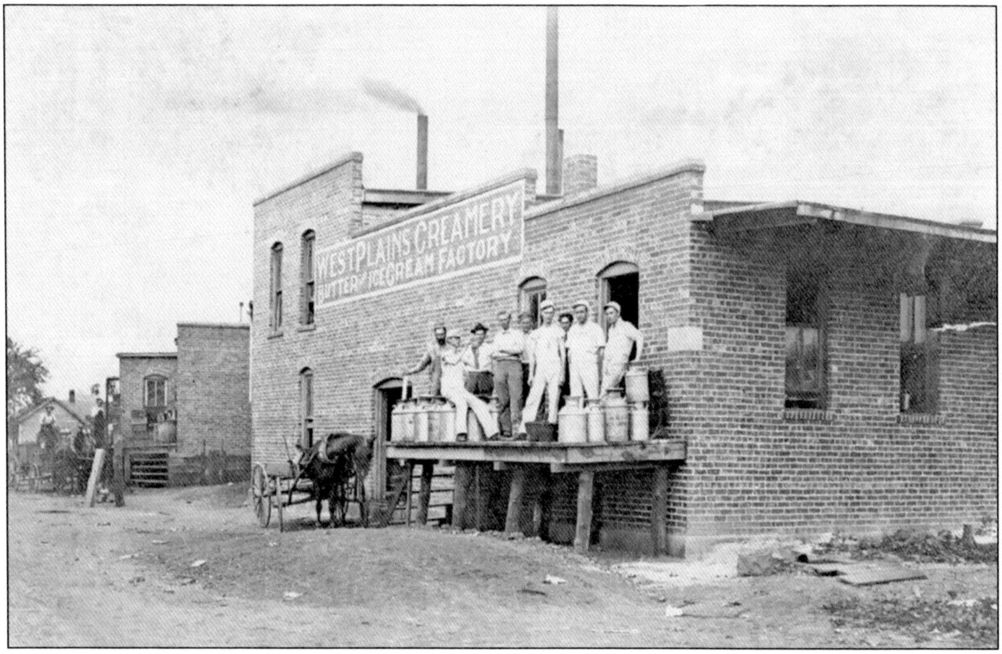

The Hammond Brothers built the West Plains Creamery on West Second Street in 1910 adjoining their ice plant. It was 50 feet by 80 feet and built of brick with concrete floors. When it opened in May, 5,000 people came to watch the machinery work and to receive free ice cream and soda pop. West Plains was the largest cream shipping station on the Frisco Railroad.

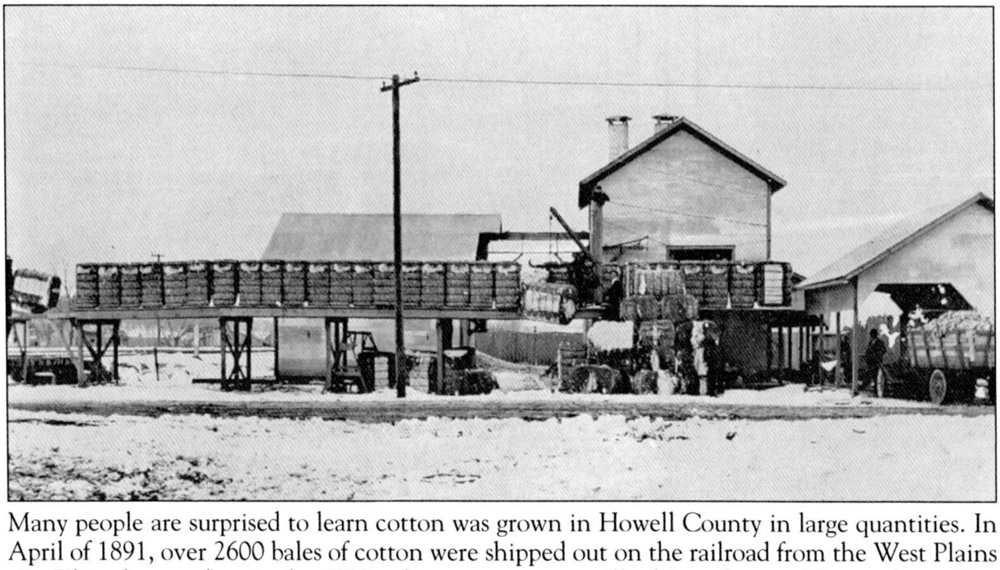

Many people are surprised to learn cotton was grown in Howell County in large quantities. In April of 1891, over 2600 bales of cotton were shipped out on the railroad from the West Plains gin. This photo, taken in the 1920s, shows cotton was still a big cash crop 30 years later. The gin was on Railroad Avenue, east of St. Louis Street.

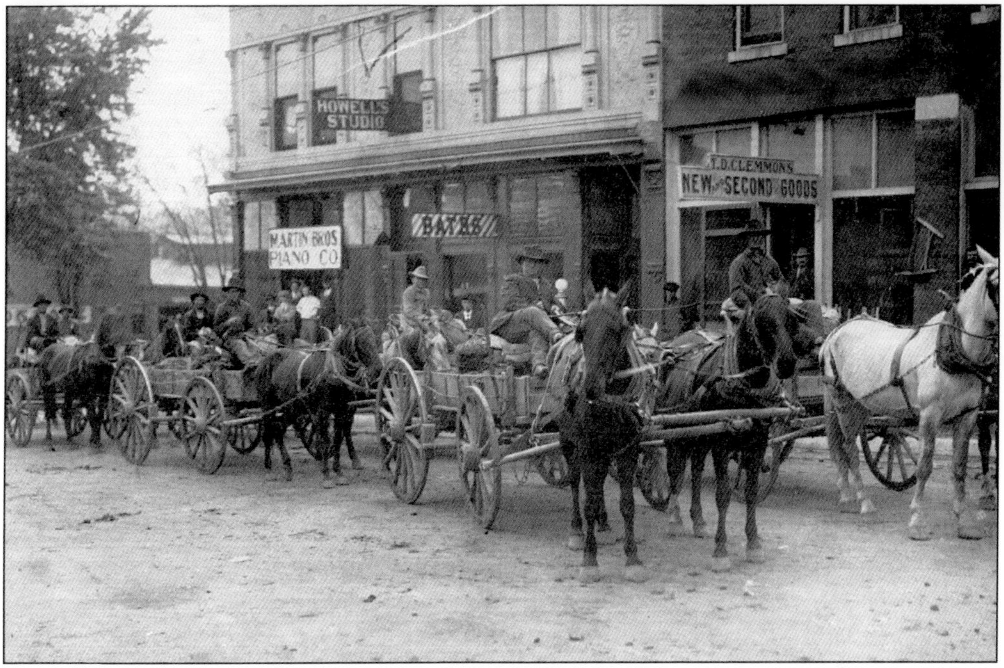

The Springfield Wagon was the basic vehicle of the farmer in Howell County. Here, four of them are lined up just off the Square on East Main in 1910. In the background, from left to right, are Spring Park, Walnut Street, the Halstead building with Howell's studio on the second floor, and the Bond Building, scene of the dance hall explosion in 1928.

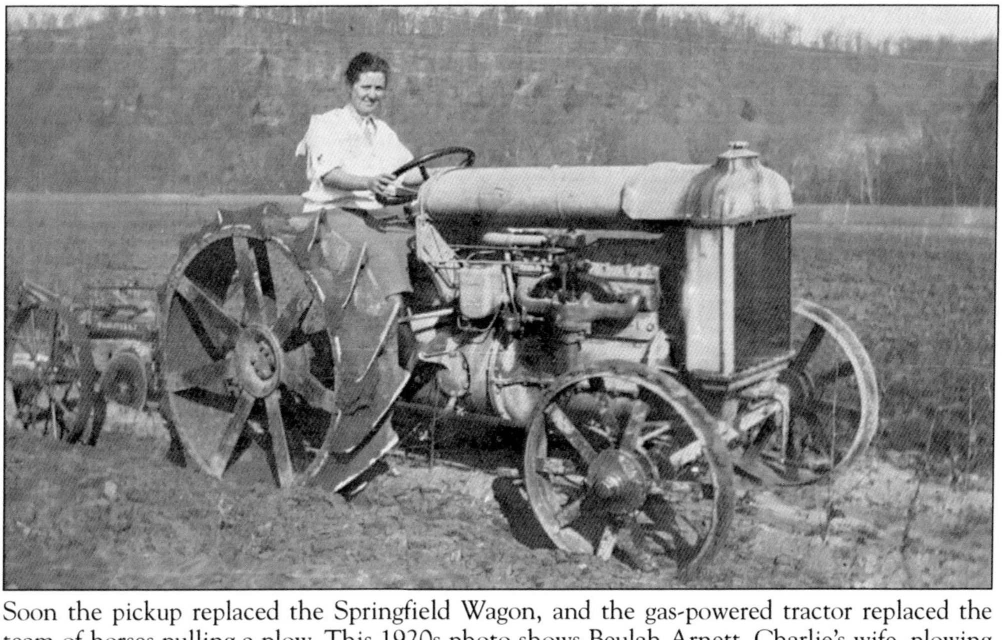

Soon the pickup replaced the Springfield Wagon, and the gas-powered tractor replaced the team of horses pulling a plow. This 1920s photo shows Beulah Arnett, Charlie's wife, plowing on their farm below Bakersfield on the Bennett Bayou. The switch from horsepower to gasoline engines changed things in town as much on the farm. Stables converted to garages, and hay dealers opened gas stations.

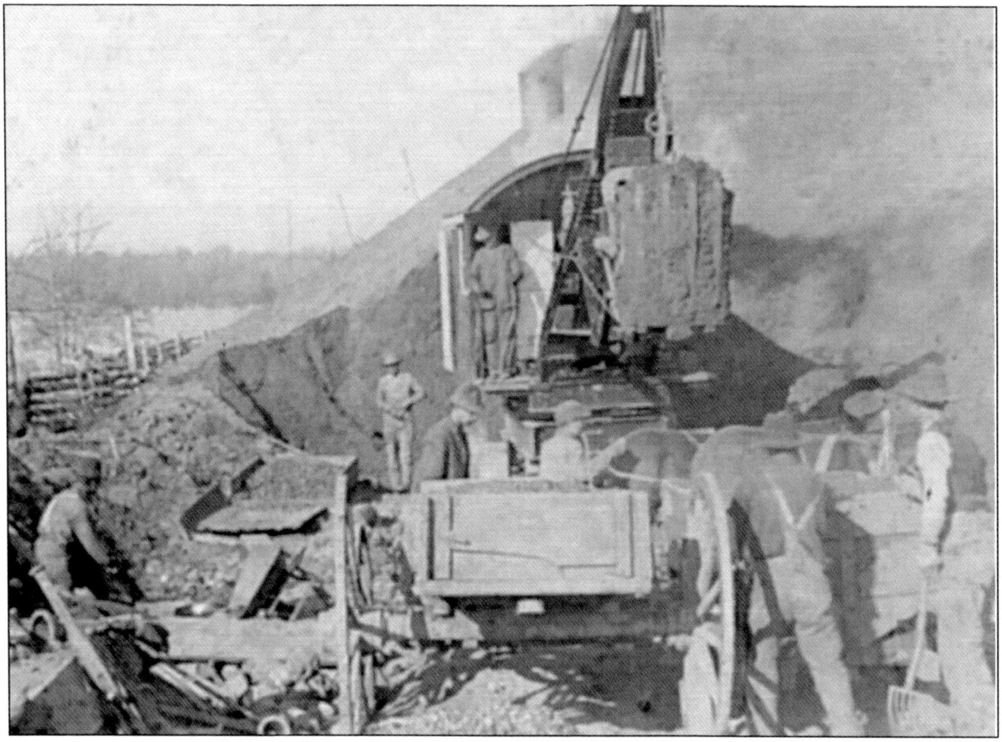

Only three stereo views are known to exist of West Plains. They are all of iron mines. Most of the ore mined in Howell County was dug by hand, hoisted out of the pit in large buckets by a steam derrick, and then moved to the railroad on a narrow gauge rail line in cars pulled by horses. This view shows an unidentified mine with a steam shovel.

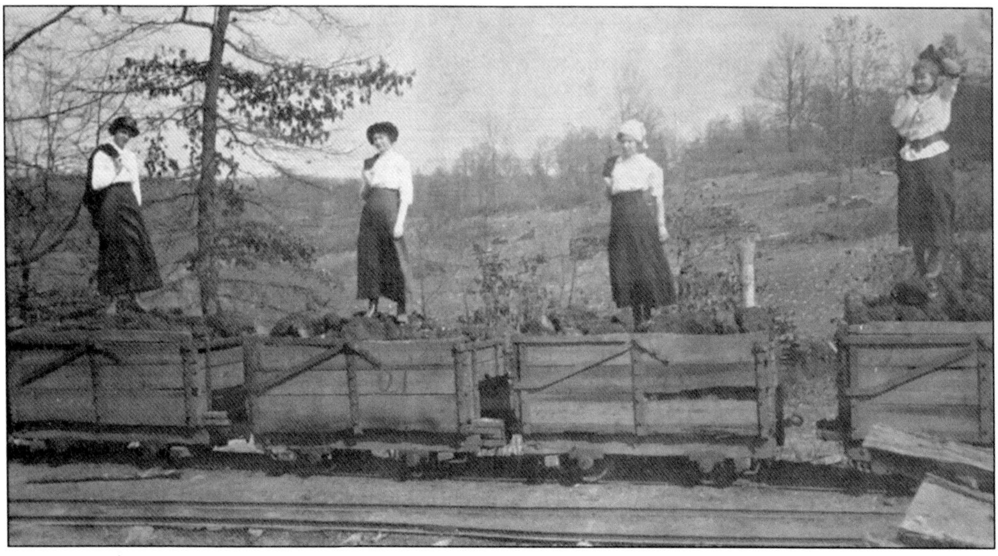

J.C. Kingsbury owned two iron ore mines southeast of West Plains in 1910. The Kingsbury Mine was near the County Highway PP-U.S. 63 Junction. The Carson Mine was on U.S. 63, west of Mustion Creek. Kingsbury's daughter, Olive, took this photo of her friends on an outing. They are standing on one of the narrow gauge ore cars used at his mines.

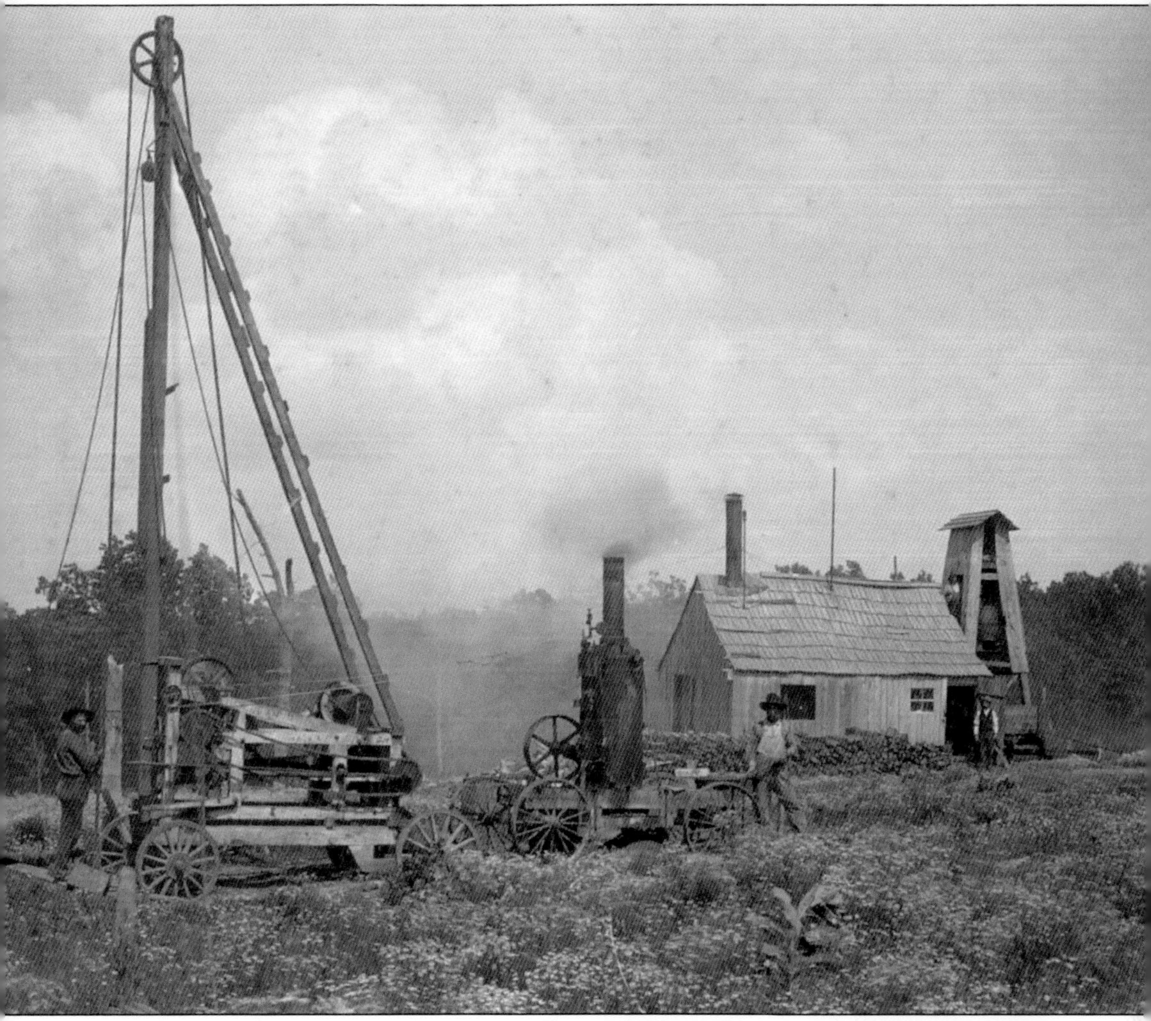

Zinc was also mined in the West Plains area. This is the Rex Mine near Caulfield. A steam-powered derrick is running to bring ore out of the pit. At the nearby Alice Mine, a similar steam engine exploded in 1934 killing one man and severely injuring others. For a short time at the turn of the century West Plains had a zinc oxide plant to process ore.

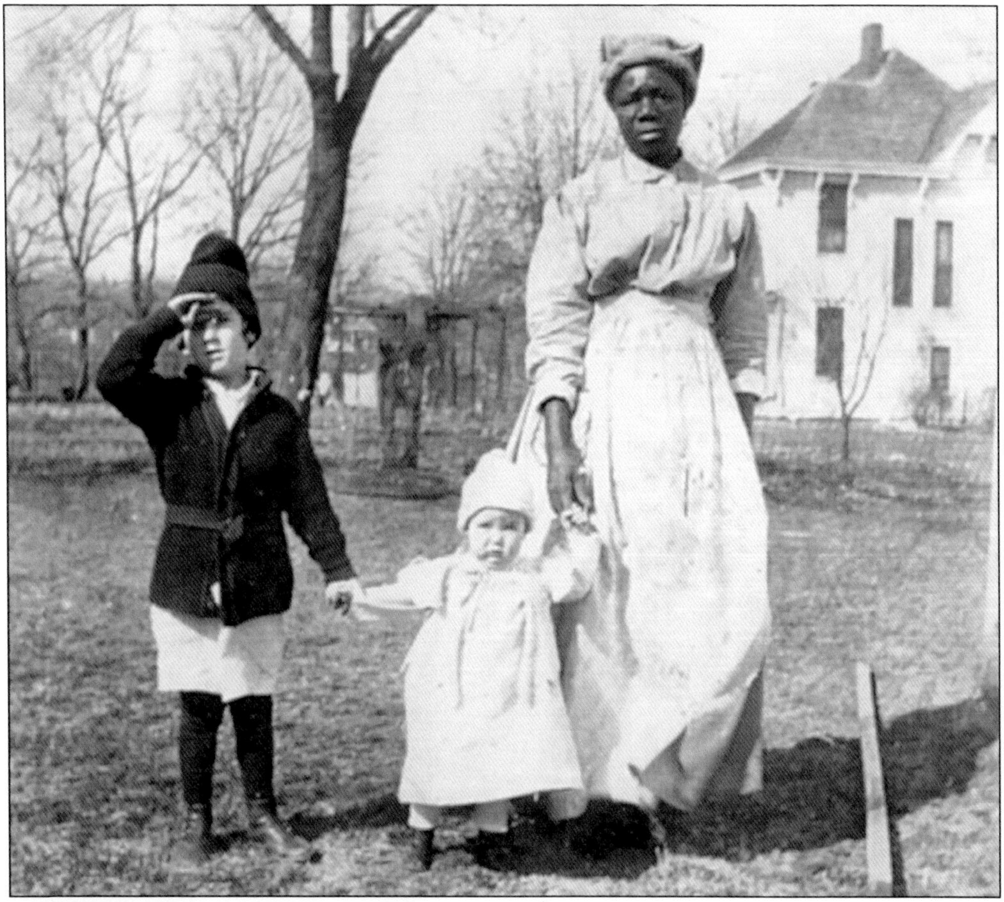

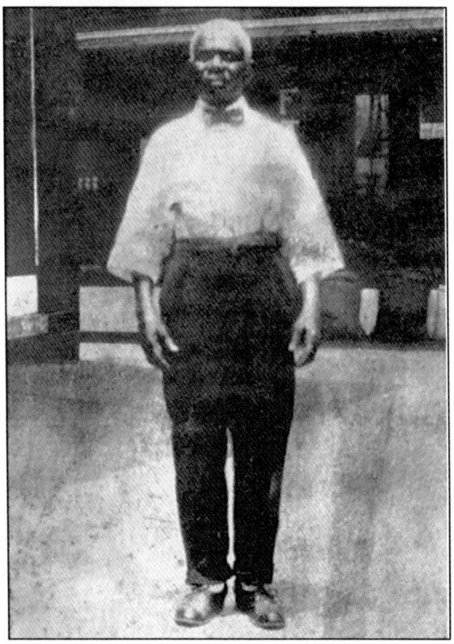

(*above*) Black women filled many domestic jobs in West Plains. Nancy Wade is shown here working as the nursemaid of Joe and Peggy Lou Aid. The history of blacks in West Plains is a long and interesting one. The Howell family, our county's first settlers, brought slaves with them. Black families in West Plains lived in "Illinois Town" on the hill north of the Depot (Chapter Six).

(*left*) "Good Morning Missy, the fire's out, the kindling's damp and a good man is hard to find," was the favorite saying of Pony Thomas. He worked at the Clark Barber Shop and as a janitor at the West Plains Bank and other businesses. His wife, Liza, was a maid and cook at Dr. Hogan's home, Parkview, on Broadway. Discrimination against blacks is evident in newspaper stories and other accounts of the time.

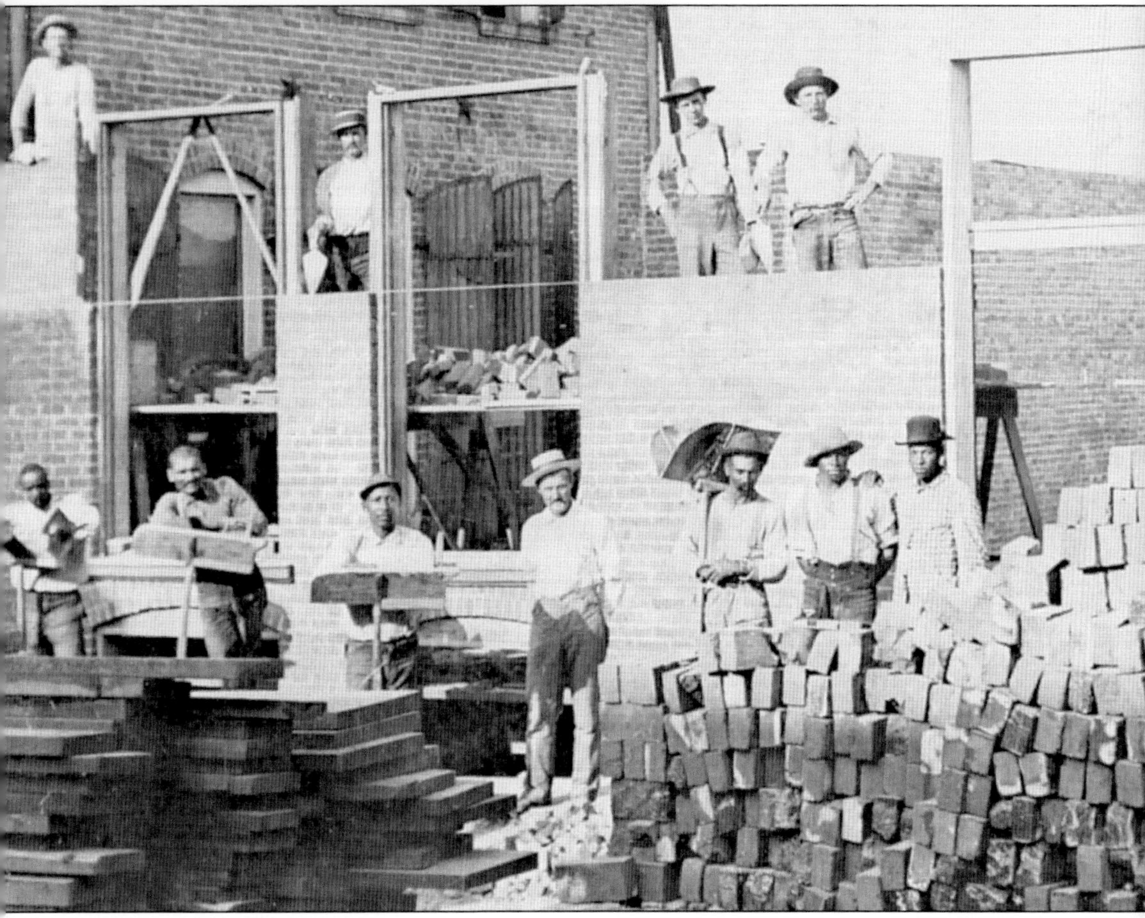

Shown here are black men working as hod carriers during construction of the Aid Building in 1914. In 1883, Dr. Olden went to Oxford, Mississippi, and hired a group of black families to help clear land for his orchards. Several of them homesteaded land near the Highway 14-63 junction and lived there for many years. The Sadie Brown Cemetery is the last sign of their presence.

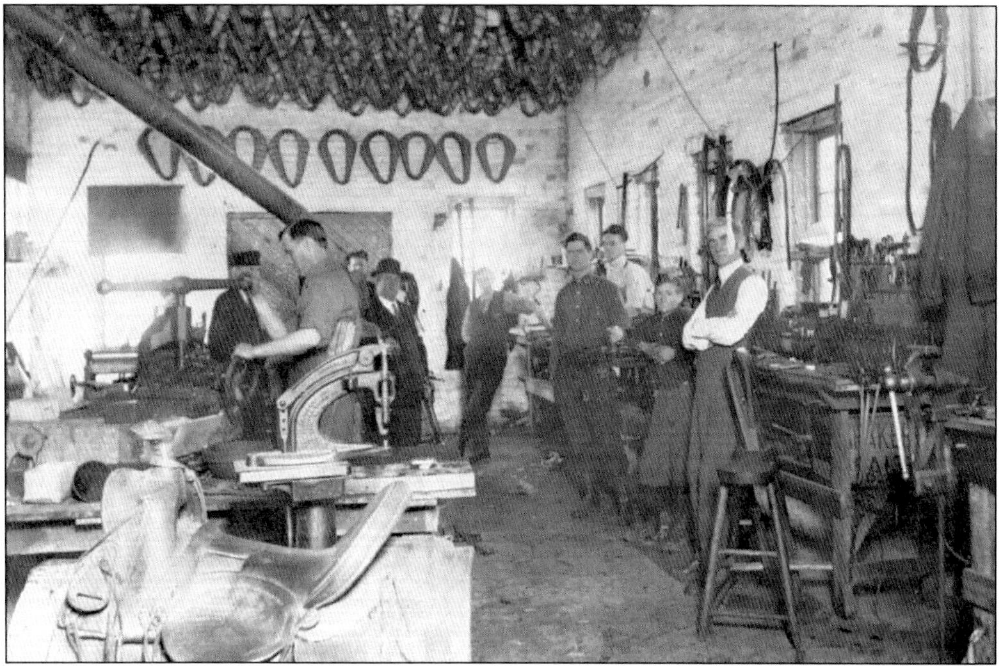

This is the workshop at the back of Ward's Leather Company, c. 1912. Leatherwork was big business before the arrival of the automobile. As demand for saddles and tack decreased, Ward's became well-known for high quality suitcases, valises, gun cases, and custom work. This building is standing today on the west side of Washington, the second door north of Cleveland. Ward's later moved to the west side of the Square.

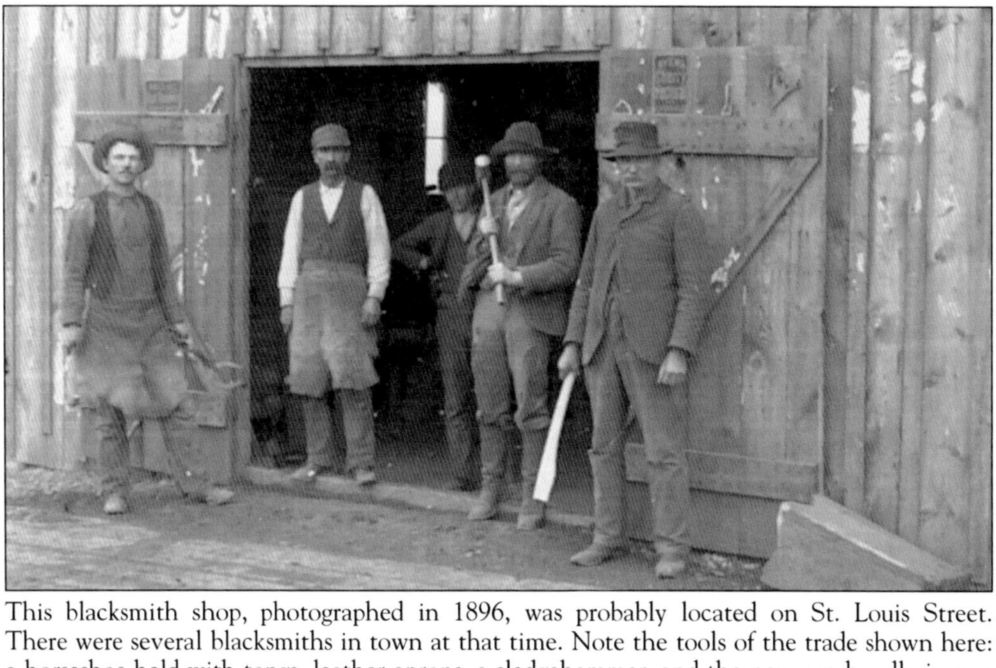

This blacksmith shop, photographed in 1896, was probably located on St. Louis Street. There were several blacksmiths in town at that time. Note the tools of the trade shown here: a horseshoe held with tongs, leather aprons, a sledgehammer, and the new axe handle in one man's hand. Blacksmiths became welders and machinists in the 1930s.

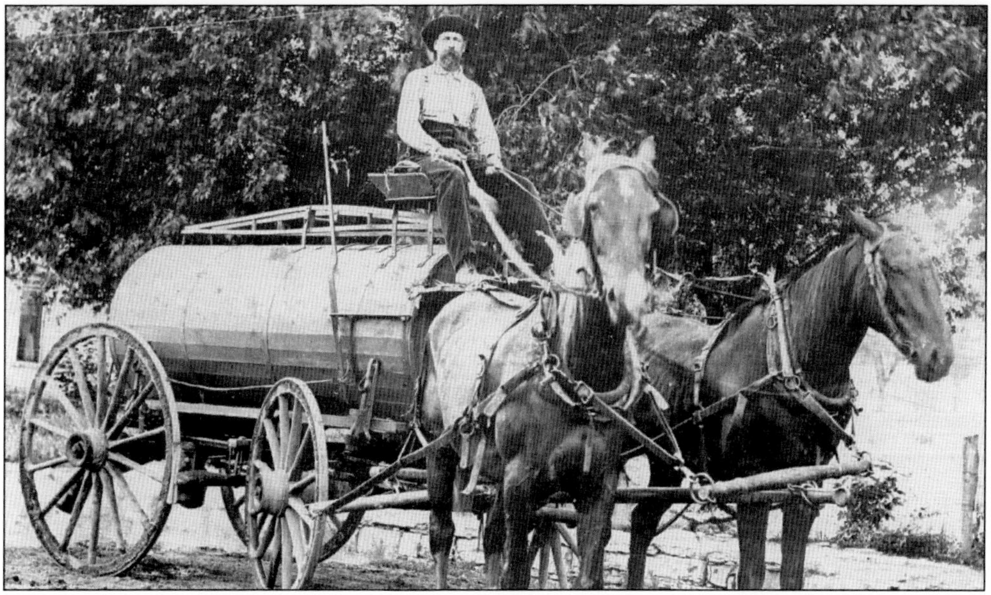

J.C. Barrett sits atop his water wagon pulled by his horses Frank and Bert. Before the Square was paved in 1917, it was a big chore to keep down dust in the summer. The city didn't have the money to pave the Square, so C.T. Aid talked all the businesses in his corner into paying to have their quarter paved. It was so popular that all the others quickly followed suit.

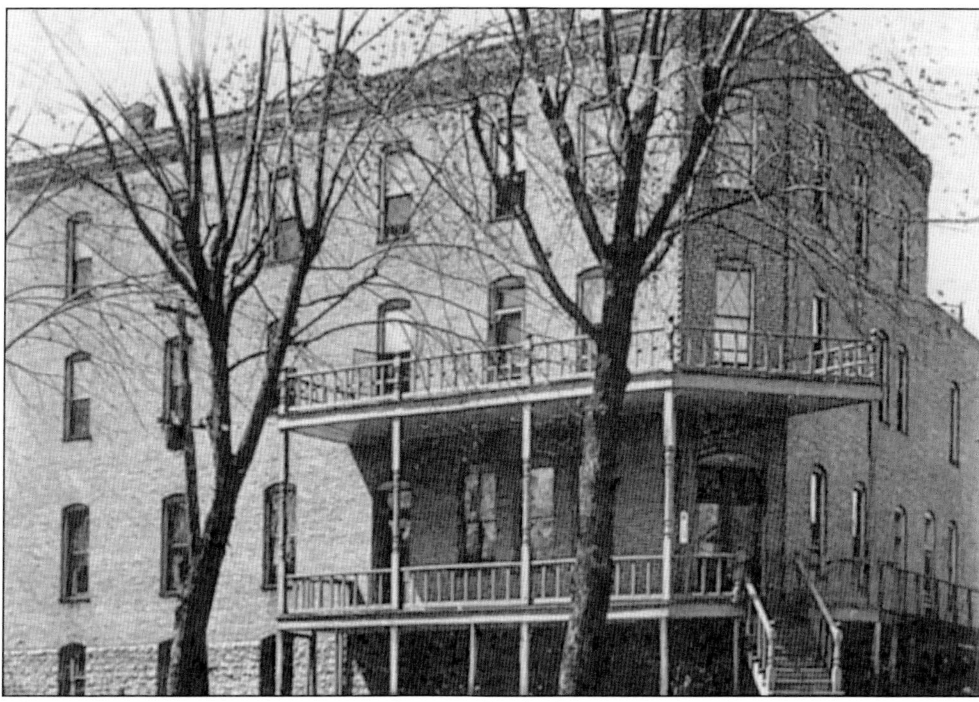

The largest hotel in West Plains was the Arcade, built in 1901 by Judge W.N. Evans. It was a three-story brick building with a large basement. It had 22 sleeping rooms, steam heat, electric lights, hot and cold water, and a signal system. Its most famous guest was "Jim the Wonder Dog" whose owner Sam Van Arsdale managed the Arcade when Jim was just a pup.

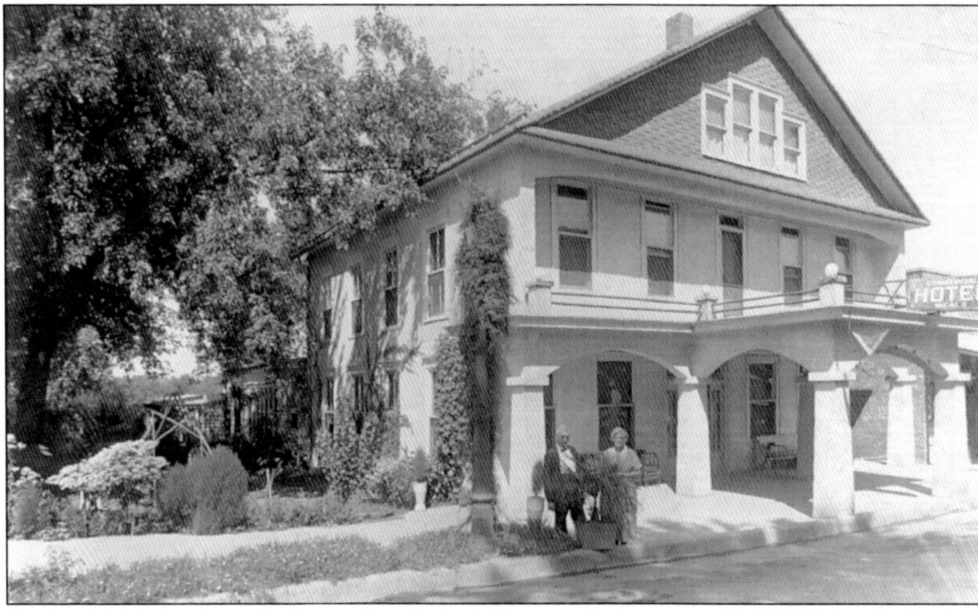

The railroad brought legions of "drummers" or salesmen to West Plains, carting a suitcase in one hand and a large leather-strapped catalog in the other. Many small hotels and rooming houses served these men and other visitors. This is the Commercial Hotel in 1924 with its proprietors Mr. and Mrs. Mark Summers. The Commercial was built around 1890 and remodeled several times; it was later renamed the Summers Hotel.

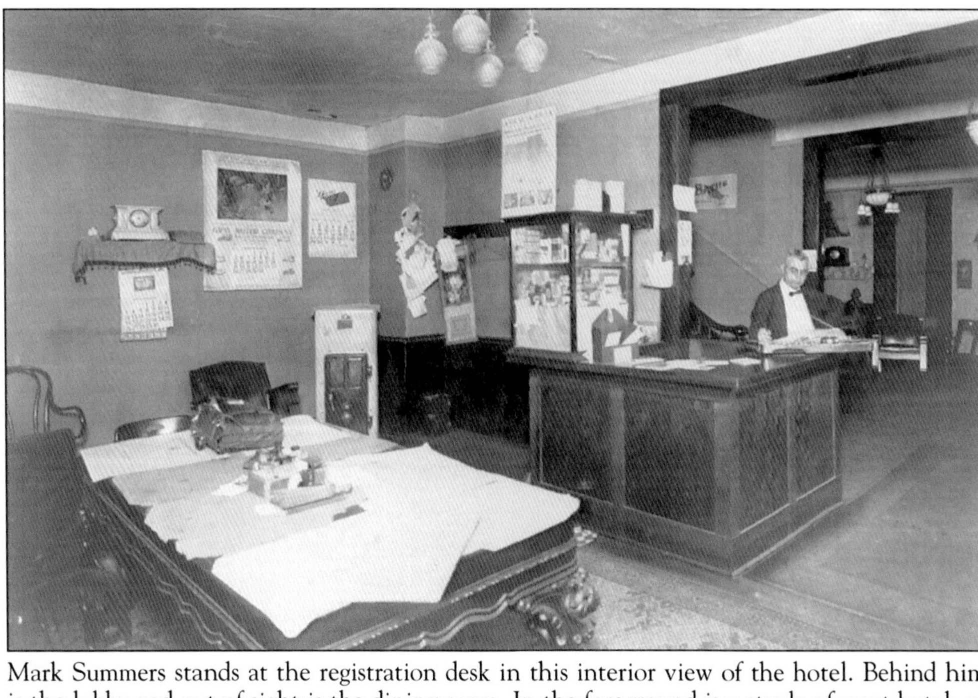

Mark Summers stands at the registration desk in this interior view of the hotel. Behind him is the lobby and out of sight is the dining room. In the foreground is a staple of most hotels of that time, the sample room with its large table and chairs. This gave salesmen a place to pitch their goods when it wasn't possible to visit their customer's place of business.

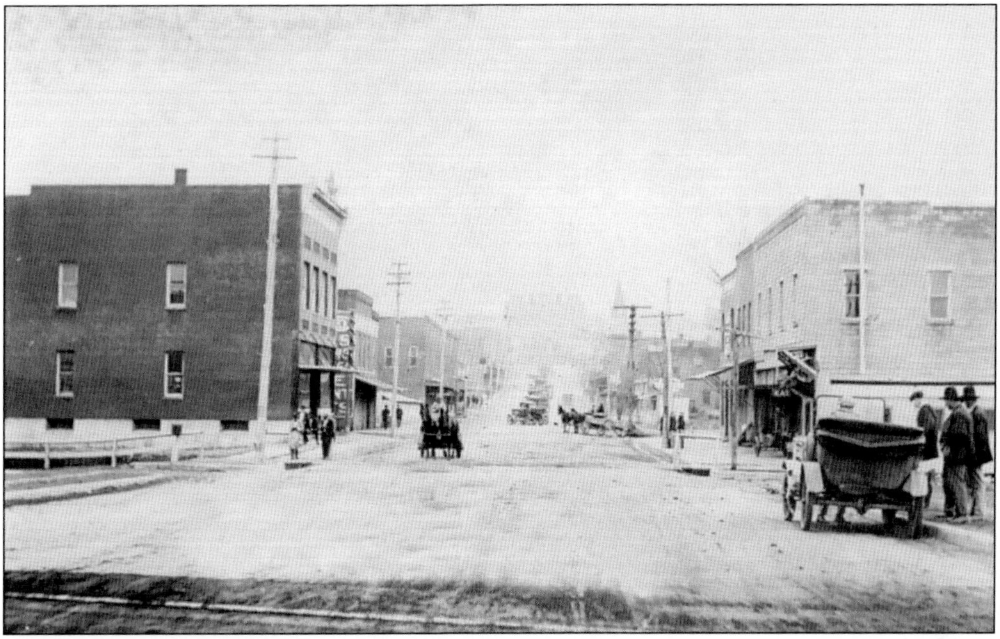

The photographer was standing on the railroad tracks when he captured this 1920 view looking south, up Washington Avenue. Note the cars parked up the middle of the street. The first building to the left is the Reed-Harlin's wholesale house. It was established in 1904 and soon grew to serve a territory up and down the railroad from Mansfield, Missouri, to Portia, Arkansas.

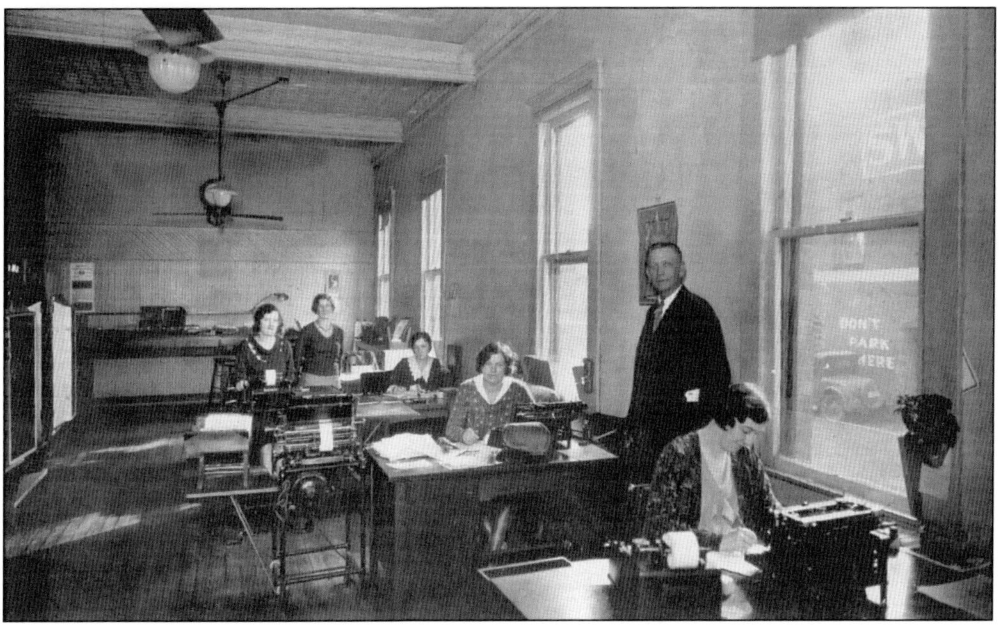

This is the bookkeeping department of Reed-Harlin in the late 1920s. Pictured from left to right are the following: unidentified, Lucille Arnett, Mildred VanWormer, Kate Riley, Frank Wood, and Phyllis Dressler. The Swanson Lumber Company, across the alley, is visible through the window. The Wood and Reed families, Gainesville merchants, started this company in partnership with the Harlins, who supplied the necessary capital.

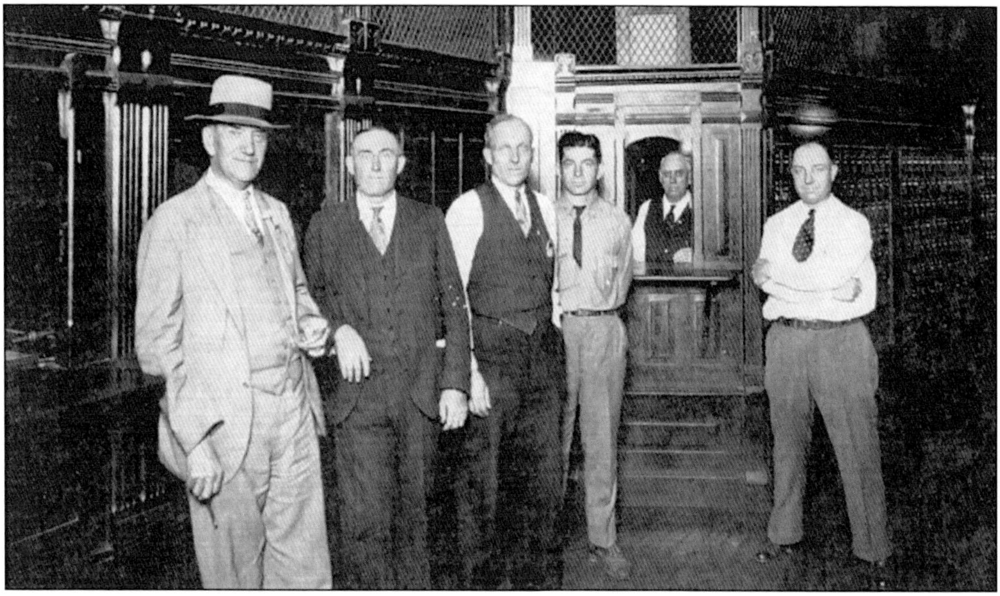

Employees pose in the post office on the first floor of the Catron Opera House. The post office was moved there from the east side of the Square in 1899. It was located there for over 30 years until the WPA constructed a new post office on East Main over the town spring. From left to right, they are: Postmaster Arch Hollenbeck; J.P. Morgan; Mont Widener; Lindsay Briscoe; A.J. Shelton; and Arthur West.

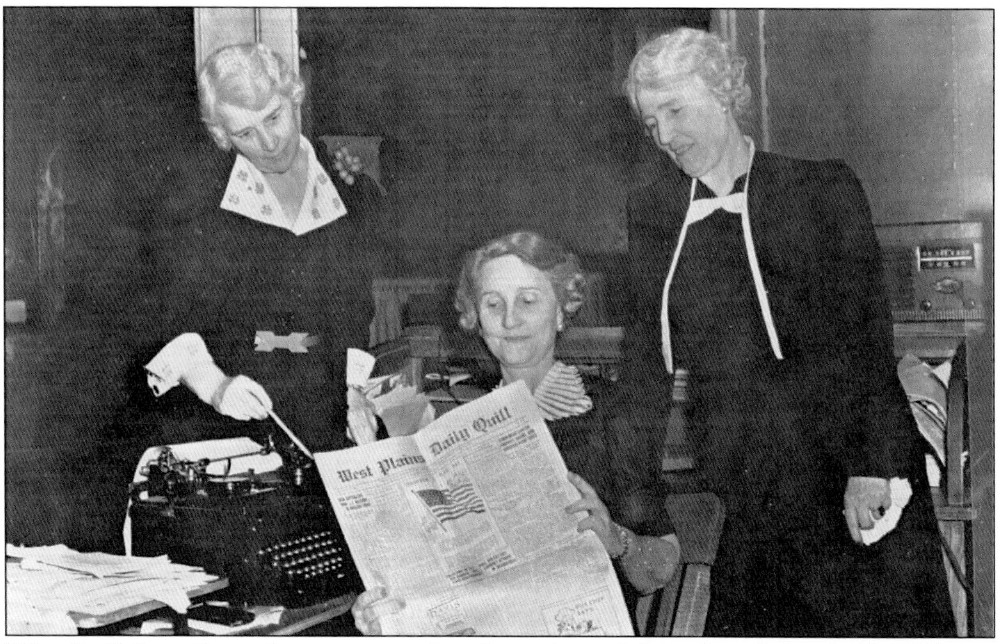

"The Quill Sisters" ran the newspaper that they inherited from their father, Mills Williams. Cleora, Ella, and Fritze gained national recognition for a business run completely by women. The *Daily Quill* was established in 1903 on Walnut Street opposite Spring Park. Later it moved upstairs in the Alsup, Risley, and Skillman block before locating in the Elledge Arcade. After that the business moved to the Zorn Building on South Main.

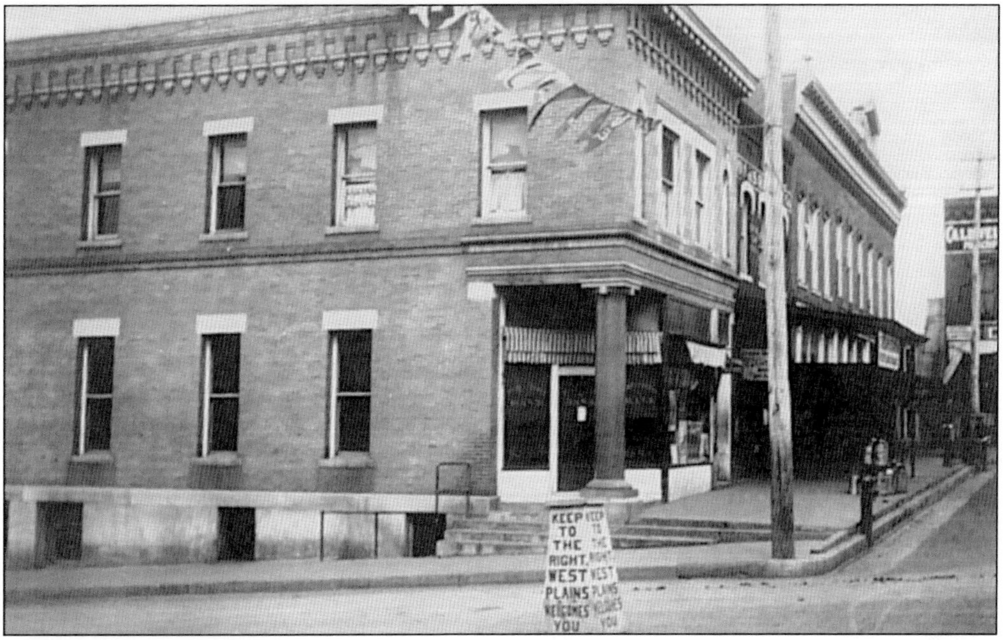

The Howell County Bank was the second bank in West Plains, receiving its charter in 1890. It faced the Square on the east side of Washington where the Wiles law office is located. J.L. Thomas, a former officer of the West Plains Bank, was its first president, D.W. Reese the vice president, and George H. Carter its cashier. When the building was remodeled in 1910 it acquired a distinctive marble column at its corner entrance.

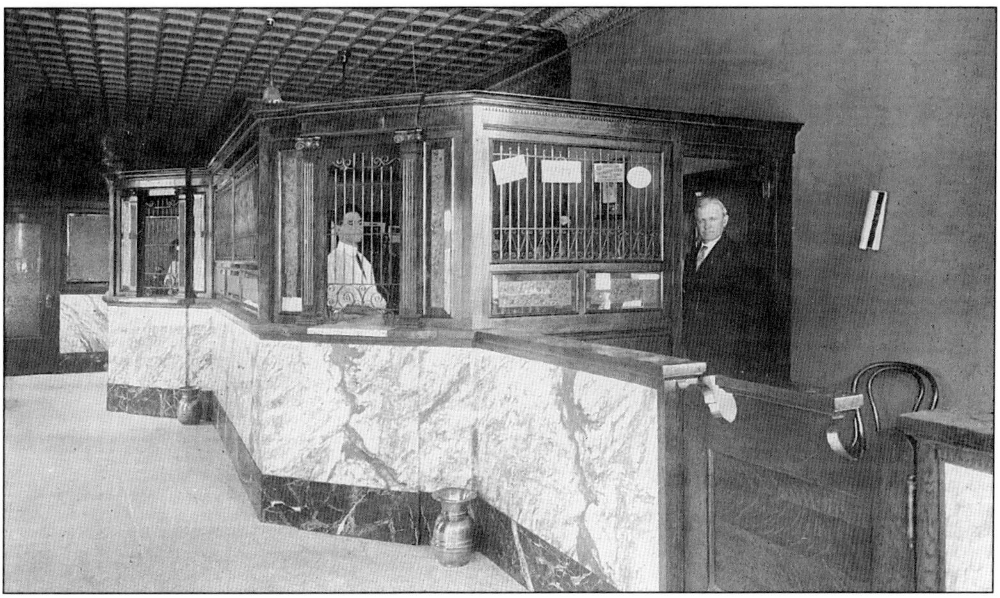

In 1908, the Harlin family from Gainesville bought a controlling interest in the Howell County Bank, and J.P. Harlin became its president. Tan Harlin, his brother, is seen at the right in this interior view of the bank. The Harlins maintained control of the Howell County Bank until 1922 when they merged its assets with those of the First National Bank, which they had recently acquired.

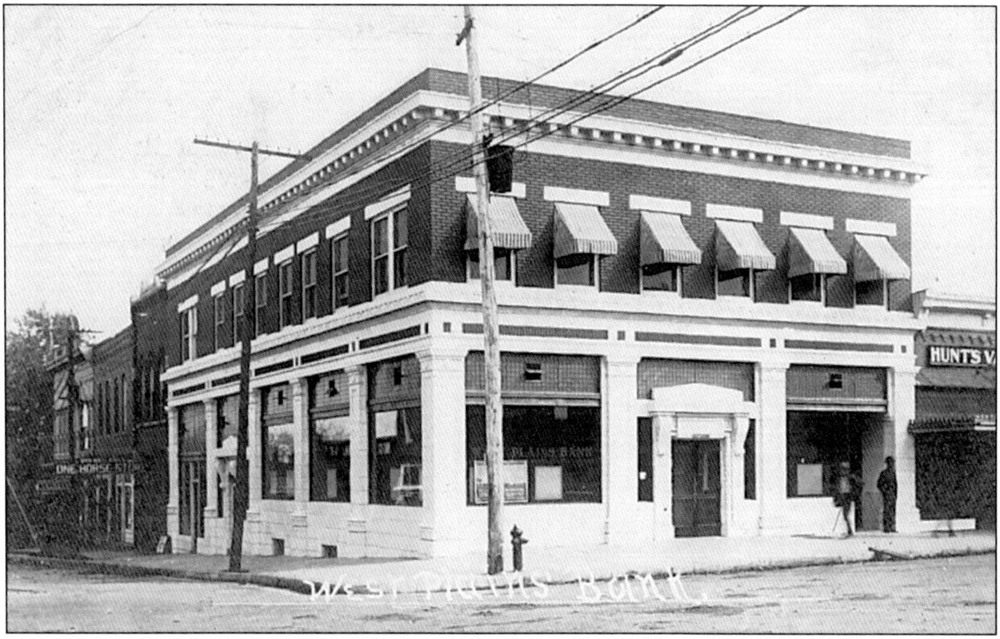

The third building the West Plains Bank built for its offices was constructed in 1916 on the site of its predecessor. The West Plains Bank occupied it for 62 years, from 1916 to 1978. During that year, its current building was constructed across East Main to the north. During the Dance Hall explosion in 1928, the back wall of the 1916 bank collapsed. You can see the replacement wall today at the back of the West Plains Savings and Loan.

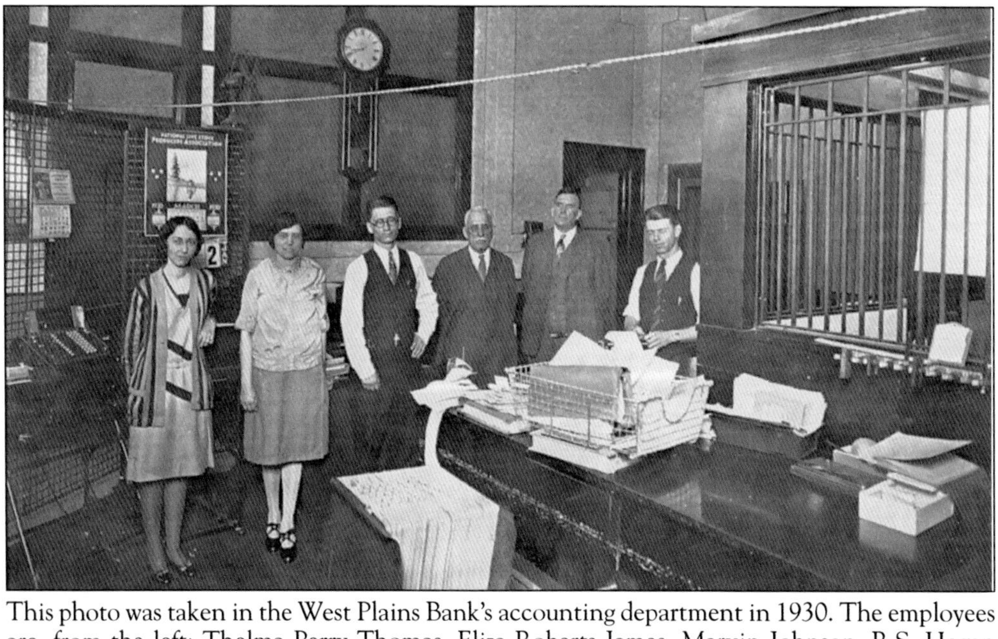

This photo was taken in the West Plains Bank's accounting department in 1930. The employees are, from the left: Thelma Perry Thomas, Eliza Roberts James, Marvin Johnson, R.S. Hogan (president), Earl Holt, and Langston Pease. Marvin Johnson worked at the bank for over 45 years. The Burroughs posting machine, to Thelma's left, was a standard piece of equipment in almost all businesses.

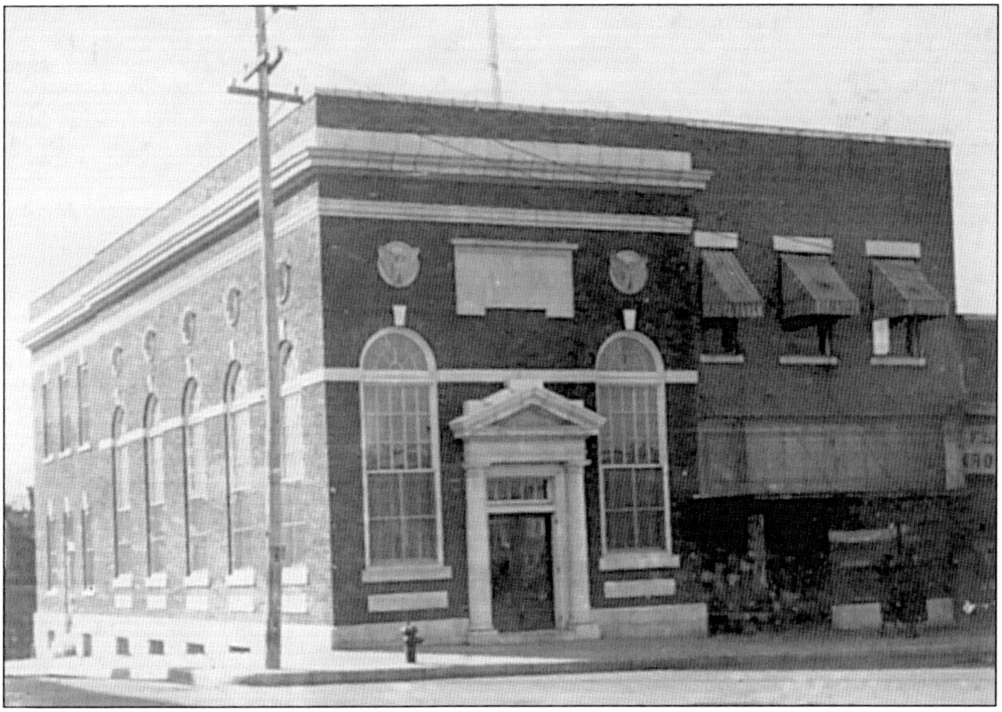

The First National Bank built this building in 1917. To the right is the Ward Leather Company. In 1952 the bank bought that building, doubling its size. The First National Bank was organized in 1895 with help from Michael Brand, a wealthy Chicago brewer who had founded nearby Brandsville. Brand was the bank's president until his death in 1897. Dr. H.T. Smith became its second president.

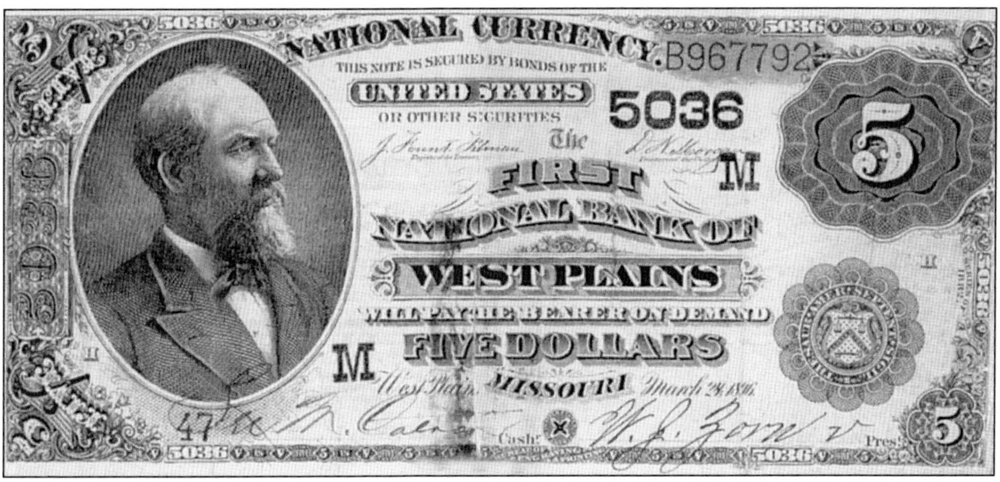

When the First National Bank was formed, it received a national charter, which allowed it to issue currency. Lee. M. Catron, as cashier, and W.J. Zorn, as vice president, signed this $5 National Bank Note issued in the late 1890s. In 1922, the Harlin family bought the controlling interest in First National, and James P. Harlin became president. The Harlins at that time owned or controlled six other area banks.

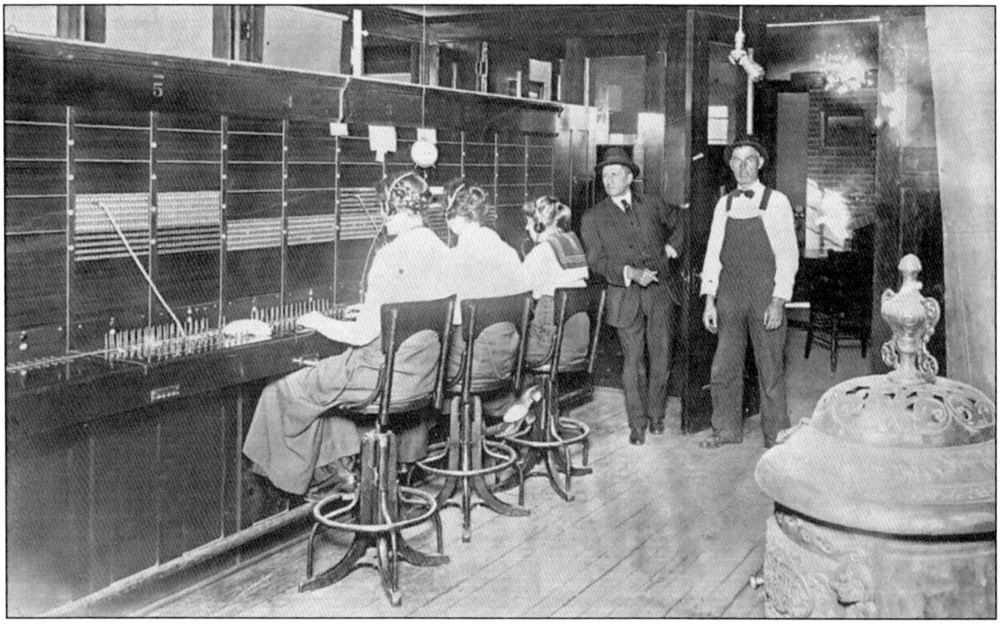

The switchboard of the West Plains Telephone Company is shown here in "Little Fruitville." That was the name of Col. Jay Torrey's town office immediately south of Spring Park. This switchboard was installed there after the old one was destroyed in the 1914 fire at Aid Hardware. The man in the suit is owner J.W. Boyer with lineman Fred Shoemaker. Marie Owens and Lorena Halstead are two of the operators.

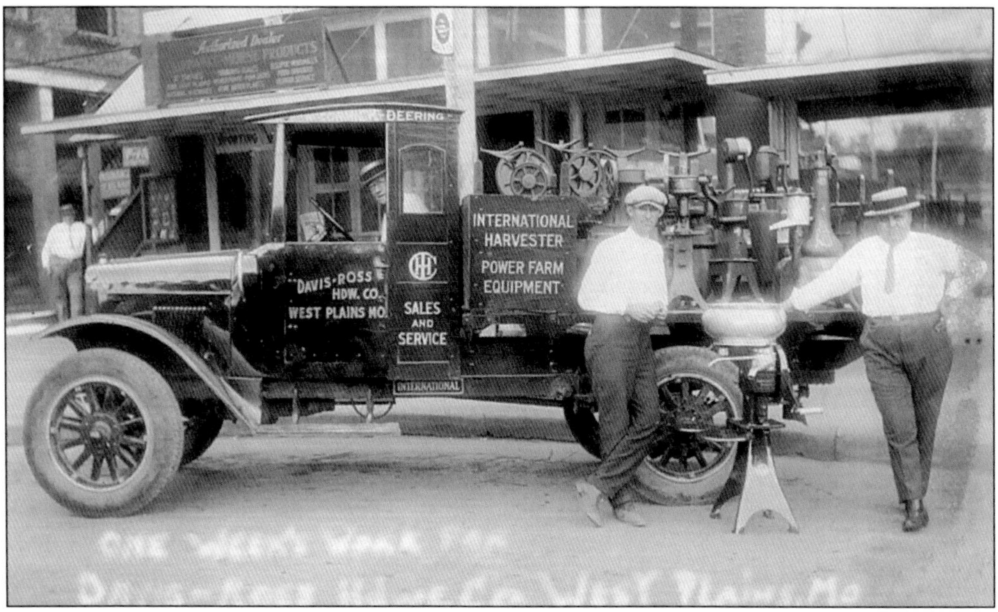

The Davis Ross Hardware Store's international delivery truck is loaded down with cream separators for delivery. The caption on the photo says "one week's work." This photo, c. 1920, shows their store in the background beside the entrance to the Catron Arcade. By 1915, there were arcades in all four corners of the Square, the Catron in the southwest, the Elledge northwest, the Evans southeast, and the Luster in the northeast.

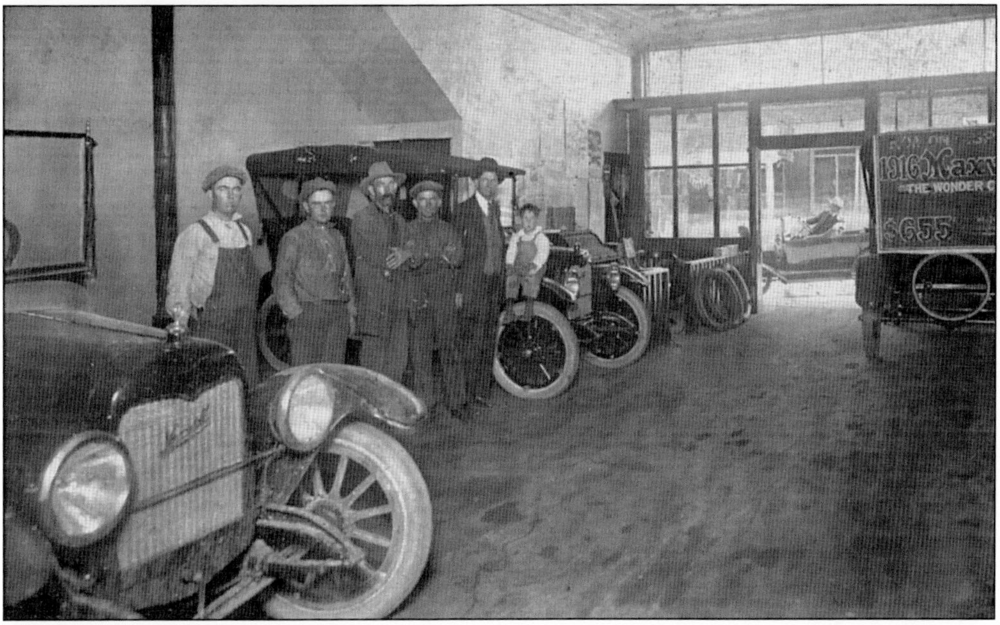

The Maxwell car dealership of Will McBride was located on Washington Avenue in 1916. The sign advertises the Maxwell as the "Wonder Car" and states you can purchase one for $655. Not long after this photo was taken, this building burned with a loss of five new Maxwells. McBride, in the coat and tie, also worked in the A.P. Clark barbershop.

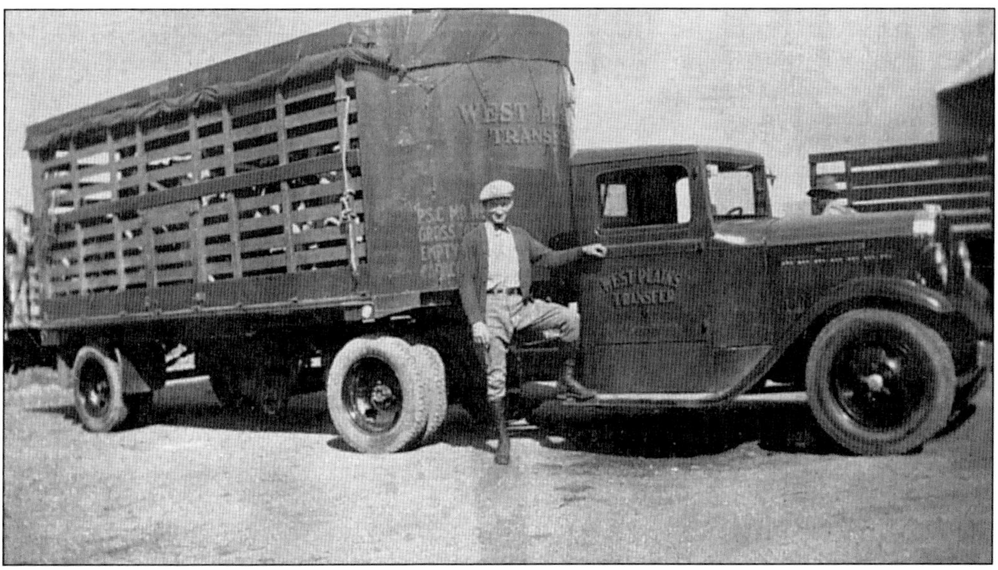

The West Plains Transfer and Storage Company was in business as early as 1909 with horse-drawn freight wagons. T.M. Renfrow was the manager. Their ad in the 1915 phone book said, "Pianos moved by the latest improved piano dollies." They also boarded horses and ran a feed barn. This trailer truck shows that by 1930 the company had changed with the times. Bill Jones is the driver for this load of cattle.

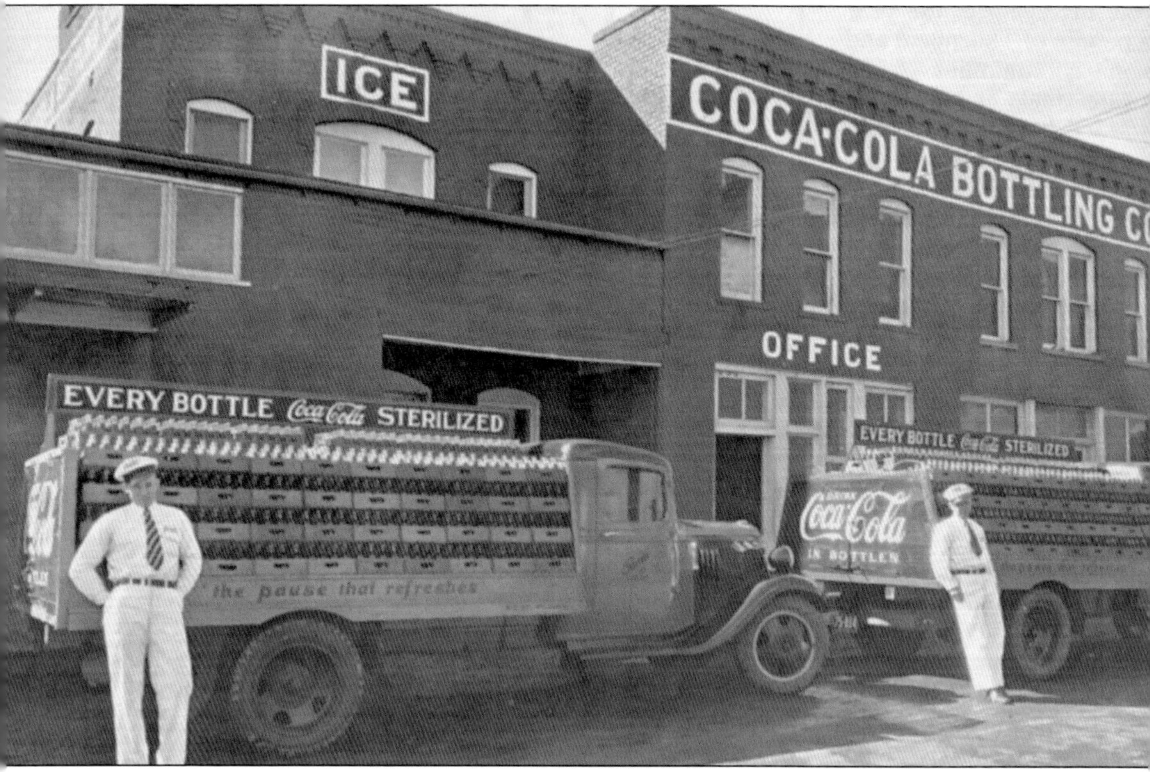

Dr. Samuel W. Paris converted the old Gulf Hotel, built around 1900, into the Coca-Cola Bottling plant and icehouse in the early 1920s. Dr. Paris moved here from Kentucky in 1920 and briefly had a Coke Plant in Willow Springs before moving it to West Plains. In 1939 he built a more modern plant for his operation on Broadway, three blocks east of the old plant. Sam's son Henry managed the new plant and expanded its capacity. Below are five early soda bottles used in West Plains. Note the 'Paris' bottle in the middle.

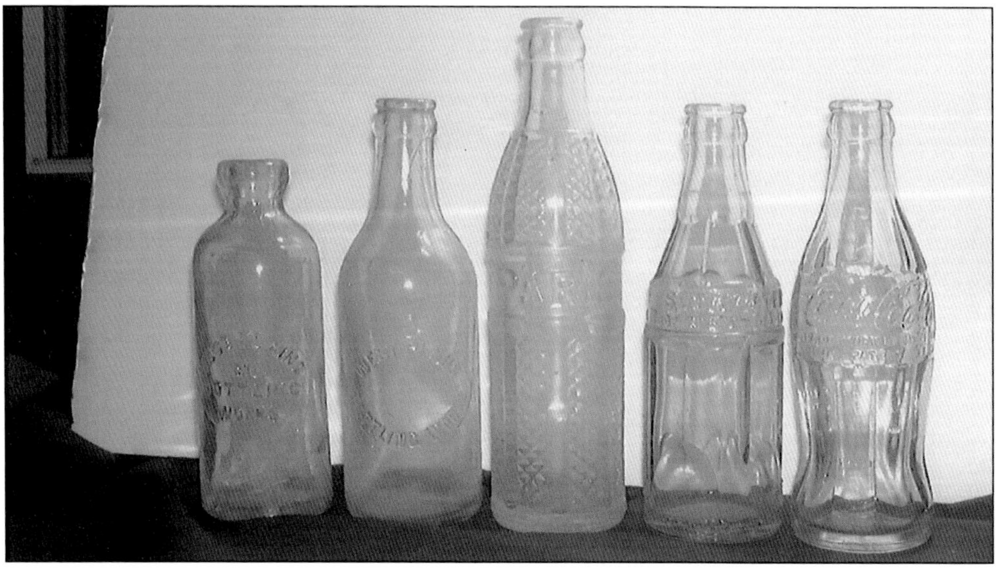

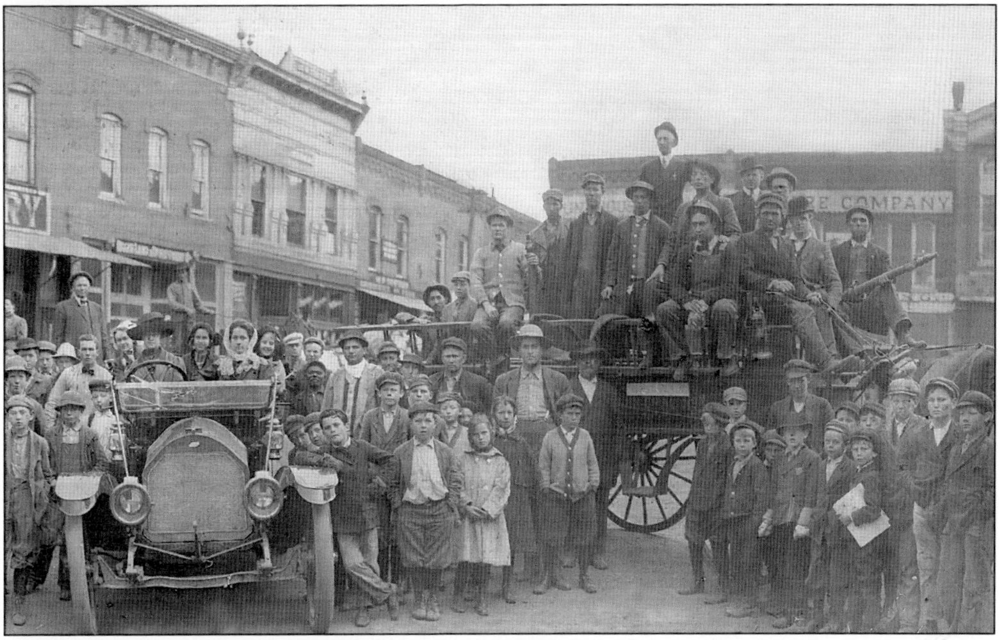

In 1896, A.C. Trowbridge built this horse drawn hook-and-ladder for the volunteer fire department. They reported that it threw a good stream of water, if water could be had nearby. There were no waterworks in West Plains until 1901, so wells were relied upon. Two years later, the fire department hung a locomotive wheel and a mallet on a tower beside the Courthouse to use as a fire alarm. Formerly, pistols had been fired as an alarm.

This is Fireman's Badge No. 5 from the first volunteer fire department in West Plains. It belonged to Joe Aid Sr. around 1905. In the photo above, Joe is sitting in the wagon with both legs hanging over the ladder. He is holding a kerosene fire lantern. Mayor J.P. Harlin is standing in back (his head is highest). Joe Martin, the fire chief, is seated on the wagon seat holding a fire nozzle.

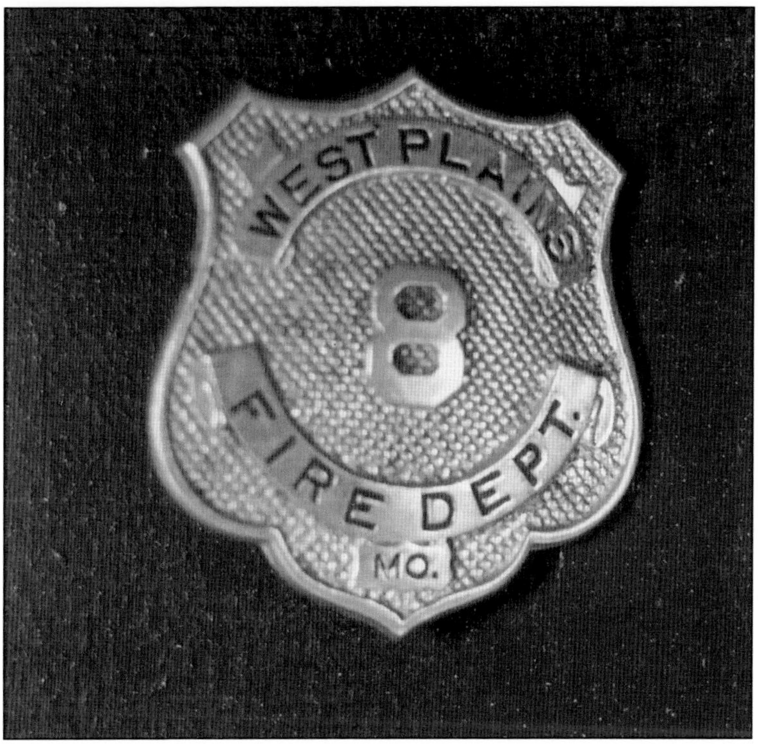

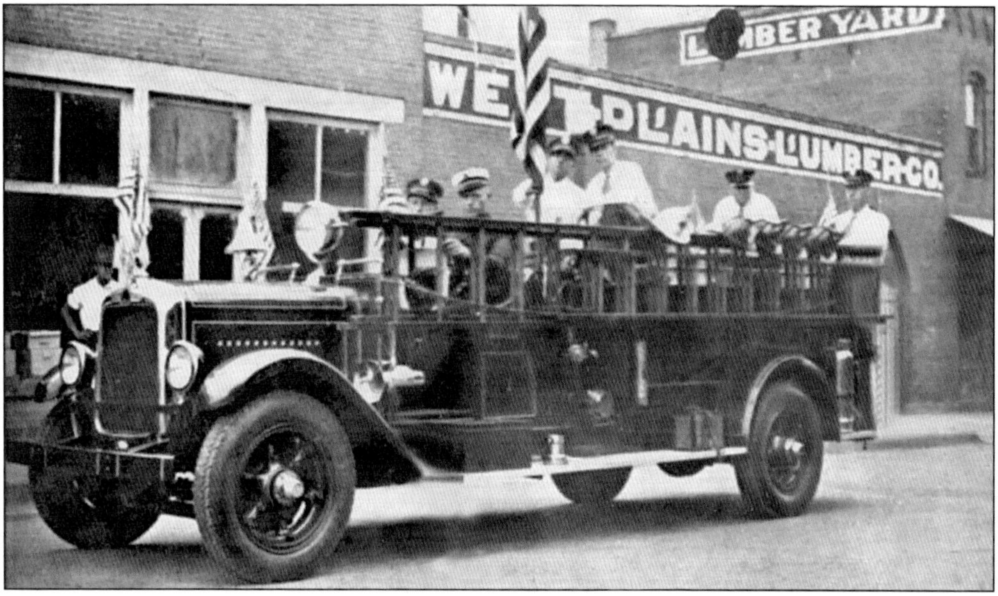

A new American La France fire truck was purchased for the fire department in 1928, a few weeks after the dance hall explosion. The first motorized fire truck was purchased before 1918 and proved to be inadequate dealing with that disaster. At the wheel of the new truck is Gus Jollif with Fire Chief Clifford Mustion seated beside him. They and the other firemen are ready to participate in the Fourth of July parade.

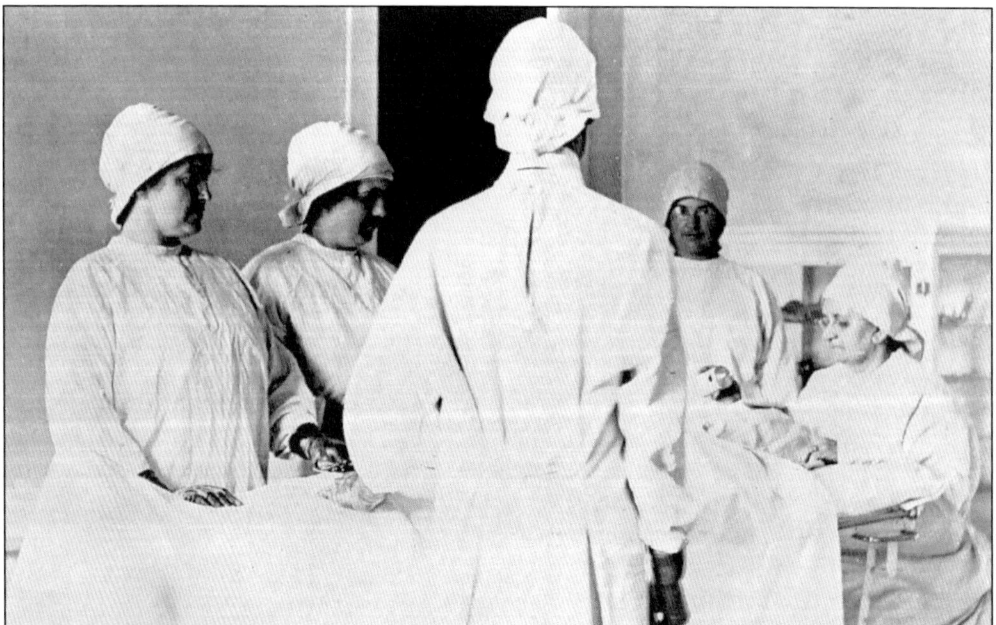

The Cottage Hospital was located at 812 Webster Street and managed by Mrs. Nan C. Torian. Is this photo, Mrs. Torian is seated administering ether to a patient before an operation. The Cottage Hospital was converted from a house into a "hospital" that specialized in handling births and minor surgery. Later, Mrs. Torian's daughter, Bess Palenske, ran a kindergarten in the same location.

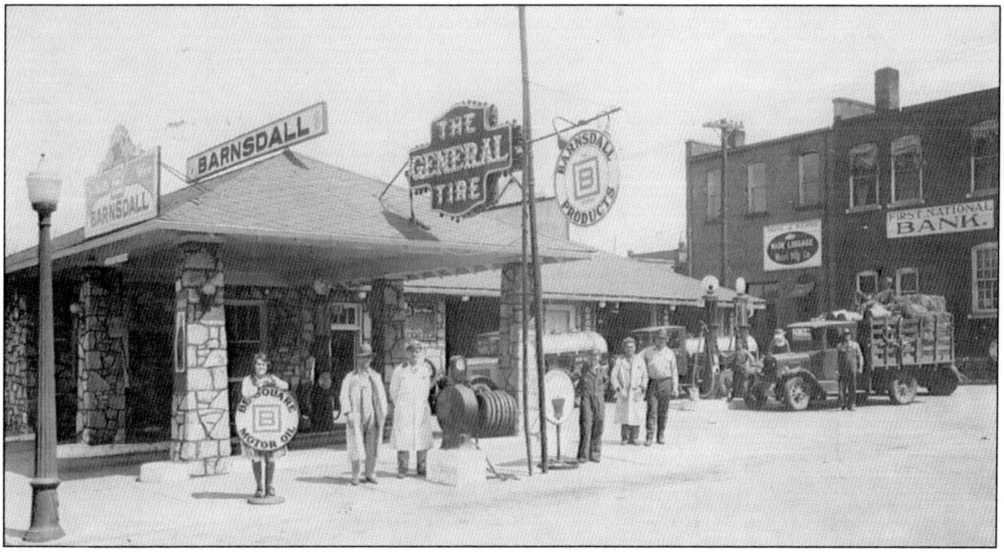

The Renfrow Service Station, seen here around 1930, featured a wide selection of Barnsdall products. It was located on West Main behind the First National Bank. Full-service gas stations became popular in the 1920s. Earlier, pumps had simply been placed in front of general stores. One of the first pumps in West Plains stood on the sidewalk in front of the Famous Grocery in the northwest corner of the Square.

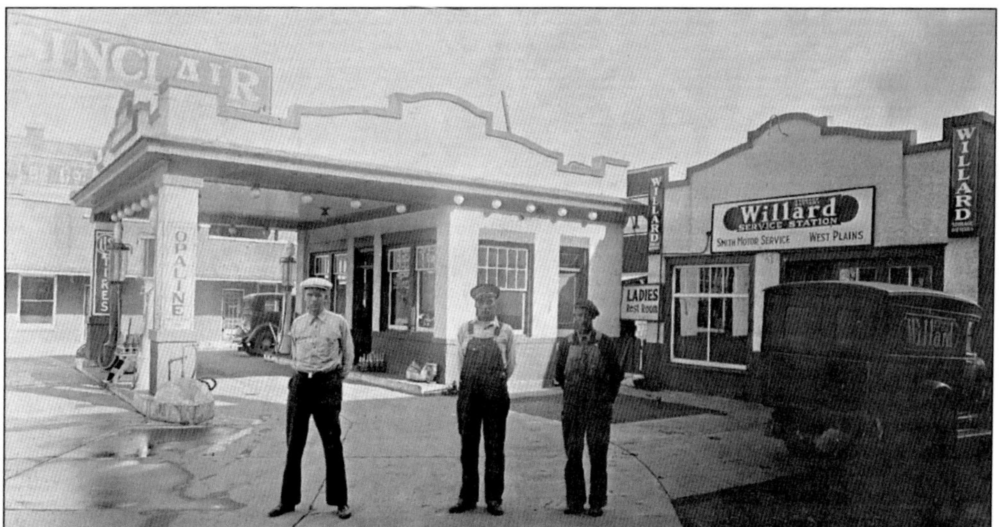

The Willard Sinclair Service Station was located on Washington Avenue in front of Swanson's Lumber Company. Smith Motor Service was part of the business. This photo, taken c. 1929, shows from the left: Willard Stephens, Kenneth Smith, and Lee Washington. The "Southwestern" architectural style was popular for Service Stations. There is a wire carrier of glass oil bottles next to the station's door.

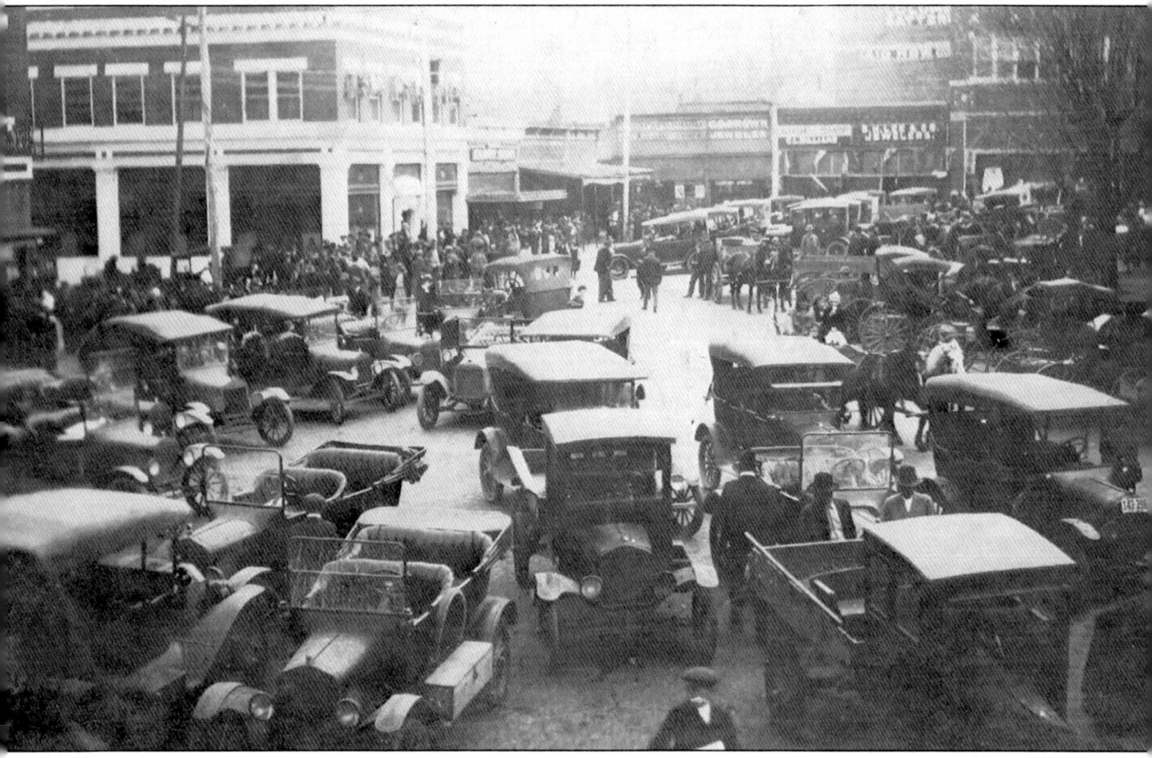

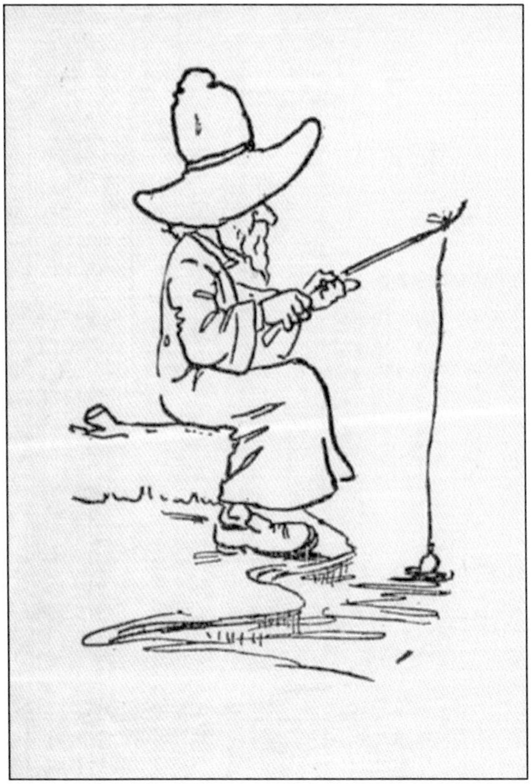

As the 1920s approached, the automobile began to replace the horse and buggy on the Square. Something big was up when this picture was taken. My best guess is that it is the last minute Christmas rush. We can see the new Langston Manse Pease store on the right (1916), the new West Plains Bank (1916), and the Square is paved (1919). Not being a car buff, I put the year at 1920–1921.

Three

West Plains at Play

From the first settlers, the people of West Plains have filled their spare time with all types of recreation. Hunting, fishing, and competitive sports were an important part of life a hundred years ago. In the era before radio and television, traveling shows and local entertainment regularly performed in the opera house and on local school stages. Plays, Chautauqua troupes, circuses, trick shooters, minstrel shows, vaudeville, and magic lantern illuminations all made their way to West Plains. Local groups were never at a loss for ways to provide entertainment, either. They held Tom Thumb weddings, tableaus, lavish banquets, musicals, and dances. They organized bands, fraternal lodges, societies, and the first local fairs. Amidst all that, they still found time to enjoy local scenic sites, rivers, mills, springs, and caves.

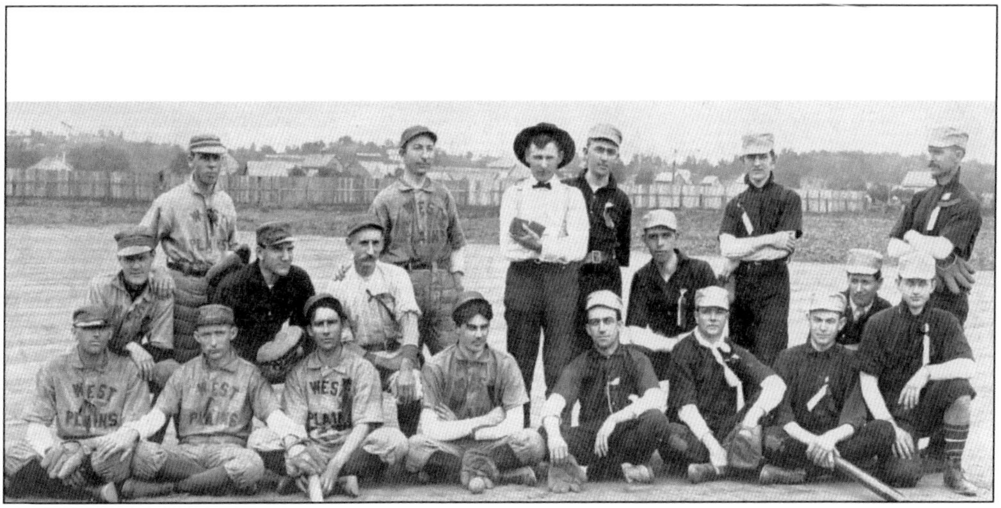

The Miami Club Baseball team of 1907 plays at the town ball field, named "Sportsman Park." The Miami Club was formed around 1903 as a men's recreational club. Pictured from left to right are: (front row) Granville Meredith, Fent Chapin, Will Langston, Ed Norton, Wayne Langston, Al Lindsay, Jim McGinty, and Tom Rhoads; (seated 2nd row) Orval Carter, A.T. Hollenbeck, C.T. Aid, and Ed Simon; (back row) Charles Mumford, Bill Zorn, Dewey Harlin umpire, Amiel Noe, Elmer Kellett, and A.B. Patterson.

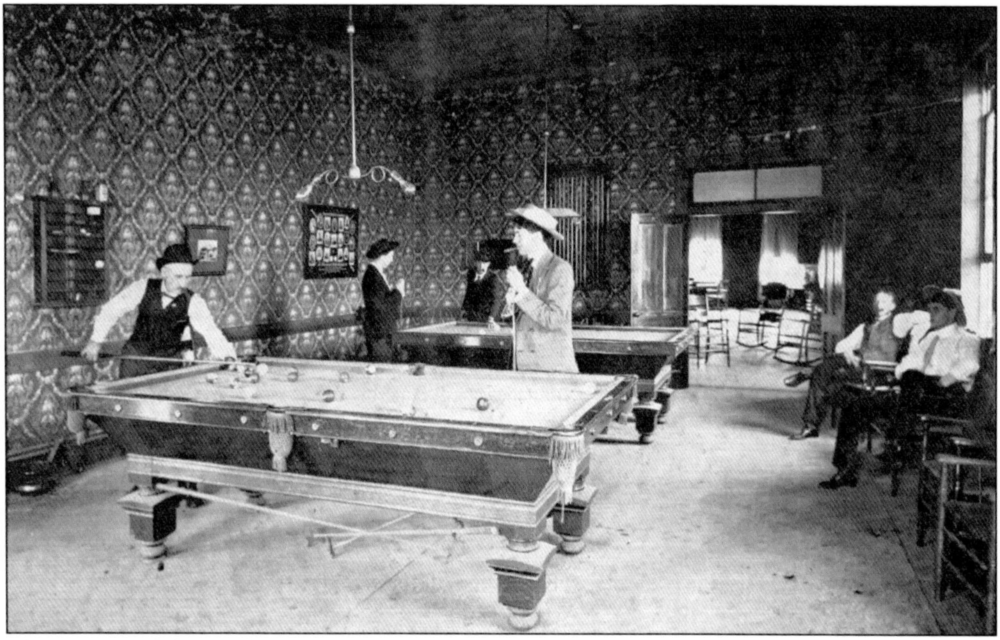

The Miami Club also had its own recreational rooms. They were a good place to relax after a hard day's work. Located on the second floor of the Halstead building on East Main (where Riverways Health Care is now), they contained billiard tables, relaxing chairs, rugs on the floors, and even a small library. The only person identified in this picture is C.T. Aid at the far left. The club disbanded around 1910.

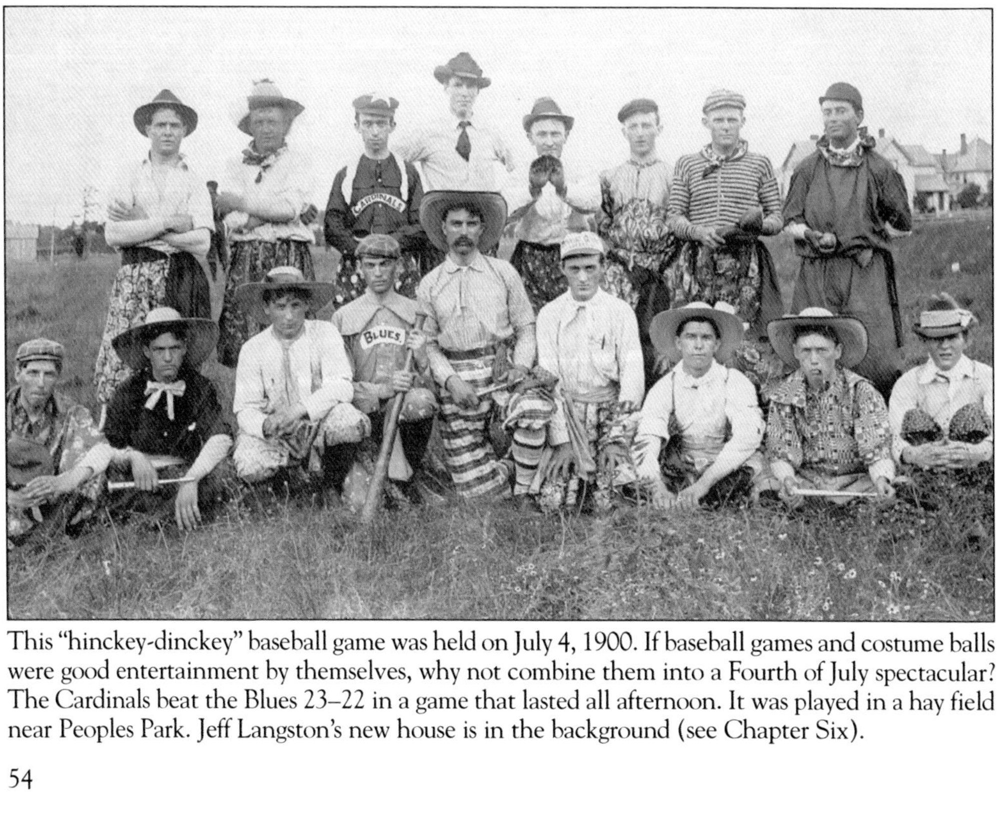

This "hinckey-dinckey" baseball game was held on July 4, 1900. If baseball games and costume balls were good entertainment by themselves, why not combine them into a Fourth of July spectacular? The Cardinals beat the Blues 23–22 in a game that lasted all afternoon. It was played in a hay field near Peoples Park. Jeff Langston's new house is in the background (see Chapter Six).

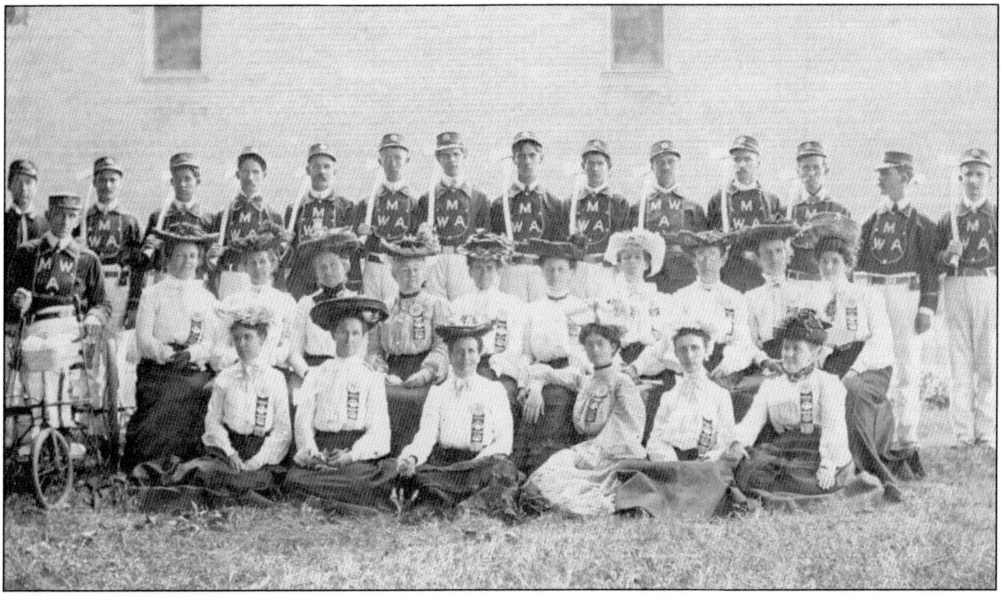

These men with axes slung over their shoulders are not out to fell a tree; they are Modern Woodmen of America. The MW of A was a fraternal organization that banded together not only for fellowship, but also as a mutual insurance group. This picture was taken at a joint meeting with the ladies auxiliary on June 12, 1904, in Spring Park. Eighteen other lodges and societies were listed in the 1912 city directory.

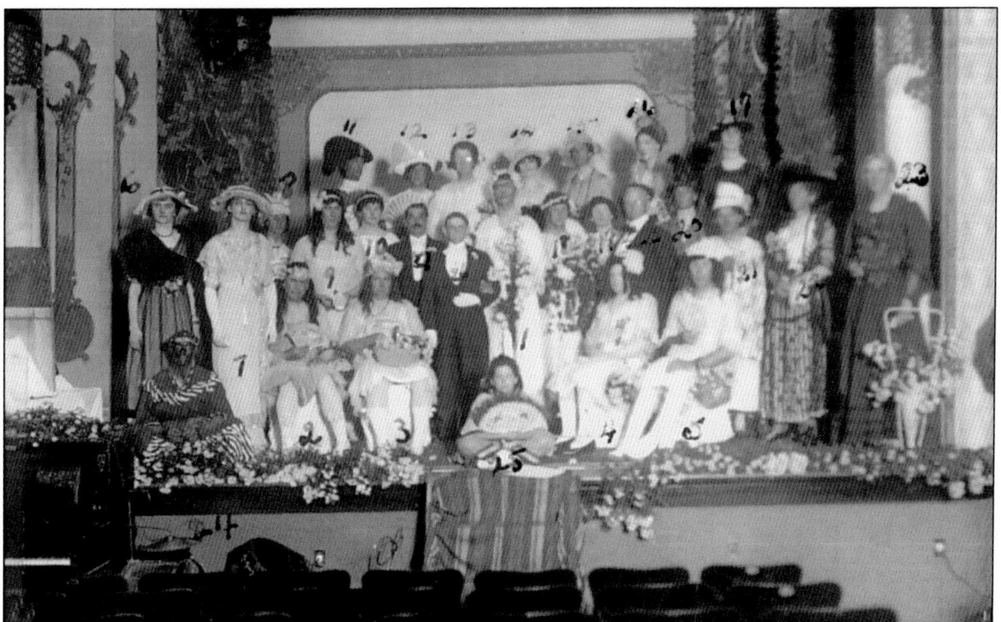

Speaking of men in funny costumes, this photo was taken of a "wedding" performed by an all-male cast at the Catron Opera House. It had 28 parts, but only three for male characters: the groom, the best man, and the preacher. The rest of the cast performed in female roles, from flower girls to the bride. Included in the cast were J.P. Harlin (mayor), Charles Bohrer (doctor), Arch Hollenbeck (postmaster), and many other community leaders.

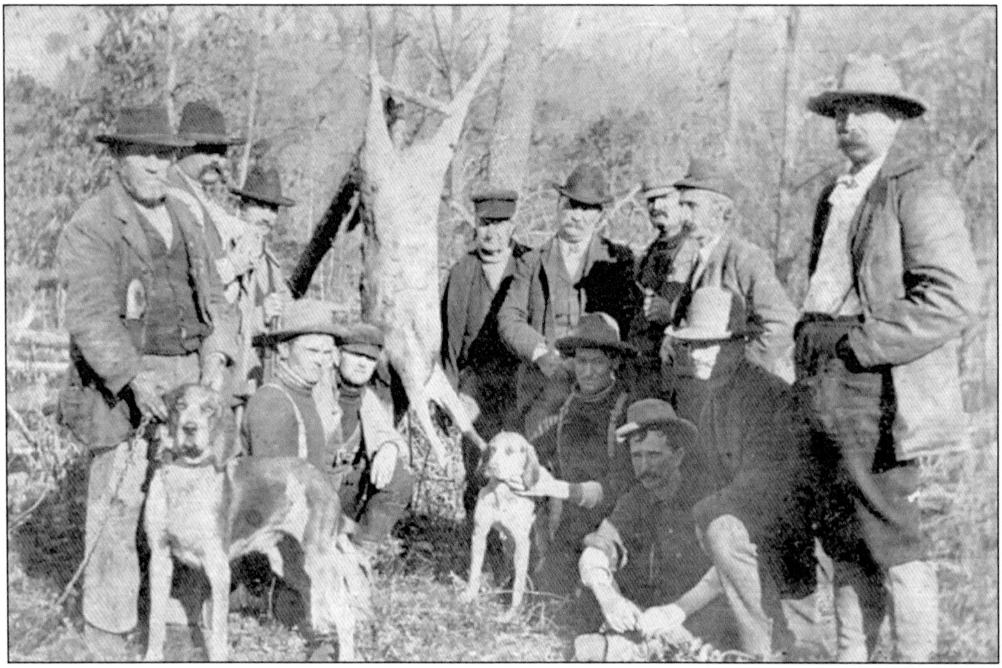

A fall deer hunt was as exciting in the 1890s as it is today. However, finding a deer was not nearly as easy. Before modern conservation methods, deer were nearly hunted to extinction in the Ozarks. This group of hunters managed to take a buck by traveling to the "Irish Wilderness" in Oregon County. Then, as now, companionship was the main goal of the outing.

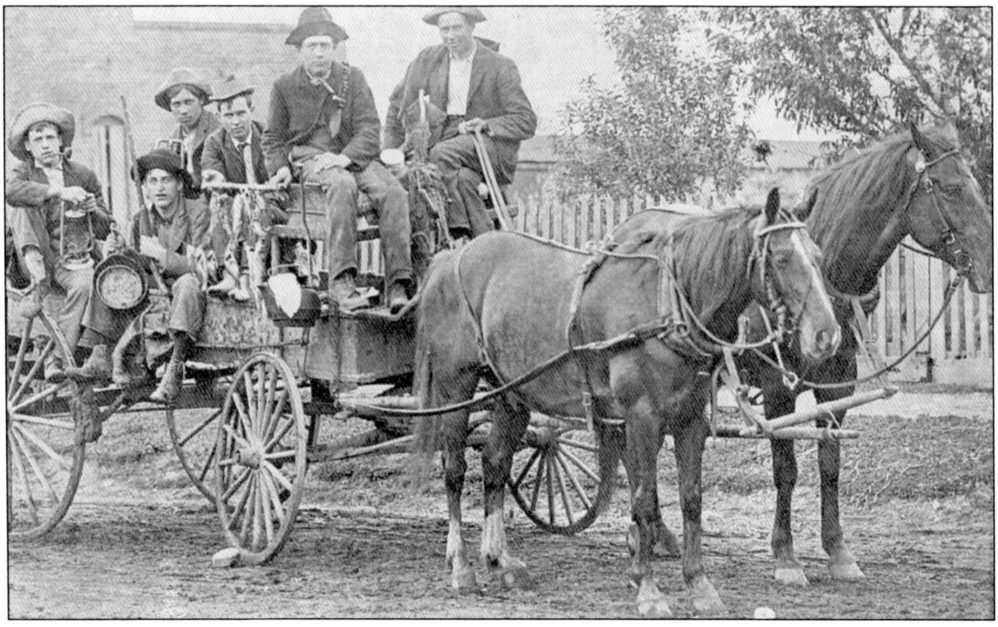

Fish were not as scarce as deer, and a fishing trip was almost always successful. These young men have returned from a triumphant outing in 1904. They are, from the left: Clarence Johnson, Jack Hogan, Ed Hogan, Humpy Thomas, Frank Green, and Will H.D. Green. It looks like that frying pan could use a good scrubbing.

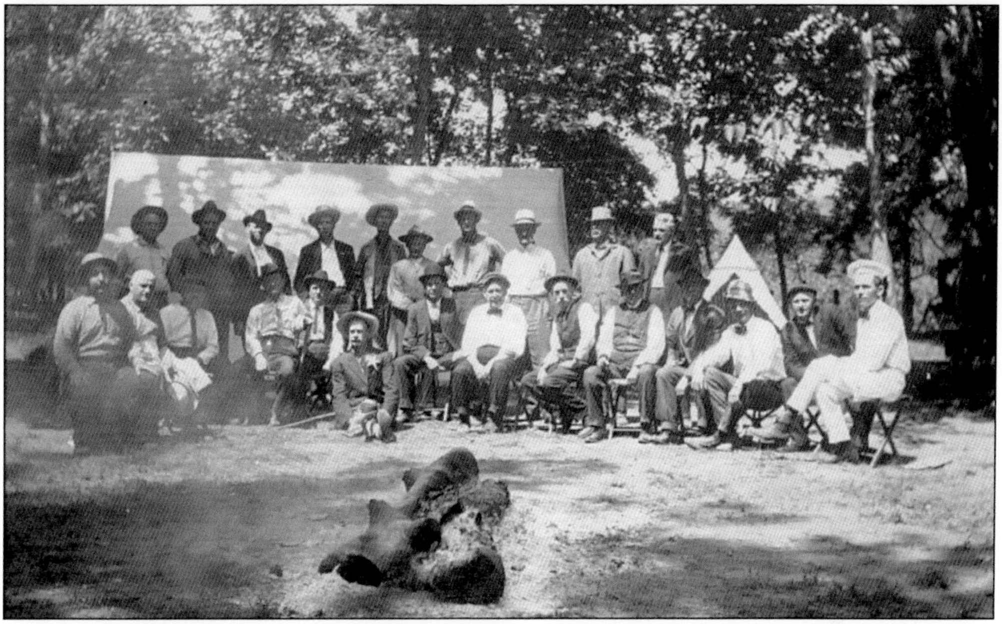

Derived from hunting and fishing clubs, a group of West Plains businessmen established the "Old Timers" Club in 1909. The goal was a week-long reunion and campout each summer solely for the sake of fun and relaxation. The club continued into the 1940s, when both it and the Old Timers began to fade away. In this photo the Old Timers are encamped around 1915.

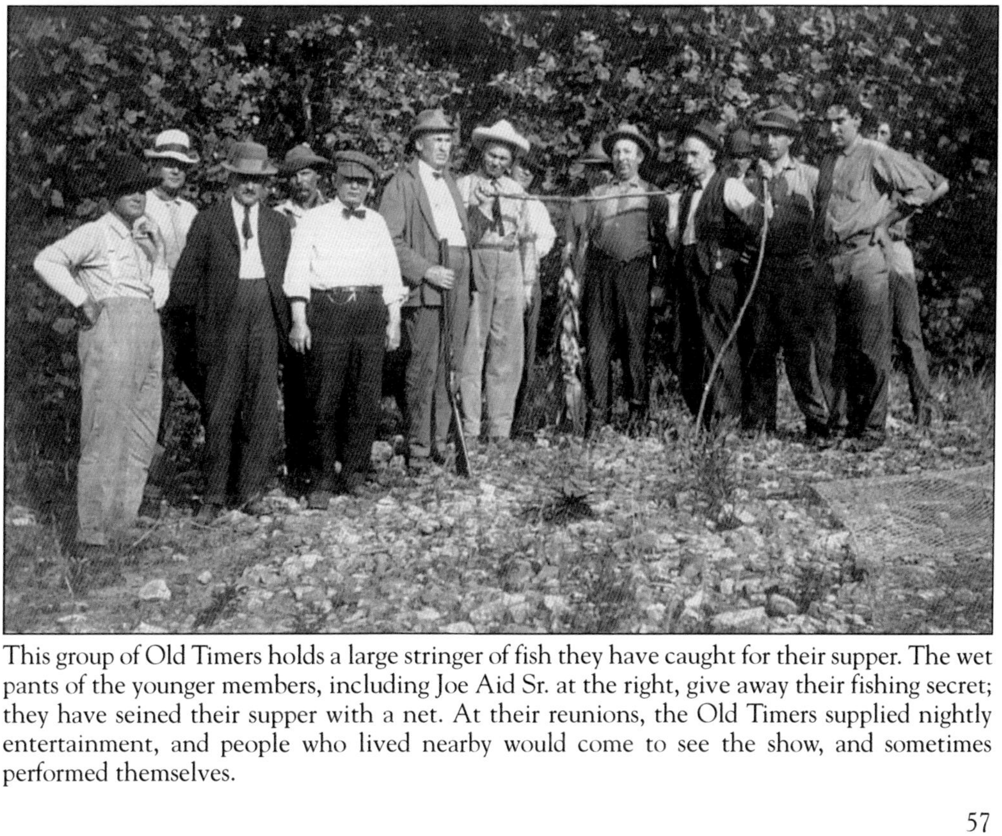

This group of Old Timers holds a large stringer of fish they have caught for their supper. The wet pants of the younger members, including Joe Aid Sr. at the right, give away their fishing secret; they have seined their supper with a net. At their reunions, the Old Timers supplied nightly entertainment, and people who lived nearby would come to see the show, and sometimes performed themselves.

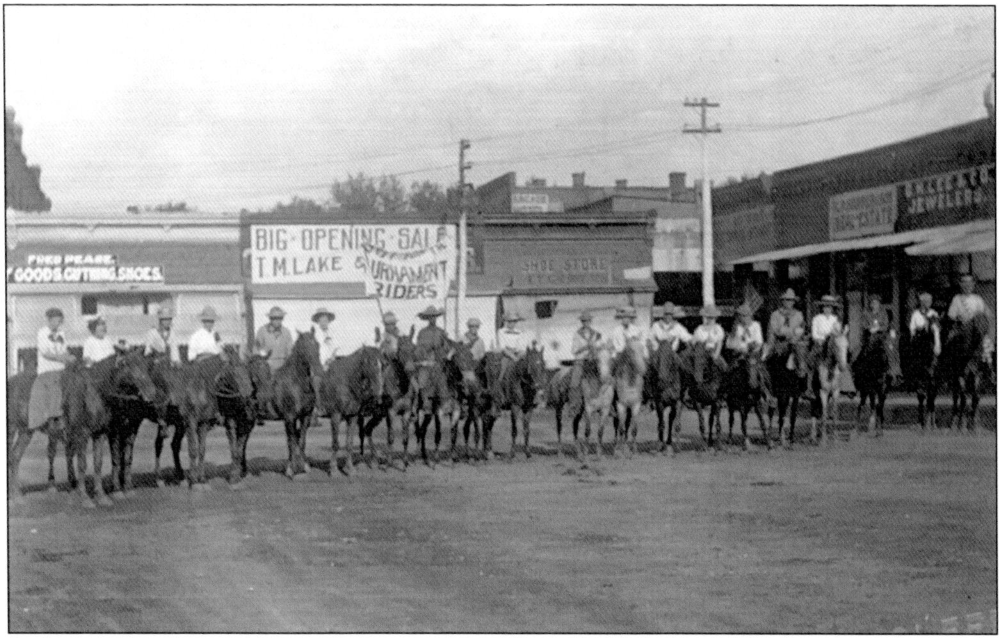

The banner this group of horseback riders is holding says "...for the Tournament Riders." W.T. Gleerup took this photo in the southeast corner of the Square *c.* 1912. Most of the riders have wide-brimmed hats and kerchiefs on. This is probably a local riding club. "Saddle clubs" and trail rides are still popular in Howell County.

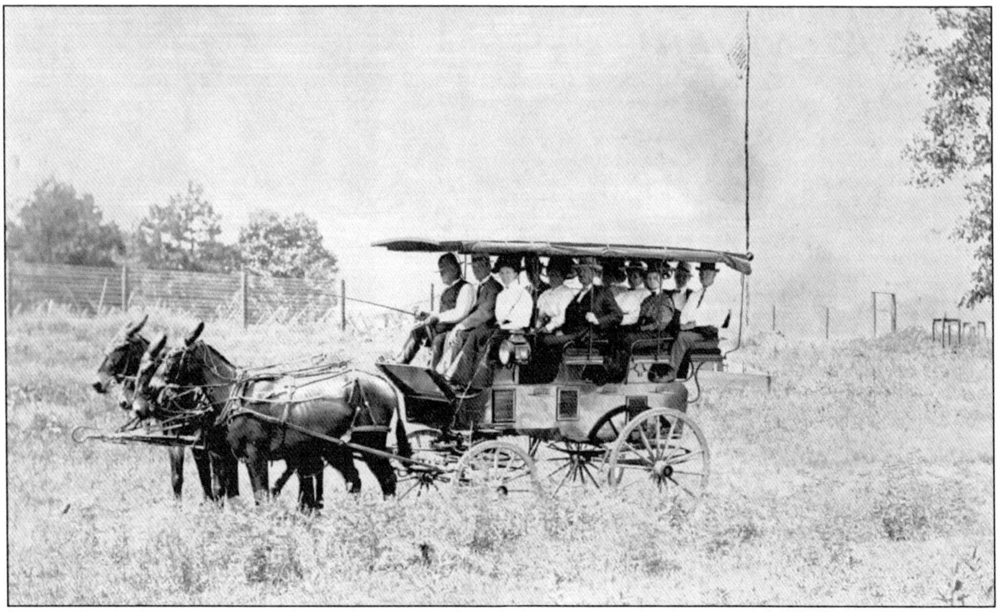

Colonel Jay L. Torrey liked to take visitors for a ride in his twelve-passenger Talley-Ho carriage. He is holding the reins to a four-mule team in this photo from around 1910. Torrey tirelessly promoted real estate in the Ozarks, sending out brochures extolling the healthful climate and cheap land. Those who answered his ads received a free train ticket to see his properties and perhaps a ride in the Talley-Ho.

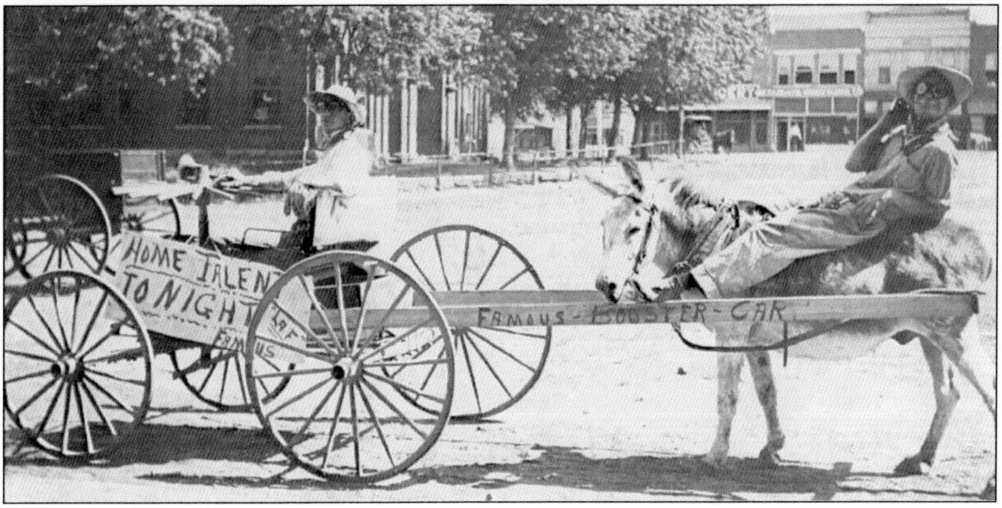

If things got boring you could always have a parade. The sign on the Famous Booster Car declares "Home Talent Tonight." J.L. Elledge opened the Famous Theater in his newly built arcade in 1914. It was the first movie theater built for that purpose in West Plains. If the movies weren't too good you could always have a talent show, just "don't get the cart before the horse."

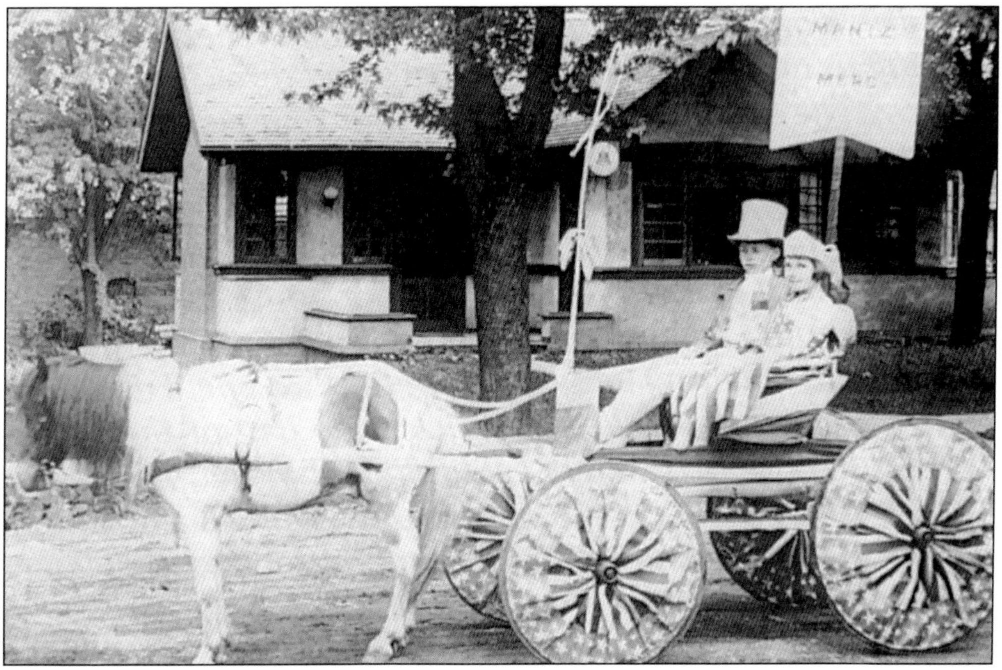

Langston Pease and Mabel Mantz have their pony wagon ready for the 1914 Fourth of July parade. They are waiting for it to start in front of Col. Torrey's Little Fruitville office. If you look on the far right you can catch a glimpse of the porch of the West Plains House Hotel. Dick Van Dyke, the TV actor, was born there. His parents were actors passing through West Plains.

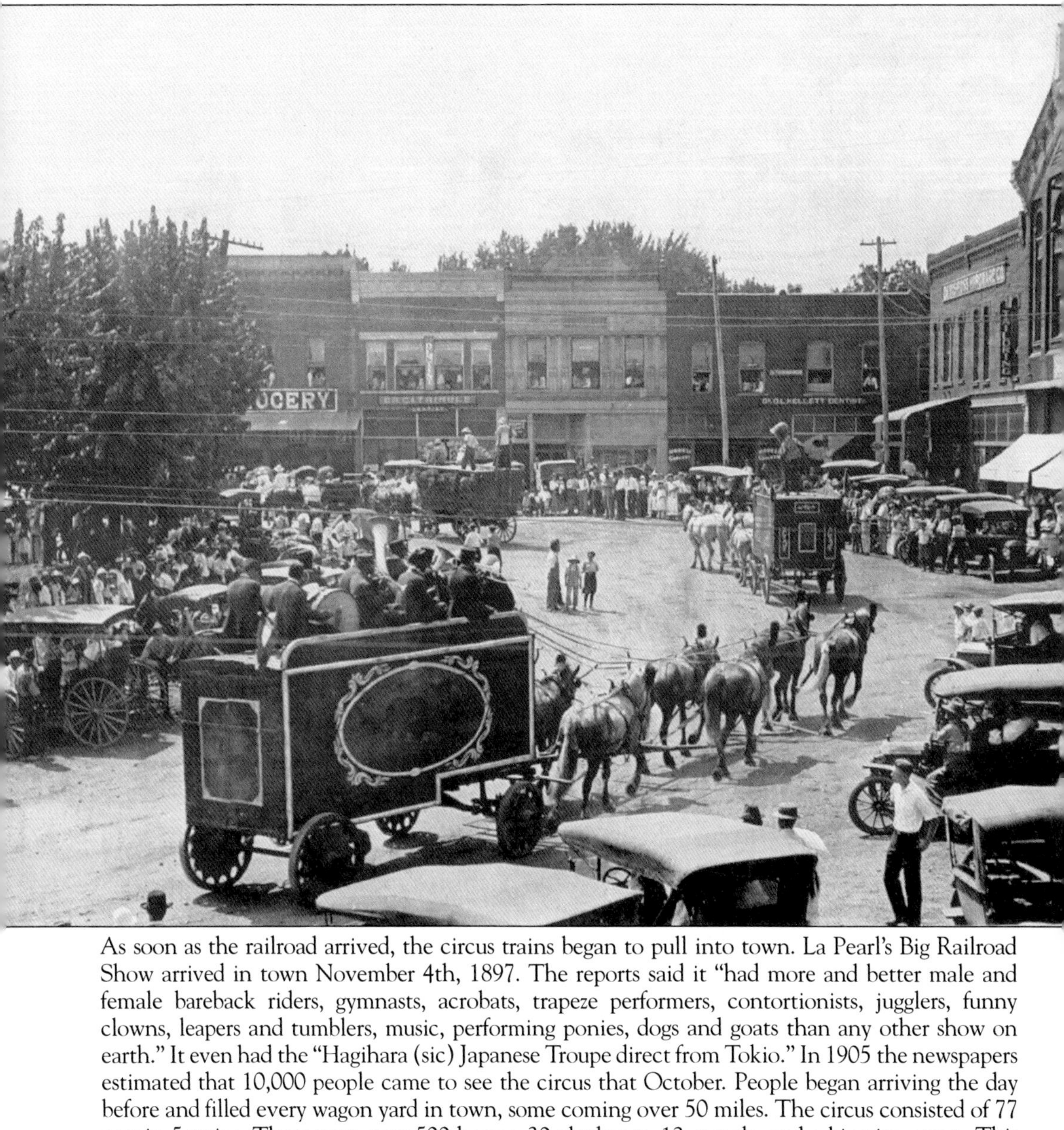

As soon as the railroad arrived, the circus trains began to pull into town. La Pearl's Big Railroad Show arrived in town November 4th, 1897. The reports said it "had more and better male and female bareback riders, gymnasts, acrobats, trapeze performers, contortionists, jugglers, funny clowns, leapers and tumblers, music, performing ponies, dogs and goats than any other show on earth." It even had the "Hagihara (sic) Japanese Troupe direct from Tokio." In 1905 the newspapers estimated that 10,000 people came to see the circus that October. People began arriving the day before and filled every wagon yard in town, some coming over 50 miles. The circus consisted of 77 cars in 5 trains. There were over 500 horses, 30 elephants, 12 camels, and a big pipe organ. This photo, of a circus in 1916, shows every sidewalk and window full of spectators.

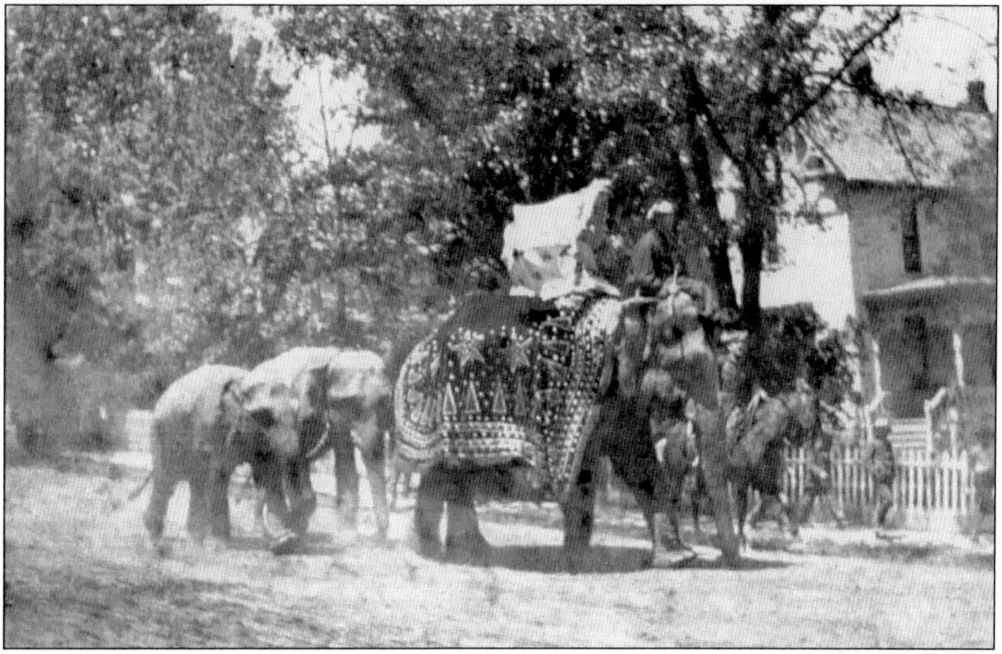

Dr. A.H. Thornburgh, the man holding a camera on this book's cover, took these photos of a circus parading down West Main Street two blocks from the Square around 1912. You can see a troupe of small boys on the sidewalk escorting the elephants down the street. The house in the background still exists, moved one-half block north to make way for Robertson-Drago's parking lot.

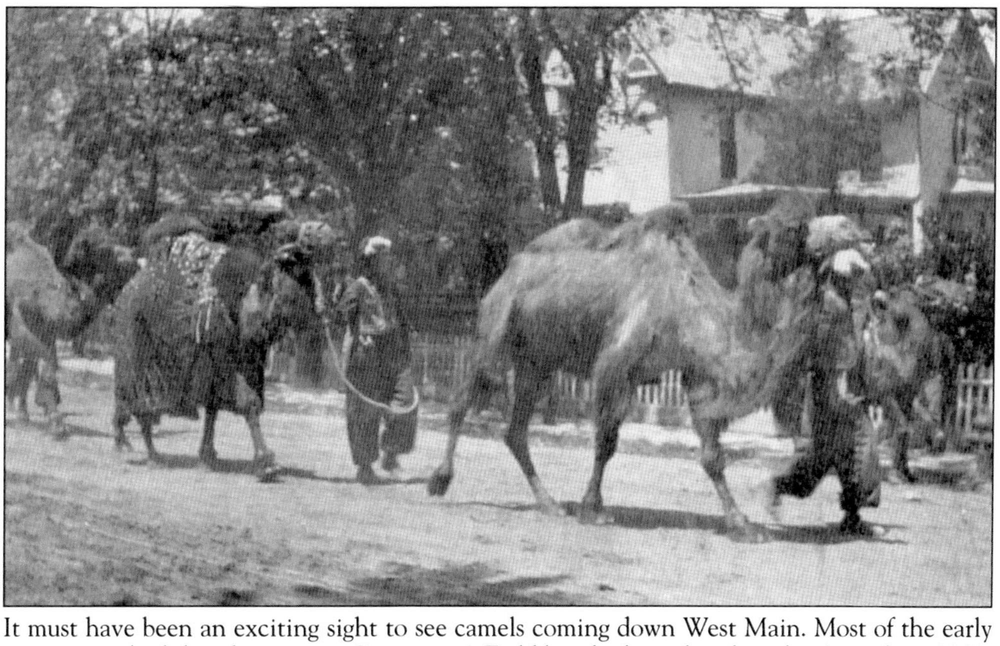

It must have been an exciting sight to see camels coming down West Main. Most of the early circuses pitched their big tops on Sportsman's Field beside the railroad tracks. As early as 1881, the county court set the tax on circus performances at $20. Horse shows were only $5. Other shows regularly stopping in West Plains were minstrel shows and vaudeville acts.

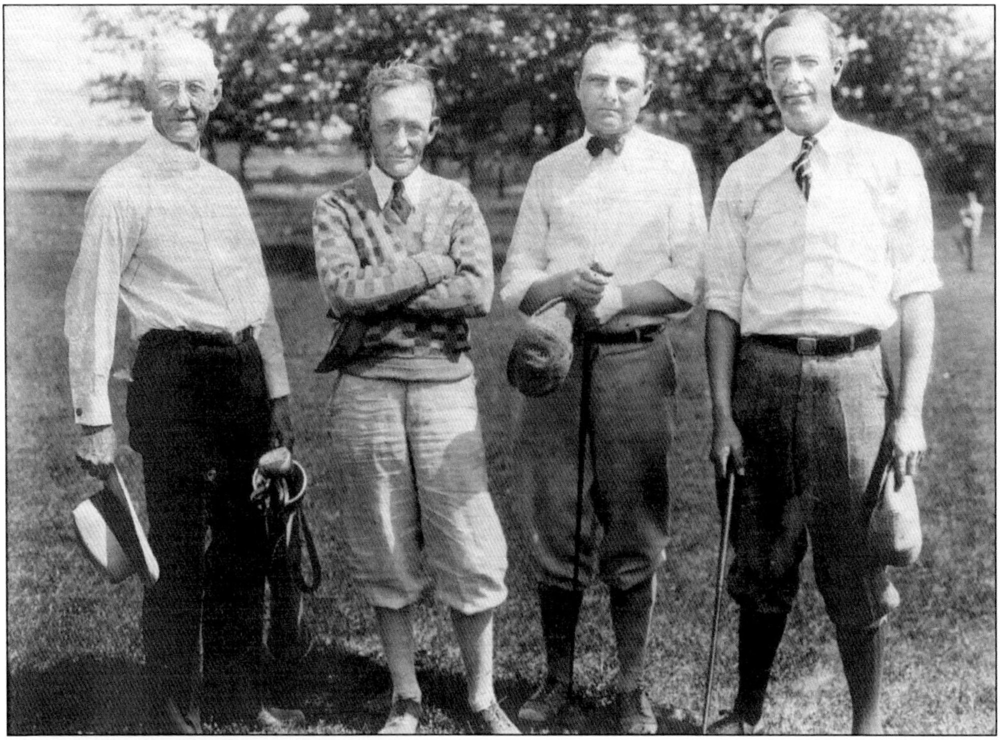

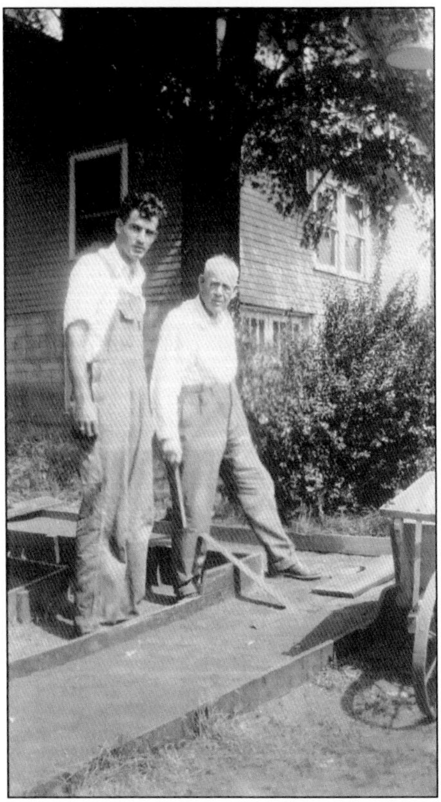

(*above*) The West Plains Country Club was founded in 1926. Before the first match could be held, the new members held rock picking parties to clear the fairways. One early fundraiser was a nighttime match. Members lined the fairways with flashlights as the steadiest shooters played nine holes. The early club members pictured here, from the left, are Mayor J.P. Harlin, Dr. L.E. Toney, C.E. Armstrong, and Paul Johnson.

(*left*) For the less athletically inclined, miniature golf arrived in the late 1920s. Pictured here are Joe Aid Jr. and his grandfather, E.D. Mumford, building "Juniors Miniature Golf." Unfortunately, Joe built his course in a residential area, and the neighbors didn't like his loudspeakers playing music until 11:00 p.m. A court order silenced his speakers and doomed his business. Another more successful course was located on Cleveland Avenue.

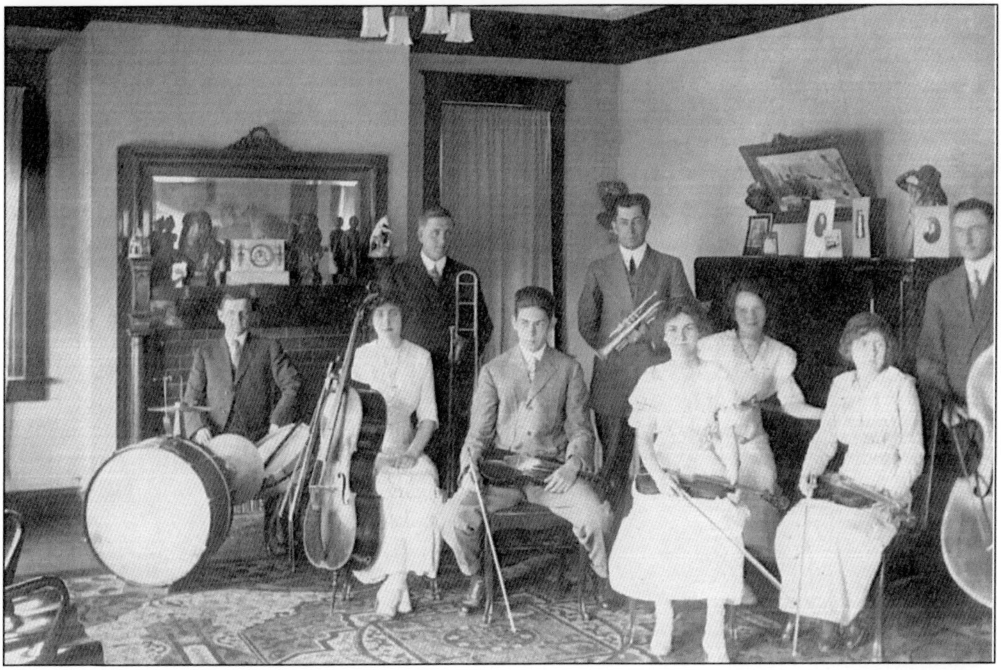

Dance bands and dancing were always popular in West Plains. This is Charlie Brown's Orchestra. Charlie, seen at the drums, was a local jeweler whose shop was one door west of the Red Apple Drug Store. Pictured from left to right are: Charlie, Ruth Catron, ? Rainey, Herbert Mantz, Harry Marquis, Alexa Whitmire, Fay Knowlton, unidentified, and ? Rainey. They are practicing in Charlie's house on Grace Avenue.

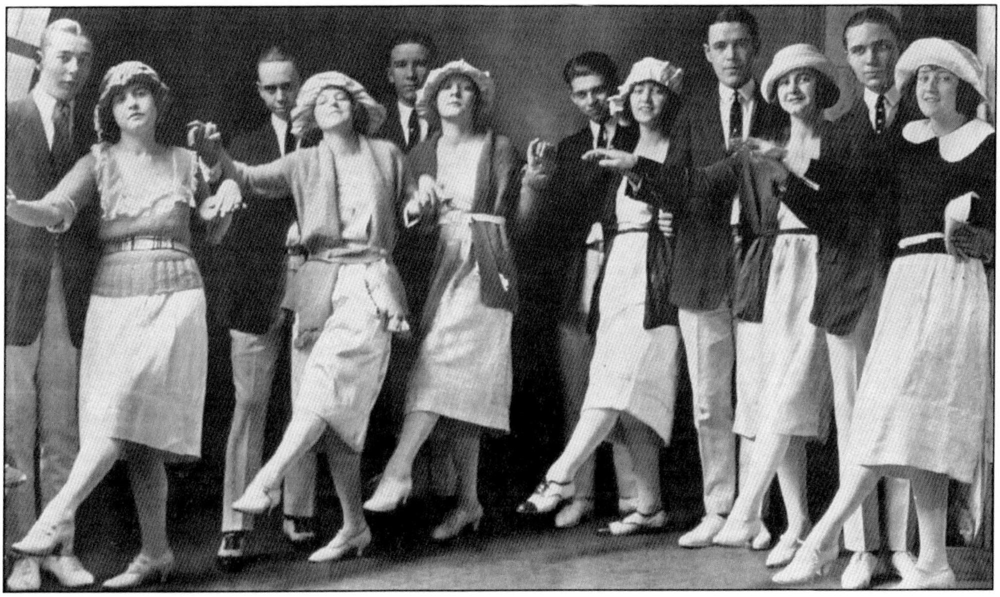

This group of dancers is "tripping the light fantastic" at the Catron Opera House in 1917. From left to right are Cecil Conkin, Jacque Dixon, John Riley, Nelly James, Everett Stover, Dorothy Bohrer, Lanston Pease, Thelma Evans, Bodie Martin, Marion Thompson, Jamie Carter, and Blanche Stover.

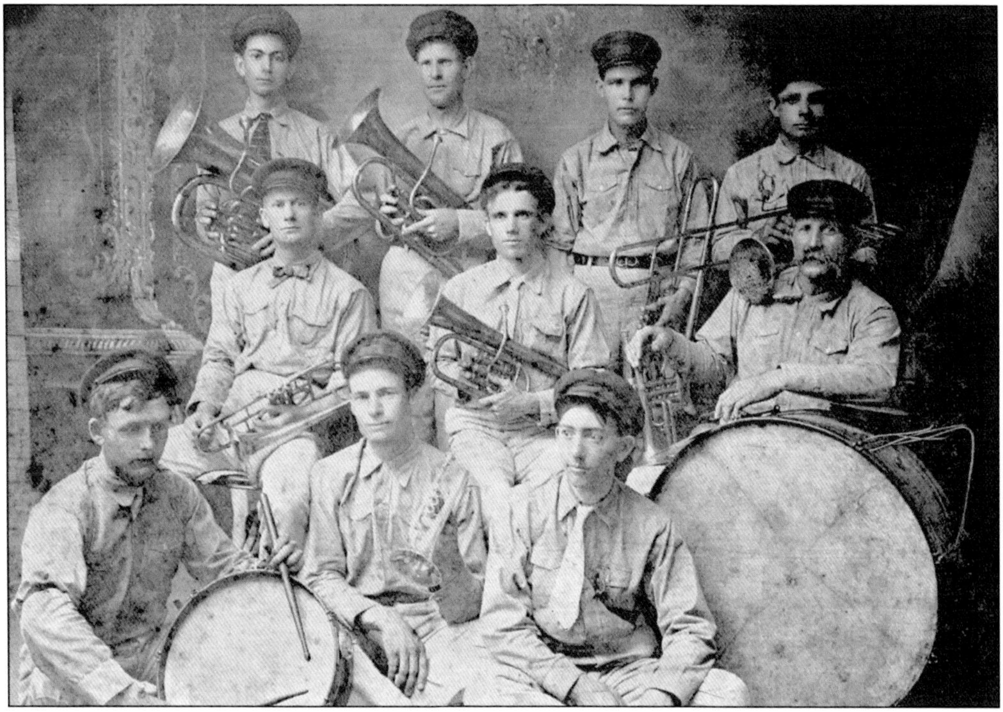

The Life of West Plains brass band was formed in 1904. Charles A. Skinner, sitting behind the bass drum, was its leader. Skinner had lost his 21-year-old son, Walter, to tuberculosis that same year. Pictured from left to right are: (front row) Matt Hard, ? Terry, and Fred Thornburgh; (middle) ? Stumbraugh, Arthur Allen, and Charles A. Skinner; (back) Ernest Thornburgh, Andrew Worstel, Wilber Worstel, and ? Aulthouse.

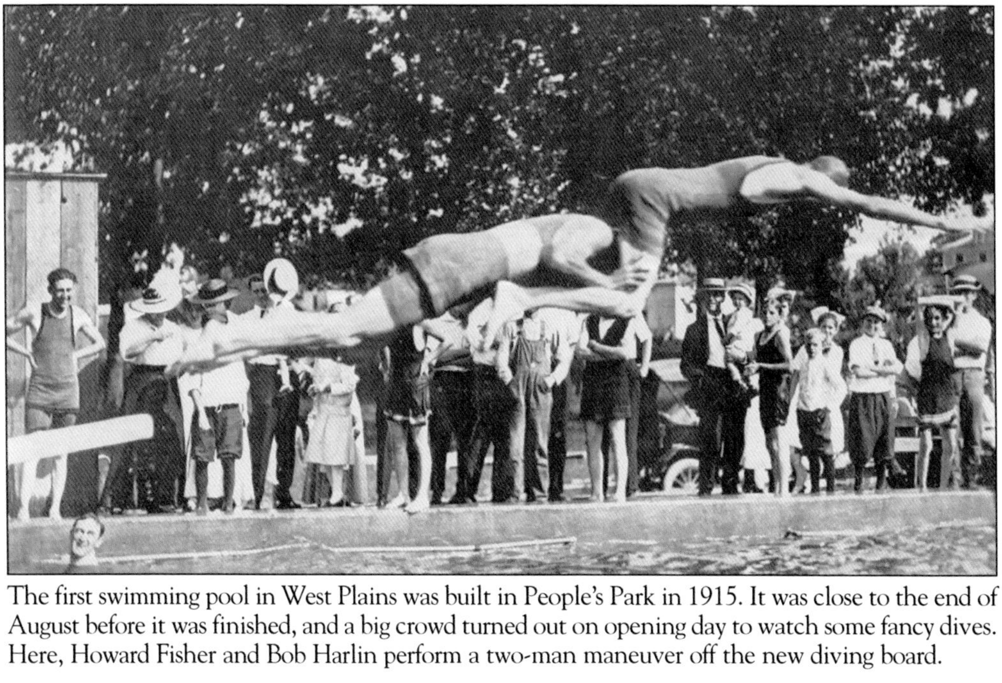

The first swimming pool in West Plains was built in People's Park in 1915. It was close to the end of August before it was finished, and a big crowd turned out on opening day to watch some fancy dives. Here, Howard Fisher and Bob Harlin perform a two-man maneuver off the new diving board.

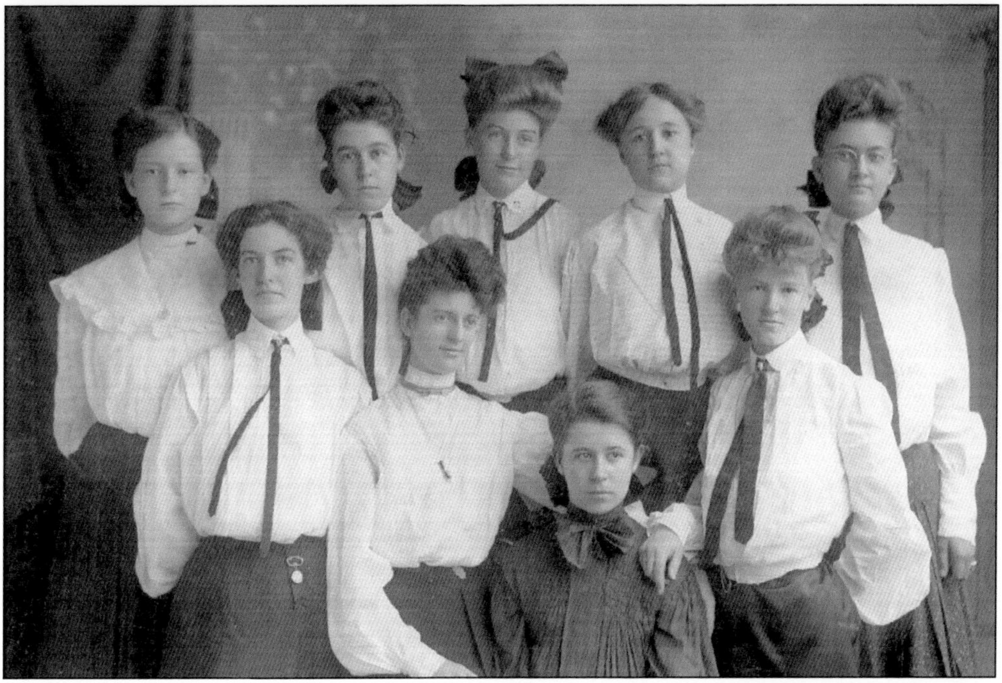

Clubs have always been a good way for friends to get together. This is the Needle and Thimble Club in 1905 made up of young women in high school. Pictured from left to right are: (front row) Rena Whitely, Alothe Pope, Elinore McCulloch, and Flossie Gilliam; (back row) Daucy Hill, Kate Mumford, Gertrude Farmer, Henrietta Hale, and Agnes Whitmire.

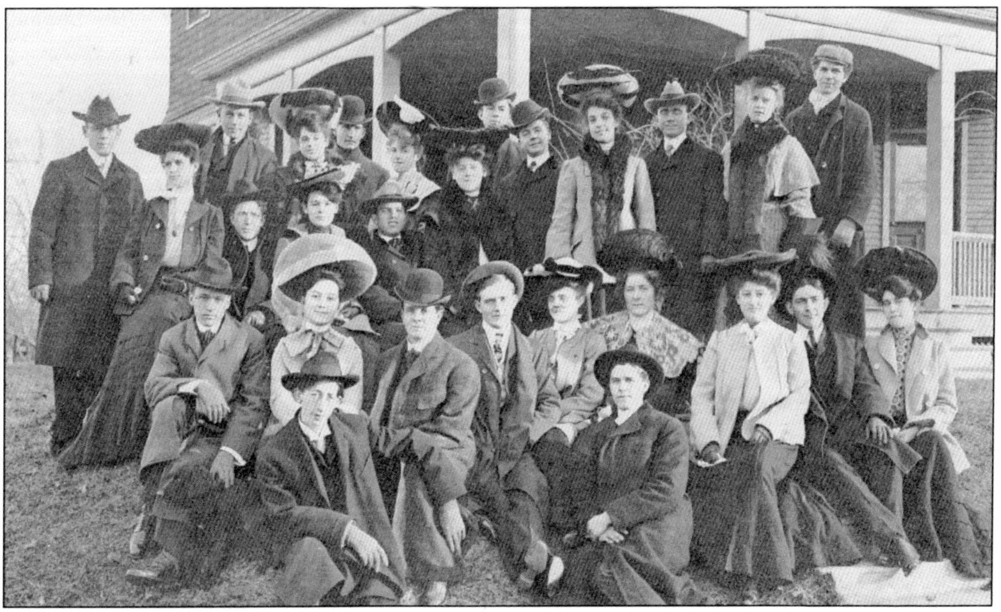

There was nothing like a nice hat to turn a fella's eye in 1903. Of course, if you were a gentleman, you knew that your hat was important too. This group is gathered on the front lawn of Fern Hines' home, one block up Summit Street from West Main. Lists of early West Plains merchants included numerous millinery shops, tailors, shoe stores, and clothing stores.

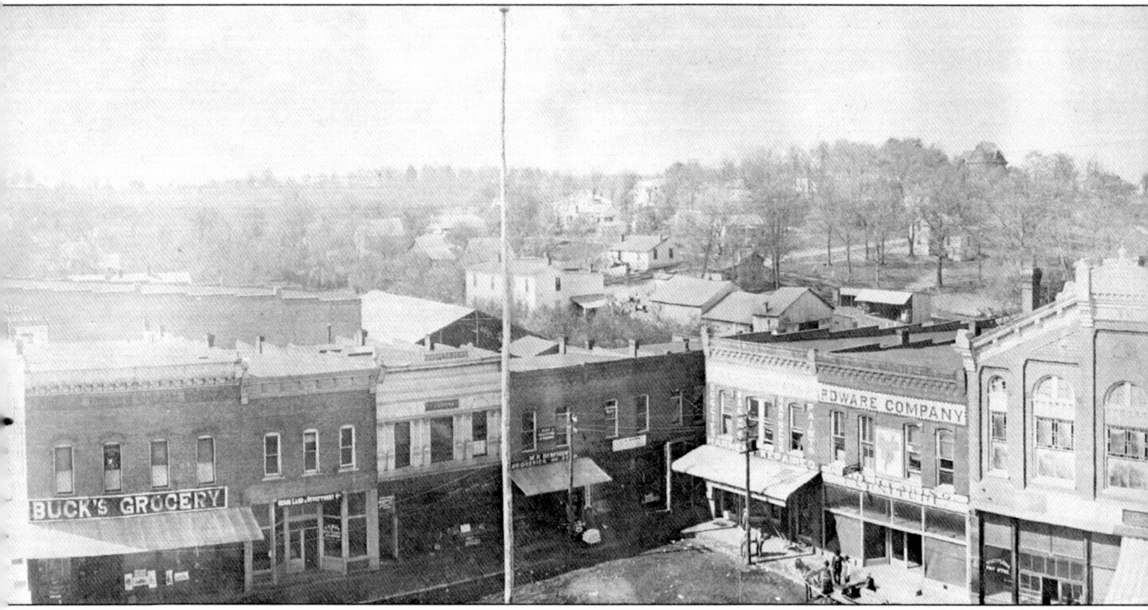

This giant 360-degree panoramic view of downtown West Plains was taken *c.* 1912 from atop the Courthouse. It was almost certainly shot by Thomas Jefferson Howell with his new panoramic camera. You could spend all day studying this photo and still not see everything in it. There is an early automobile on West Main and a house being moved in the middle of lower Washington

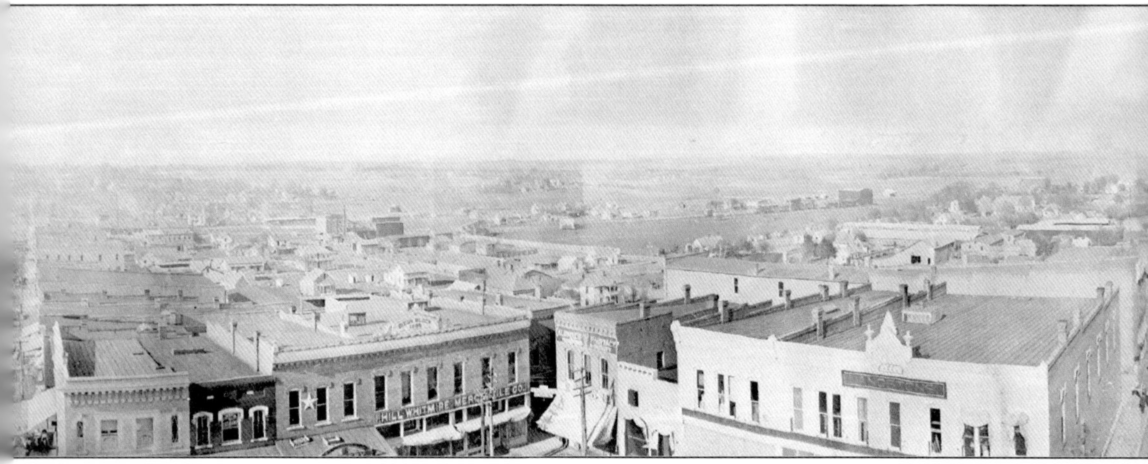

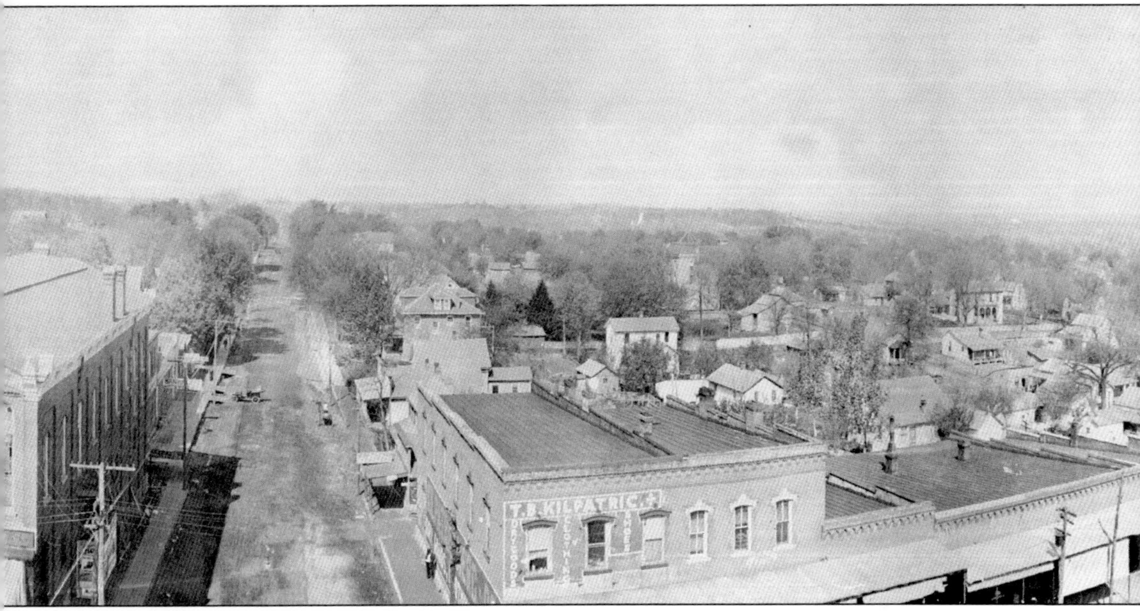

Avenue. In fact, there are two views of Washington Avenue, because one half of the shot was made in mid-morning and one in mid-afternoon. Note the shadows. One surprising detail is the size of the bleachers at Sportsman's Field just east of Pease-Moore Mill. It shows the importance of baseball as entertainment. The population of West Plains was 3,000 when this photo was taken.

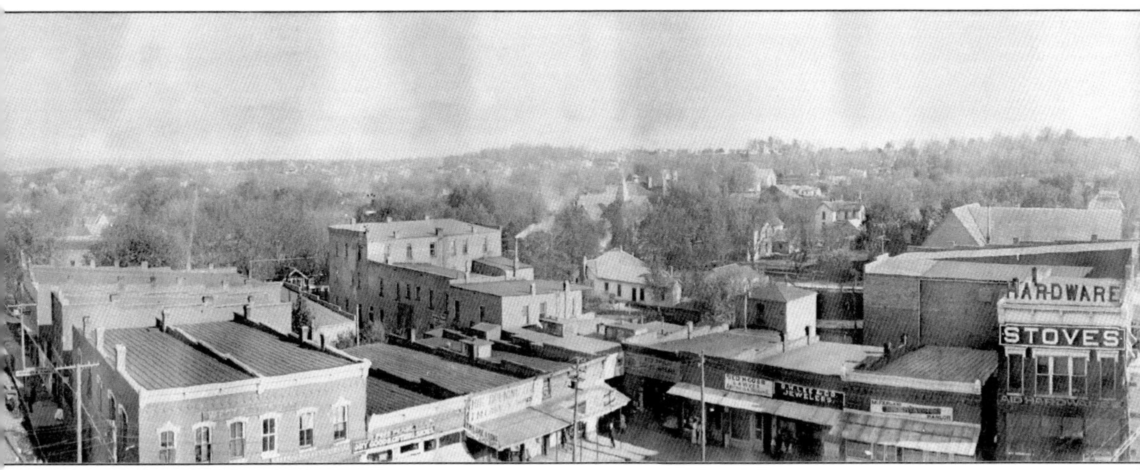

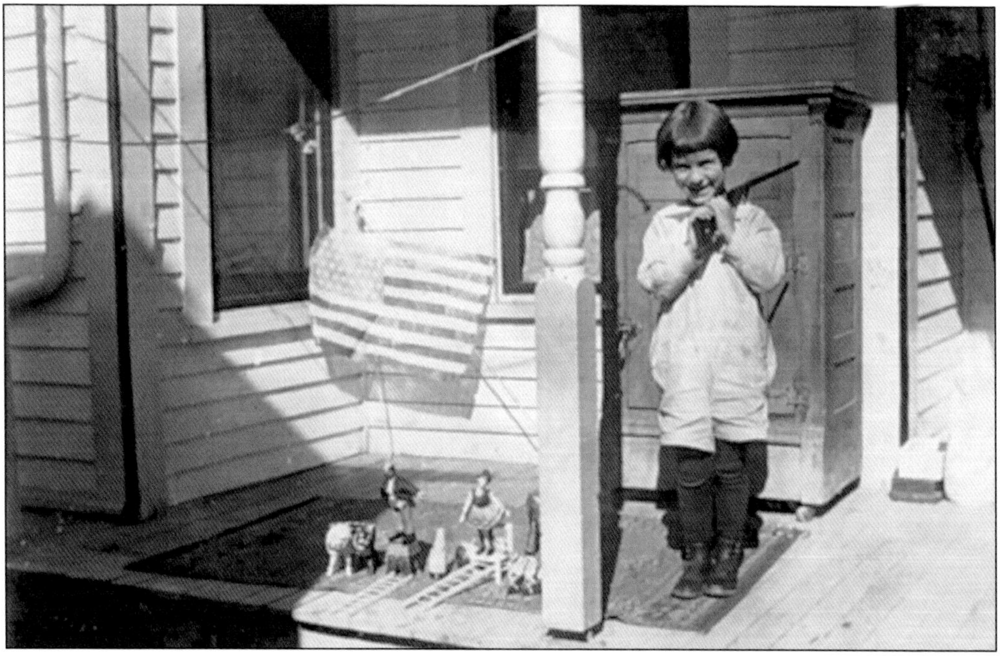

Our chapter on West Plains at play wouldn't be complete without considering children. Joe Aid Jr. proudly displays his new Schoenhut Circus toys on the back porch in 1915. With his flag and toy rifle we aren't sure if he has been to a circus parade or one for the Fourth of July. The family icebox sits on the porch behind him.

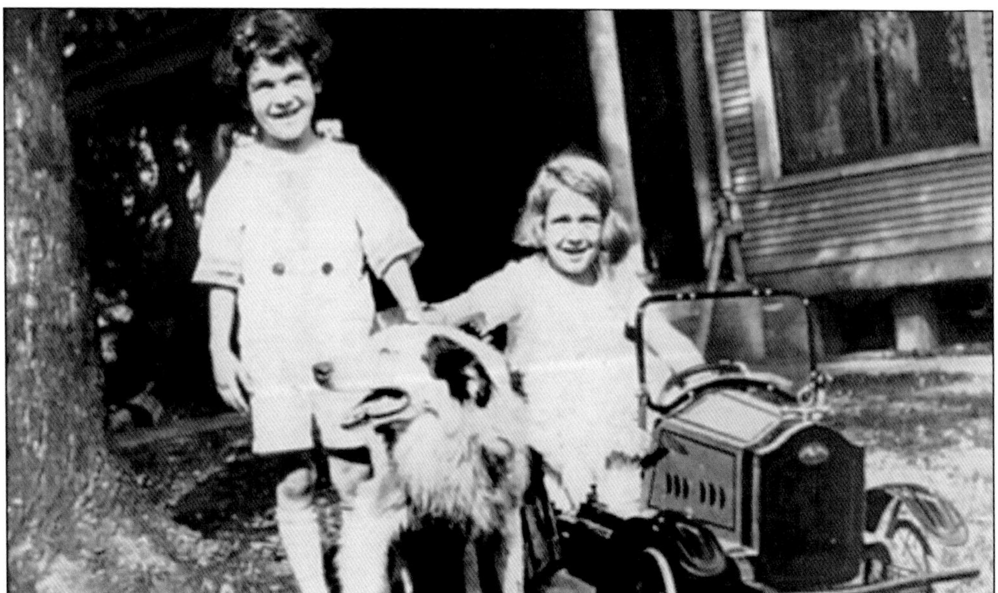

Five years later Joe's brother, Charlie, his sister Peggy Lou, and Waddles the dog show off a deluxe new pedal car. Peggy Lou died of appendicitis soon after this photo was taken. Her funeral was held in the front room of their home. Undertakers in West Plains didn't have parlors for funeral services until the 1930s. This house still stands on the southeast corner of Aid and Grove Streets.

Four

The Best Small Town Store in Missouri

There were many outstanding retail establishments in West Plains, but none lasted longer or drew as much attention as "Aid's." Its founder, Charles Theodore Aid, was a tinsmith trained in Pennsylvania who came west seeking his fortune. In St. Louis he heard of boomtowns developing along the new railroads in the Ozarks. First he tried Rogers, Arkansas, but a traveling salesman for Norval-Shapleigh Hardware, William Cook, convinced him that West Plains was the place to be. He arrived there right after the railroad and with Cook's help opened a hardware store. From a tinsmith shop to a hardware store to a department store his business grew through the years as he took advantage of new products and opportunities. His promotional skills and ability to draw huge crowds was extraordinary. In the 1920s *Hardware Age Magazine* declared Aid Hardware "The Best Small Town Store in Missouri." The store closed in 1990 after 105 years in business.

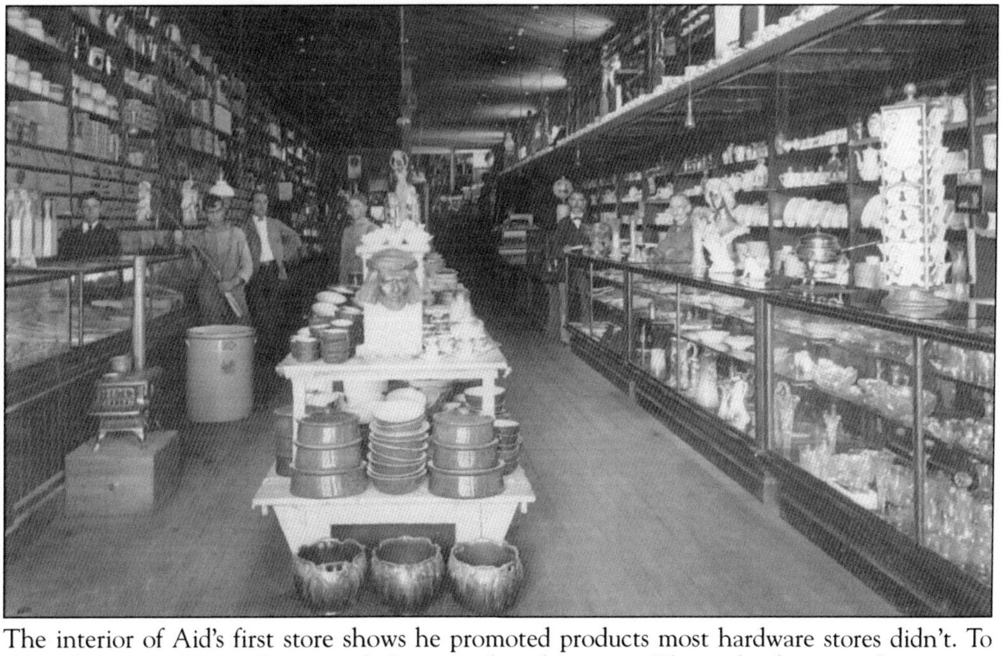

The interior of Aid's first store shows he promoted products most hardware stores didn't. To the right is cut glass and imported china in glass showcases. The rack of post cards on top is an example of another product he sold. He had photographs taken of local landmarks and sent them to post card printers in Germany. He bought thousands of these cards and wholesaled them to other businesses in the area. Aid is standing at the far right.

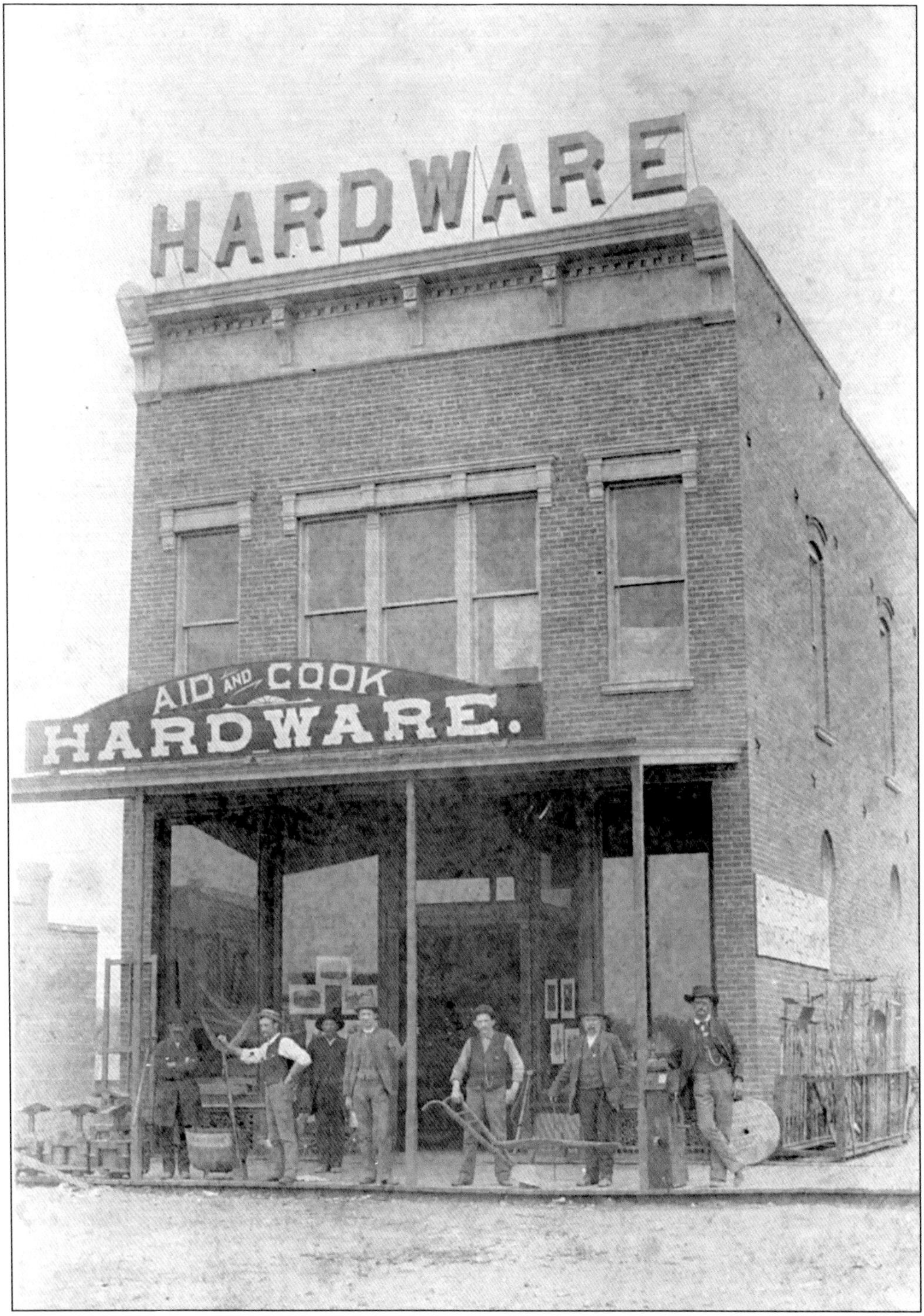

Many early products of the store are in this photo: long-handled tools, a mill stone, a cast-iron pot, and most importantly, a horse-drawn plow. C.T. took sales of plows to new heights. His annual Oliver Plow Day in March drew thousands of customers. It is amazing that among the rocky hills of southern Missouri he became one of the top Oliver Implement dealers in the country.

Most merchants offered free delivery of merchandise in 1909. That year, Aid bought an International 14-horsepower delivery truck. A salesman came from Springfield with the new truck and stayed several days to give instructions on running it. Because the International's motor was fed gasoline by gravity, one had to back it up hills to keep it running. C.T.'s son, Joe Aid Sr. is shown in the driver's seat.

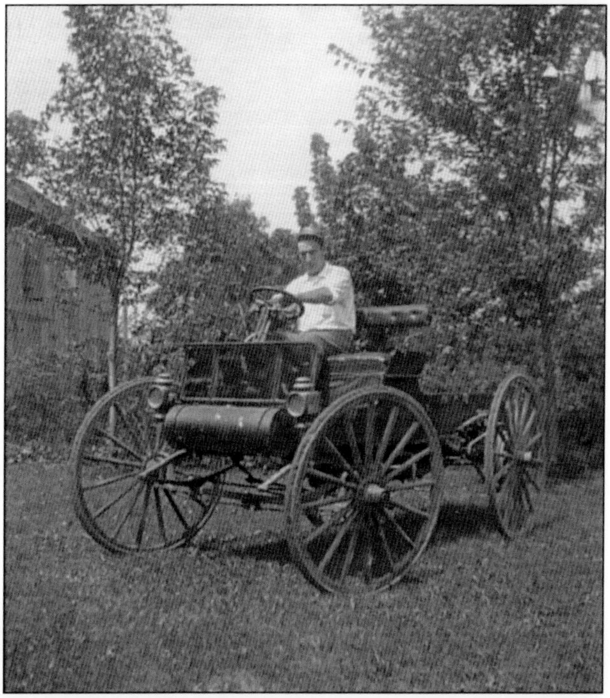

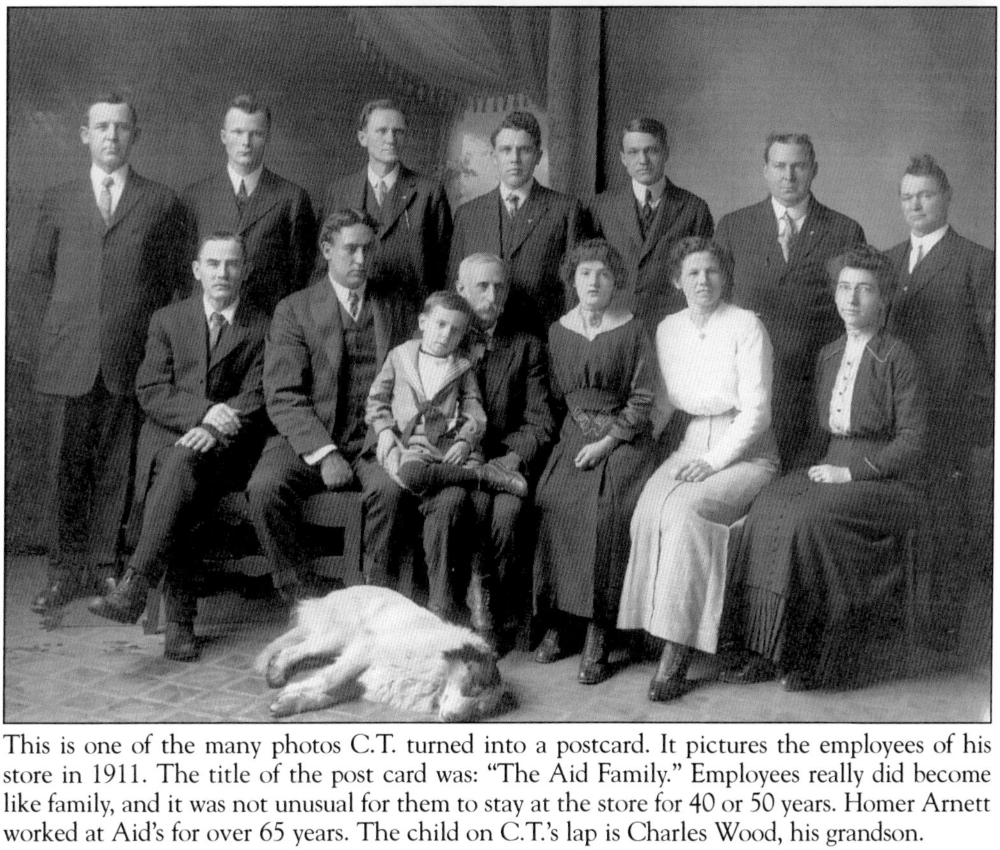

This is one of the many photos C.T. turned into a postcard. It pictures the employees of his store in 1911. The title of the post card was: "The Aid Family." Employees really did become like family, and it was not unusual for them to stay at the store for 40 or 50 years. Homer Arnett worked at Aid's for over 65 years. The child on C.T.'s lap is Charles Wood, his grandson.

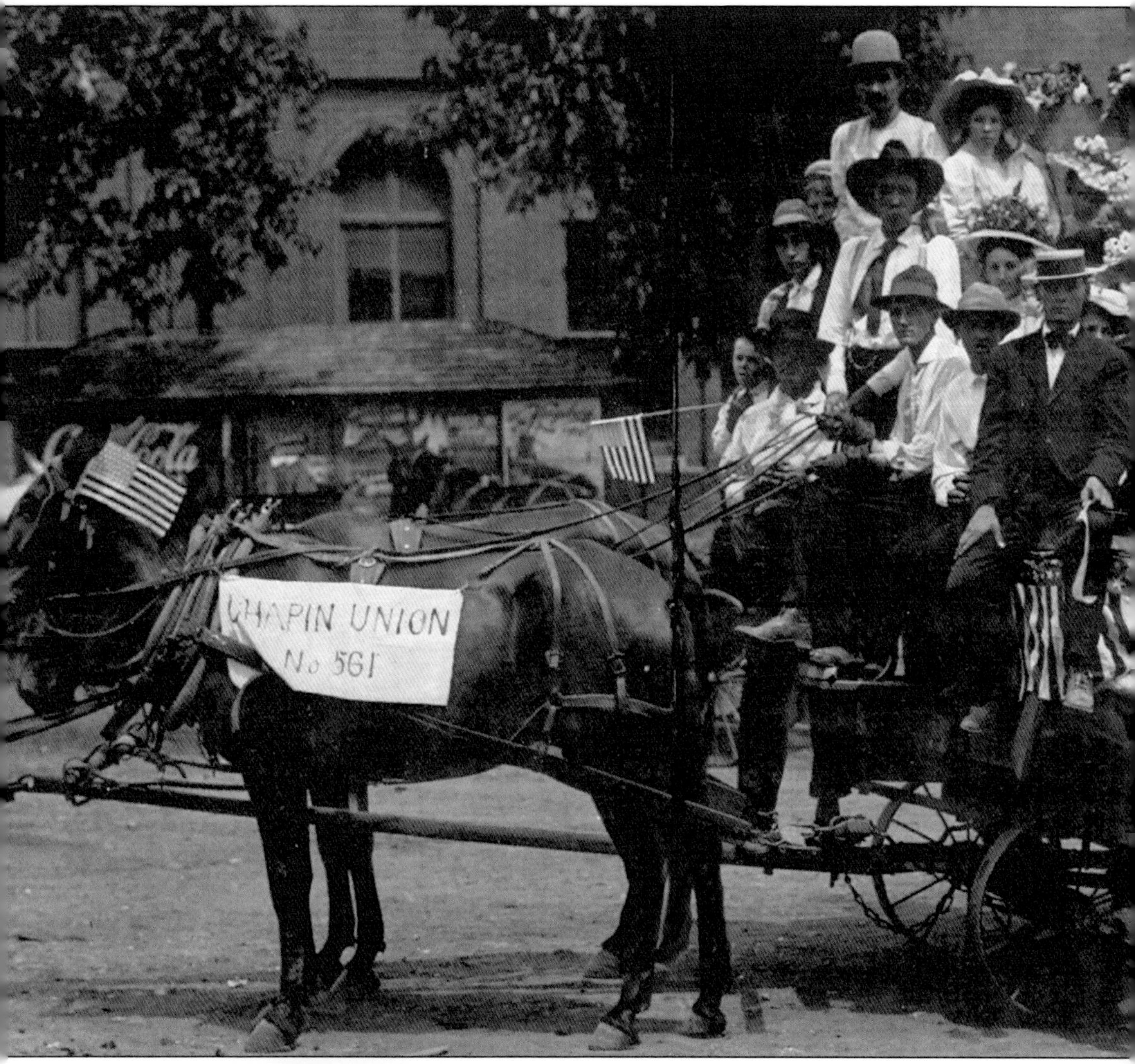

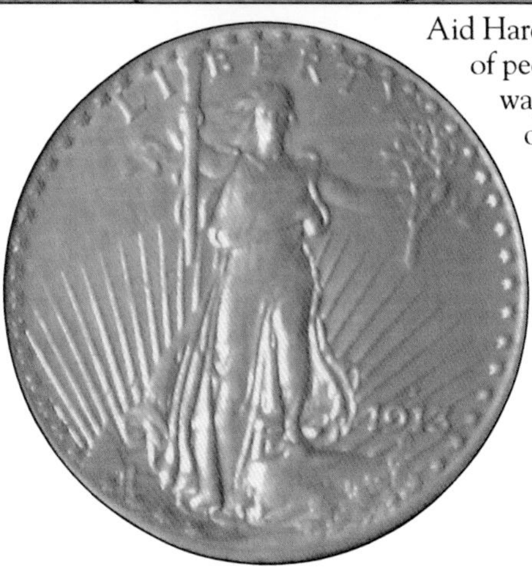

Aid Hardware offered a $20 gold piece for the largest number of people arriving at the 1908 Fourth of July picnic in one wagon. Chapin Union won with 130 people riding on one large hay wagon. To spare the mules, they walked the six miles to town, then climbed on board. In the photo, Charlie Morrison is at the reins and Joe Aid Sr. (far right) is ready to count the passengers. The

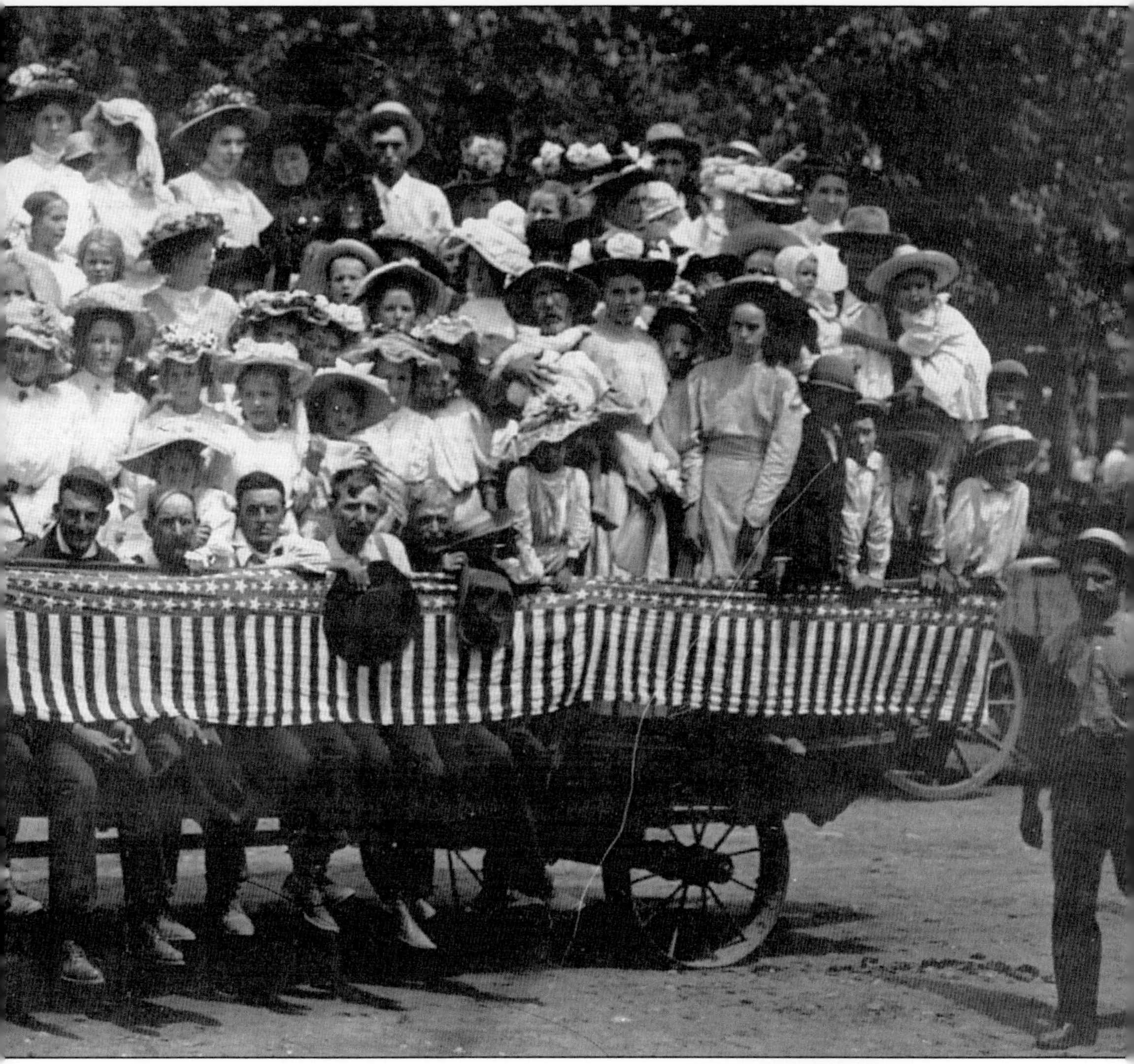

second place load had 105 riders. In another promotion, C.T. bought a train car full of hickory tool handles. He offered $5 to any man who could break one of the new axe handles. That didn't sound hard, but with no axe head on the handle and nothing to beat it on but the bare ground, no one succeeded. He sold all the handles.

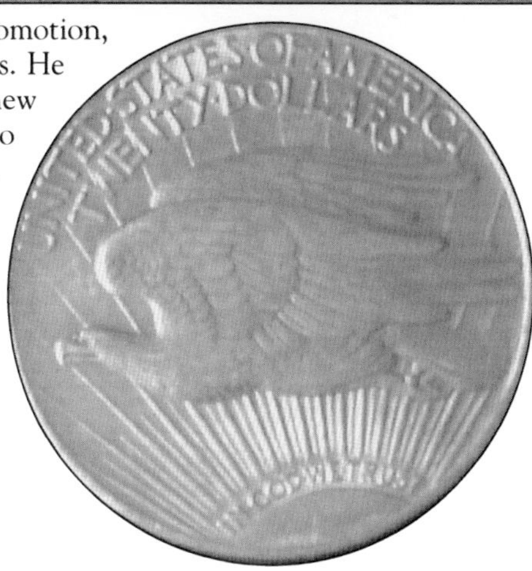

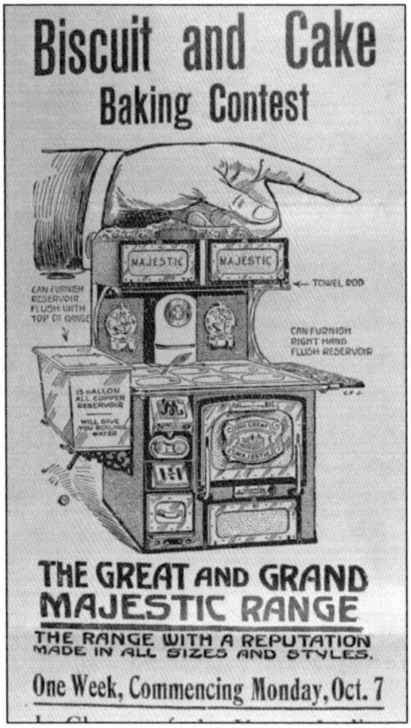

In October of 1915, the store held a week-long event designed to draw women to their new furniture department featuring the Great Majestic Kitchen Range. The sale included a baking contest with a daily $5 prize for the best pan of biscuits. Pease-Moore Milling donated Raven Brand flour for the contest. Of course, with that many biscuits around, lots of men showed up too.

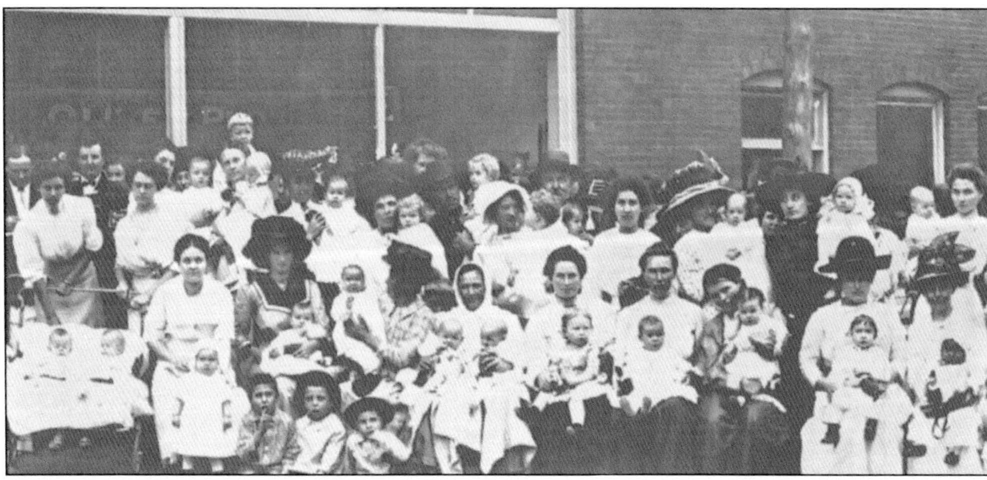

On Friday of the same week, a prize of a $20 baby buggy was offered for the prettiest baby. This group of mothers and babies is taken from a panoramic photo of the over 100 contestants. Would you liked to have been the judge for that? On Saturday a drawing was held for a $25 kitchen cabinet, and the best angel food cake won a new rocking chair.

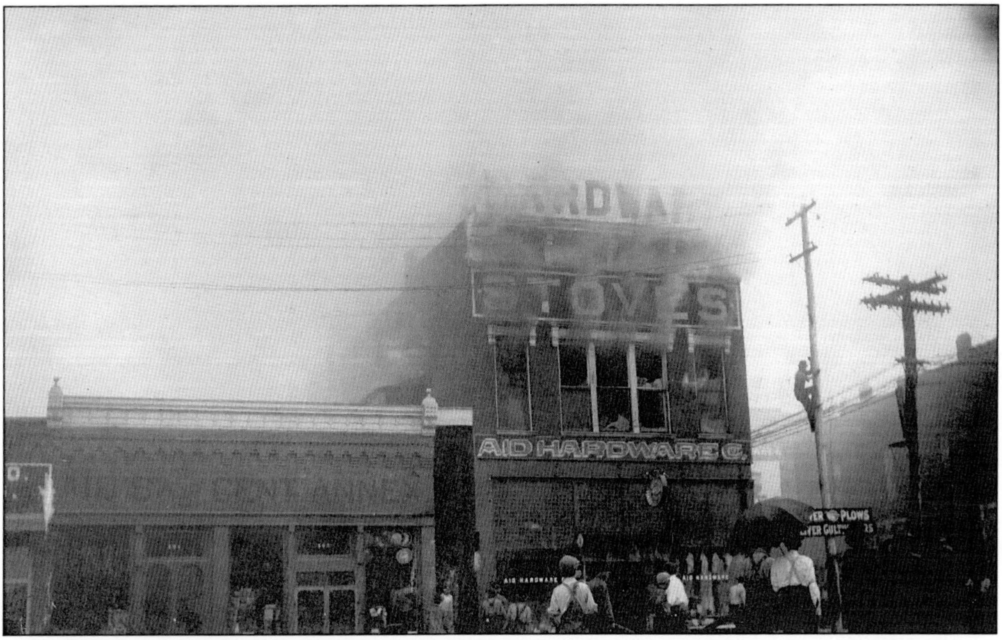

Around noon on August 27, 1914, a fire broke out behind the switchboard of the West Plains Phone Company, located on the second floor of Aid Hardware. Within five minutes the whole floor was in flames. Fire Chief Joe Martin and his men arrived quickly with their horse drawn hook and ladder. Fearing the fire would spread, other merchants began emptying their shops.

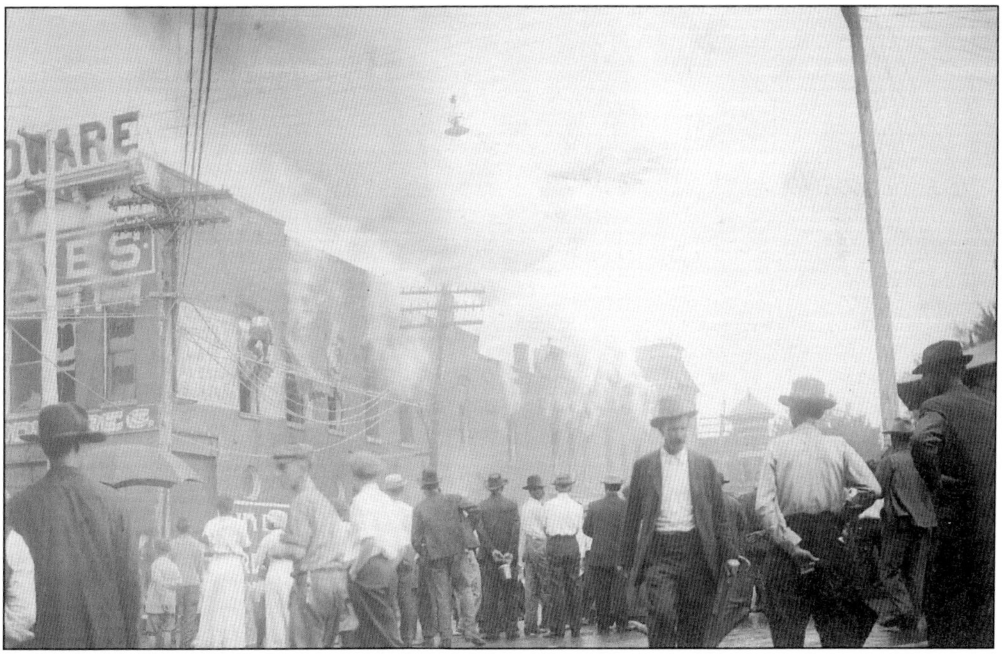
The flames entered the new annex Aid had built across the back of his building in 1906. It was full of wooden wagon parts and holiday goods brought in early because of the threat of war in Europe. Aid Hardware was a complete loss and phone service to the entire town was lost, but the water supplies held out and nearby buildings were saved. Aid lost over $50,000 in goods alone.

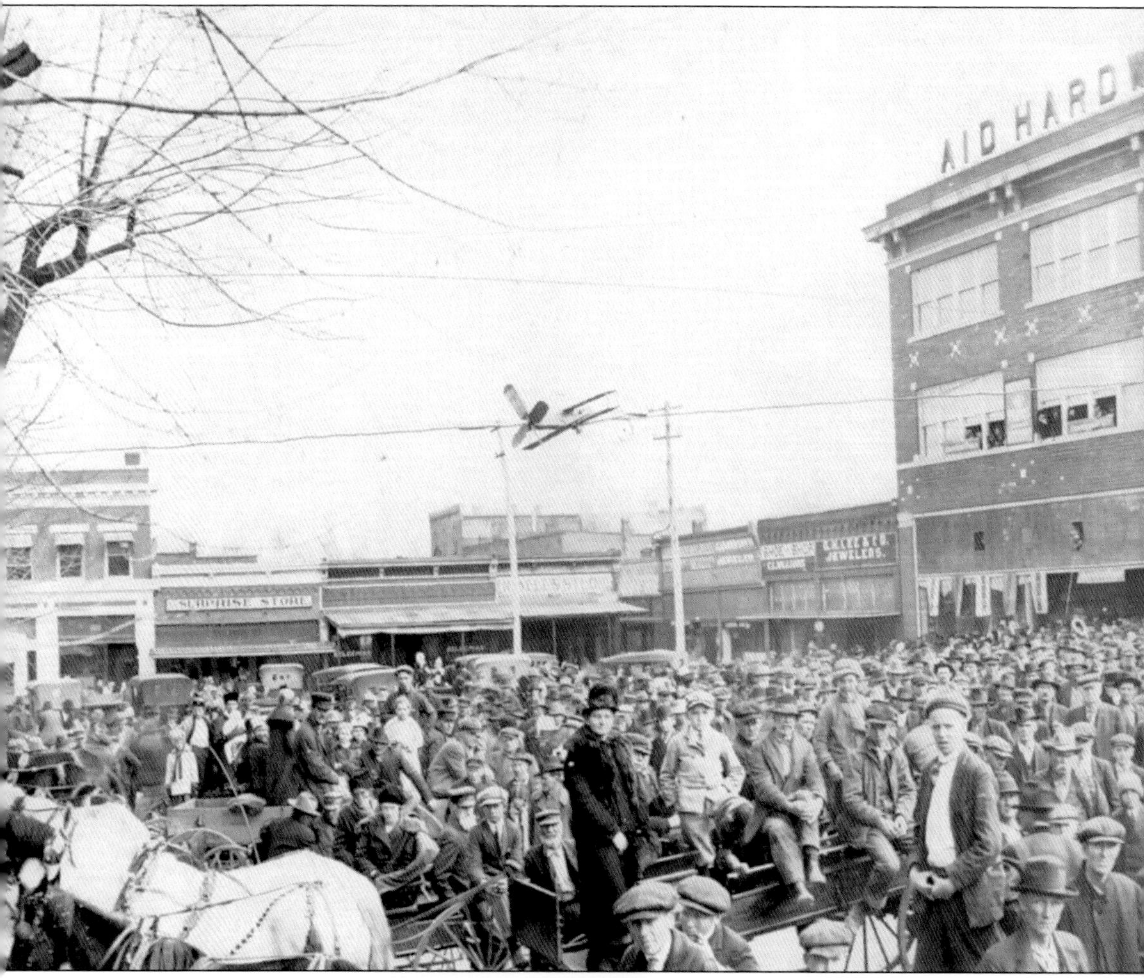

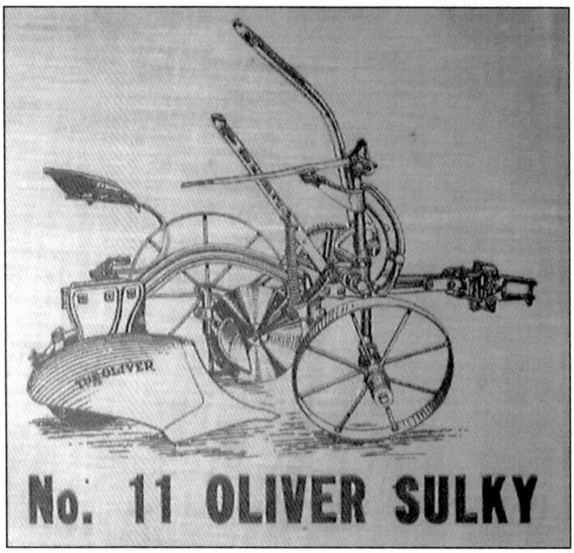

Aid Hardware's new building is the centerpiece of this Oliver Plow and American Fence Day photo from March of 1920. Following the 1914 fire, all the fire-damaged buildings were razed and this new 42,000 square foot structure built. It was made as fireproof as possible; a state-of-the-art sprinkler system was put on every floor. Paving brick was used in its exterior walls because C.T. knew they would last decades longer than regular brick. An Otis

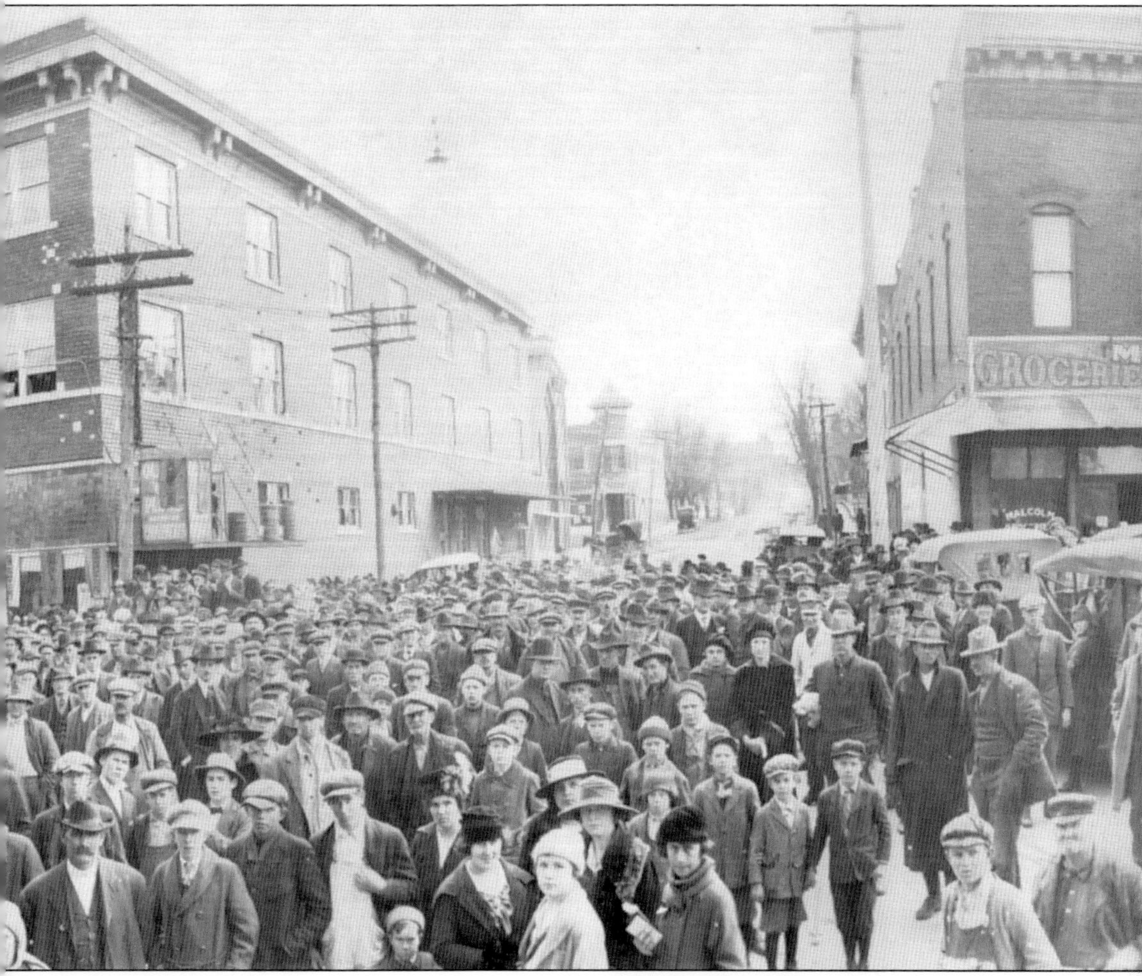

freight elevator was installed and is still in use today. Public restrooms were also included, a new idea at that time. Close to the Presbyterian Church a mirror was placed in the exterior wall for ladies to check their clothes one last time before going into church. Records from the construction reveal it cost over $25,000 to build the new store: a fortune at that time. Within ten years, sales had climbed to over $250,000 a year, proving the money a good investment.

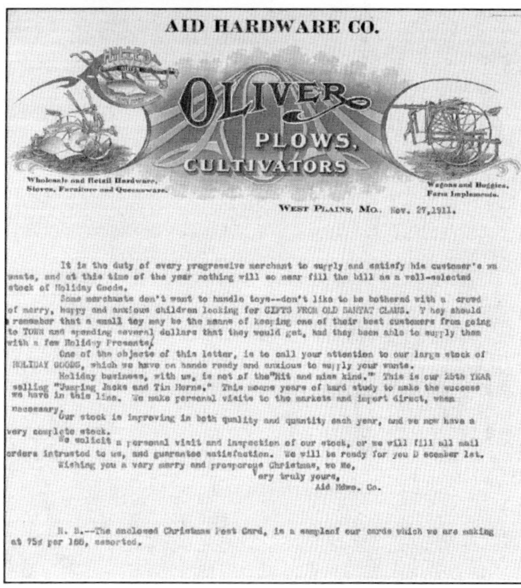

AID HARDWARE CO.

OLIVER PLOWS, CULTIVATORS

Wholesale and Retail Hardware, Stoves, Furniture and Queensware.

Wagons and Buggies, Farm Implements.

WEST PLAINS, MO. Nov. 27,1911.

It is the duty of every progressive merchant to supply and satisfy his customer's wa wants, and at this time of the year nothing will so near fill the bill as a well-selected stock of Holiday Goods.

Some merchants don't want to handle toys--don't like to be bothered with a crowd of merry, happy and anxious children looking for GIFTS FROM OLD SANTAT CLAUS. T hey should remember that a small toy may be the means of keeping one of their best customers from going to TOWN and spending several dollars that they would get, had they been able to supply them with a few Holiday Presents.

One of the objects of this letter, is to call your attention to our large stock of HOLIDAY GOODS, which we have on hands ready and anxious to supply your wants.

Holiday business, with us, is not of the"Hit and miss kind." This is our 25th YEAR selling "Jumping Jacks and Tin Horns." This means years of hard study to make the success we have in this line. We make personal visits to the markets and import direct, when necessary.

Our stock is improving in both quality and quantity each year, and we now have a very complete stock.

We solicit a personal visit and inspection of our stock, or we will fill all mail orders intrusted to us, and guarantee satisfaction. We will be ready for you D ecember 1st.

Wishing you a very merry and prosperous Christmas, we Me,

Very truly yours,

Aid Hdwe. Co.

N. B.--The enclosed Christmas Post Card, is a sampleof our cards which we are making at 75¢ per 100, assorted.

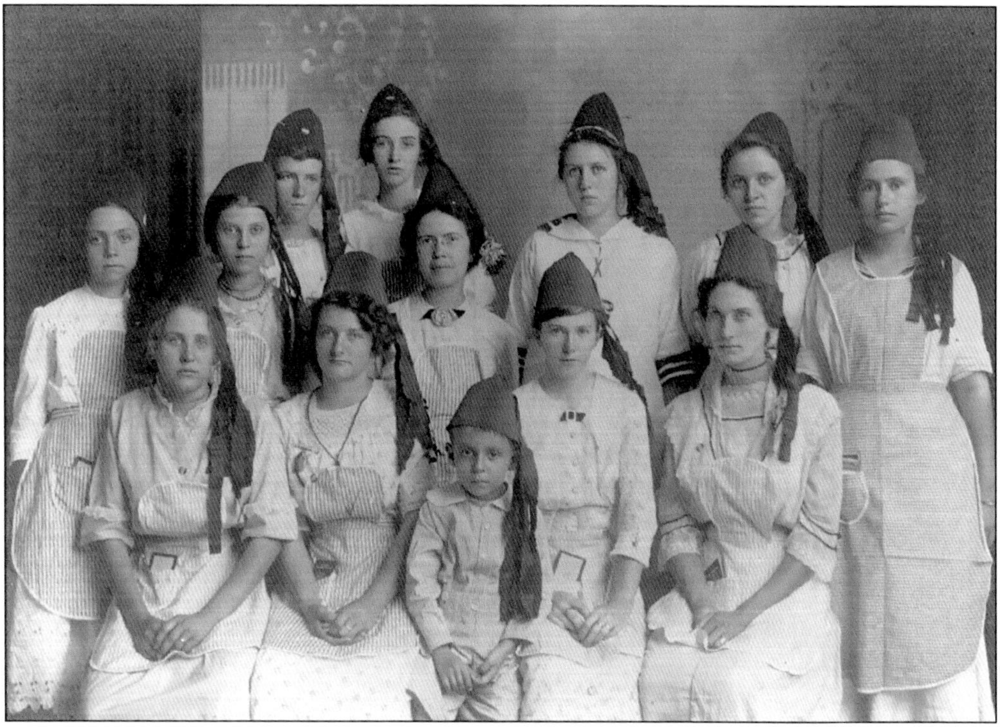

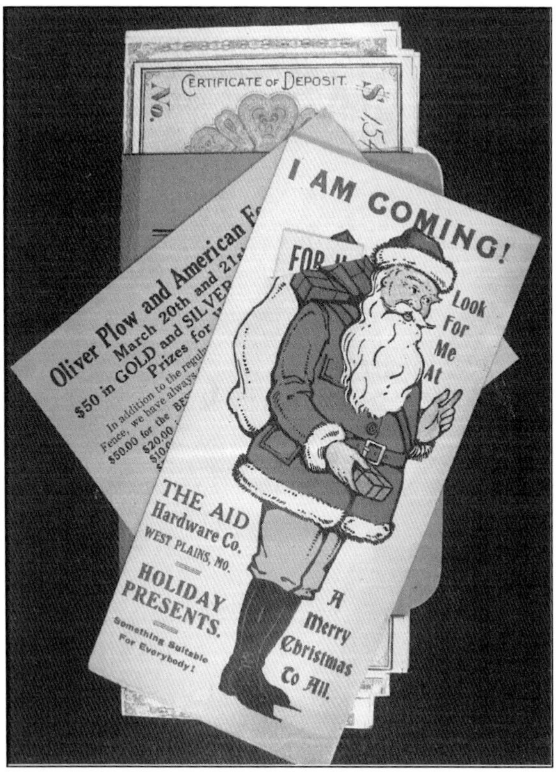

(*above*) To help with sales of this size, the Aid Hardware Booster Girls were created to act as an auxiliary to the regular store clerks. For additional help, local church groups were invited to help run the baking contests and given a percent of each day's sales. The result was crowds of customers that reached into the hundreds by the weekend.

(*left*) C.T. Aid promoted events such as his biscuit-baking contest with intense mail advertising. Cards, brochures, and flyers were mailed regularly to every rural box holder in the county. The Santa card at the left told of a bigger Christmas catalog that would be in the mail the next week. The Oliver Plow Day card offers prizes of $50 in "Gold and Silver" to be given away.

Advertising, advertising, advertising was a key part of Aid Hardware's success. Shown here is a 1922 Oliver Plow Day ticket shaped like a hand. A handshake was a symbol of trust and a deal done right. C.T. Aid's celluloid name badge from 1926 and a pocket whetstone, advertising premium from the American Fence Co. are also pictured. Manufacturers could always be depended on to help with promotions and prizes.

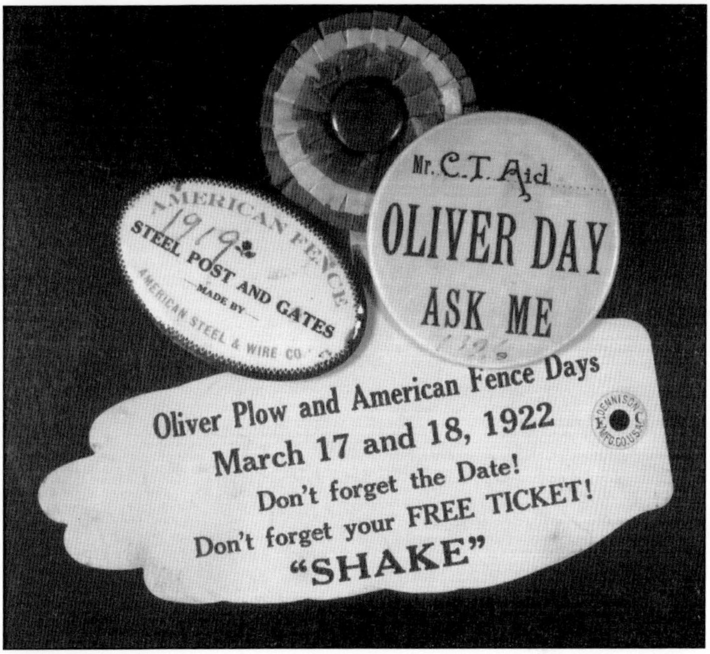

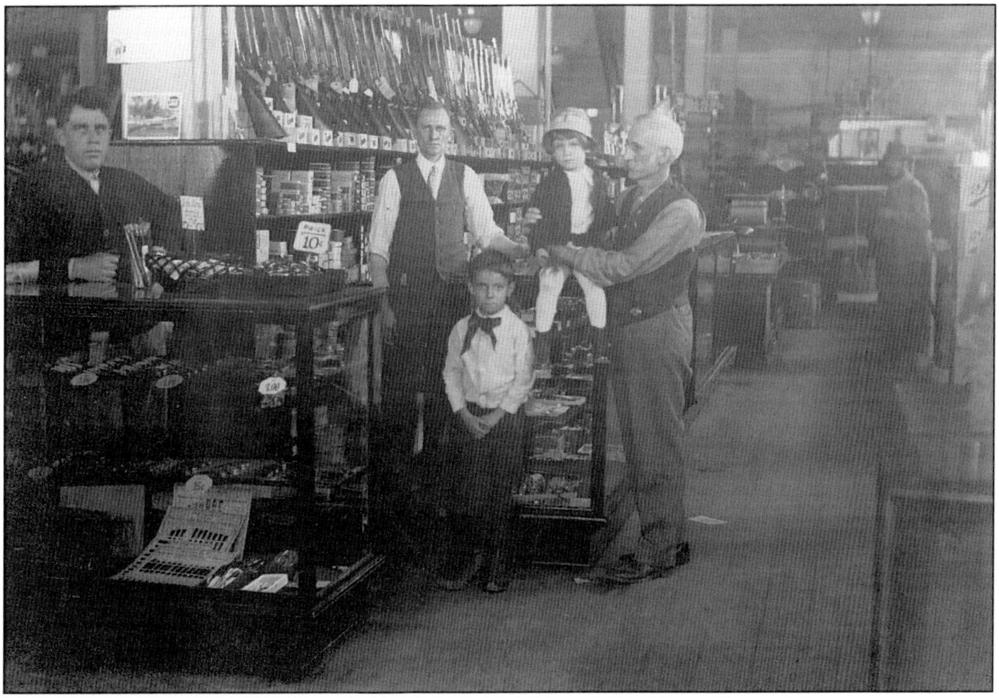

This is the first of a set of three interior views of the new store in 1915. When you entered the front door, to your right were the hardware and sporting good departments. C.T. Aid is standing, holding Joe Aid Jr. in front of a long rack of rifles and shotguns. There are even some of the new Daisy B.B. guns on the far end of the rack. The showcases are full of pocketknives and revolvers.

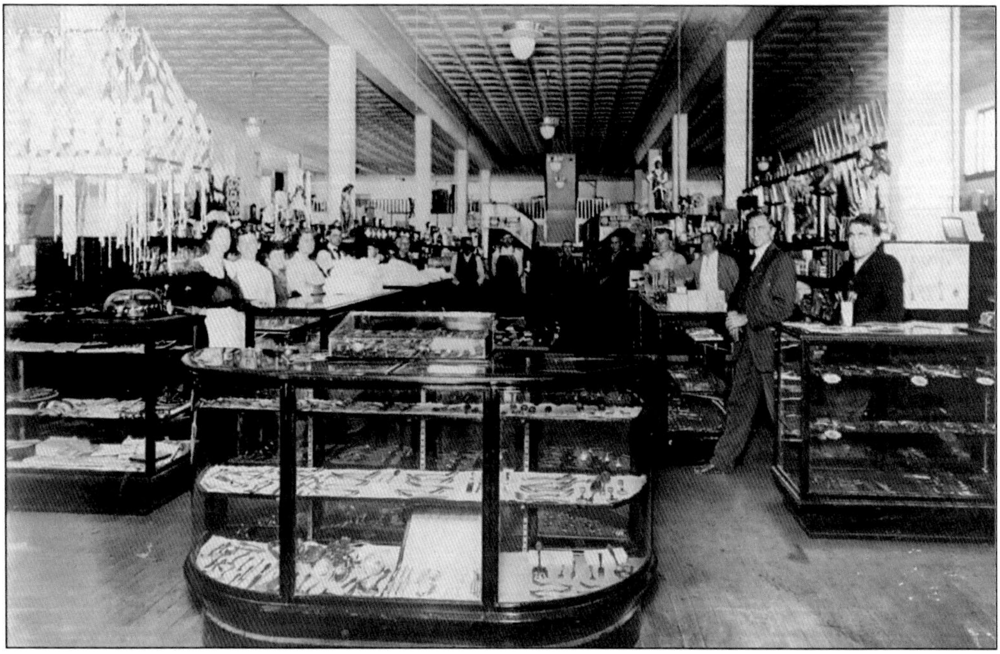

Straight ahead from the front door were higher-priced houseware items. The first showcase displays a large selection of silver ware. To the right are straight razors and to the left are ladies' silk handkerchiefs, gloves, and jewelry. Fourteen employees can be seen in this photo; later, well over 20 were employed. A worker put in six days a week from 8 a.m. to 5 p.m., and on Saturday, the store was open until 9 p.m.

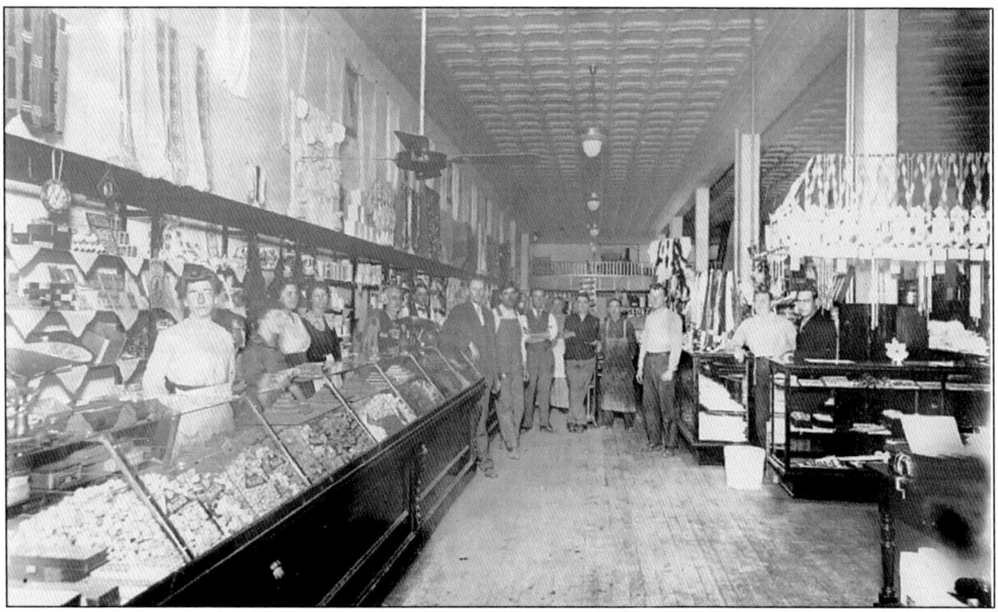

To the left of the front door was a very popular section, the candy counter. From hard candy in the hot summer to chocolates in the winter, a full-time clerk was required just to weigh up candy. Beyond the candy counter were hundreds of bolts of cloth and cabinets of dress patterns. At the back of the store, the dish department had everything for your kitchen.

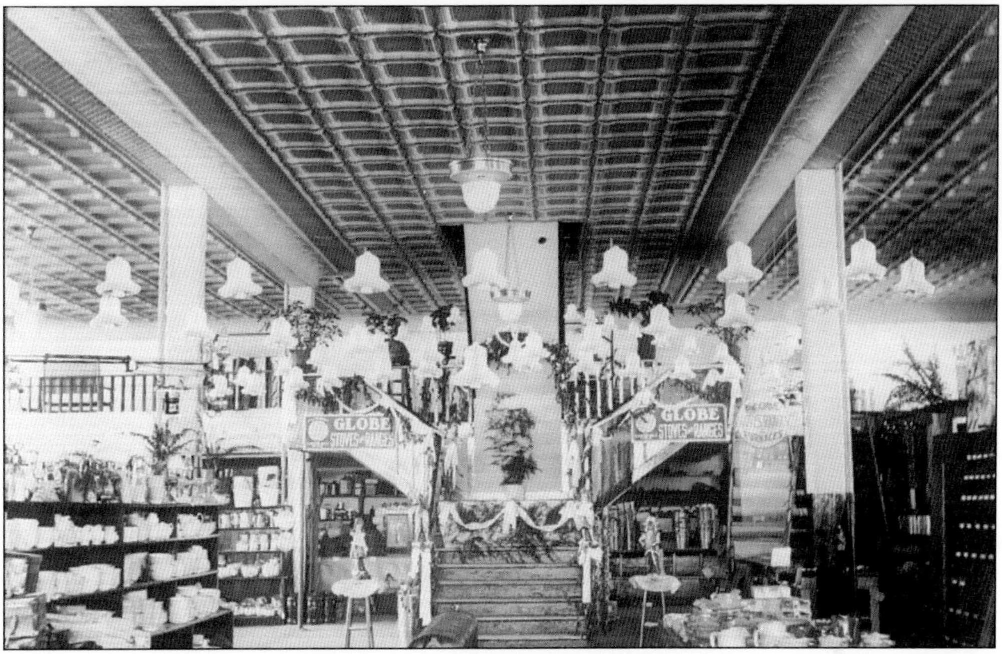

With a new store, C.T. Aid thought up a new promotion. He would offer one of his "Booster" girls credit toward a piano if she could convince a friend to get married in the store. A couple was found and their identity kept a secret until the moment of the wedding. The store was decorated with wedding bells, satin ribbons, and flowers. An overflow crowd showed up for the event.

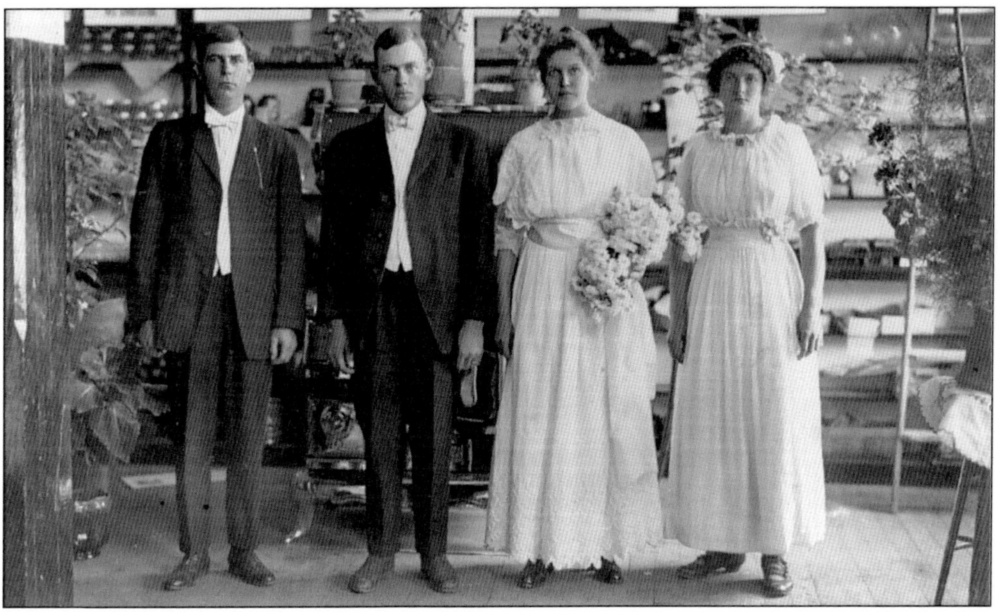

The wedding party, from the left, includes: Claude Cafferty, Best Man; William Scott, Groom; Martha Jane Yates, Bride; and Freda Pearl Bell (Taylor), Bridesmaid. The promotion was a big success. The bride and groom took home a 100-piece set of china, a set of silverware, and many more housekeeping items as part of their prize. The marriage was a big success too; the wedding couple came back and visited the store on their 60th wedding anniversary in 1975.

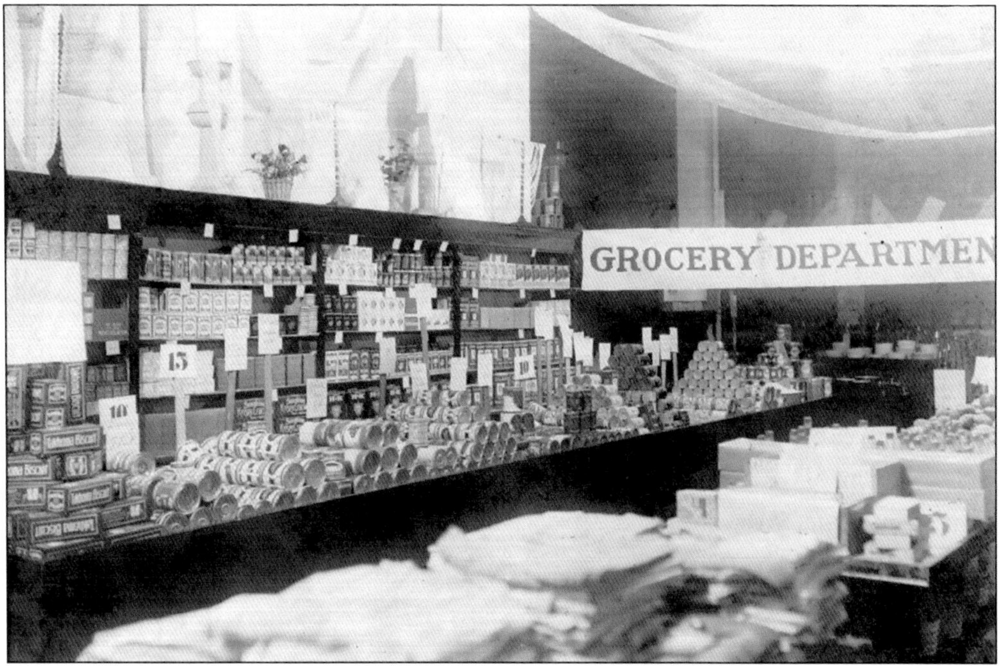

During World War I, the store opened a grocery department that was years ahead of its time. The idea was to offer groceries at very low prices, but without free delivery. Customers were required to bring their own boxes or sacks and to pick their own order from the shelves, then take it to a register to be checked out. It didn't work; people still wanted all the services the other groceries in town offered.

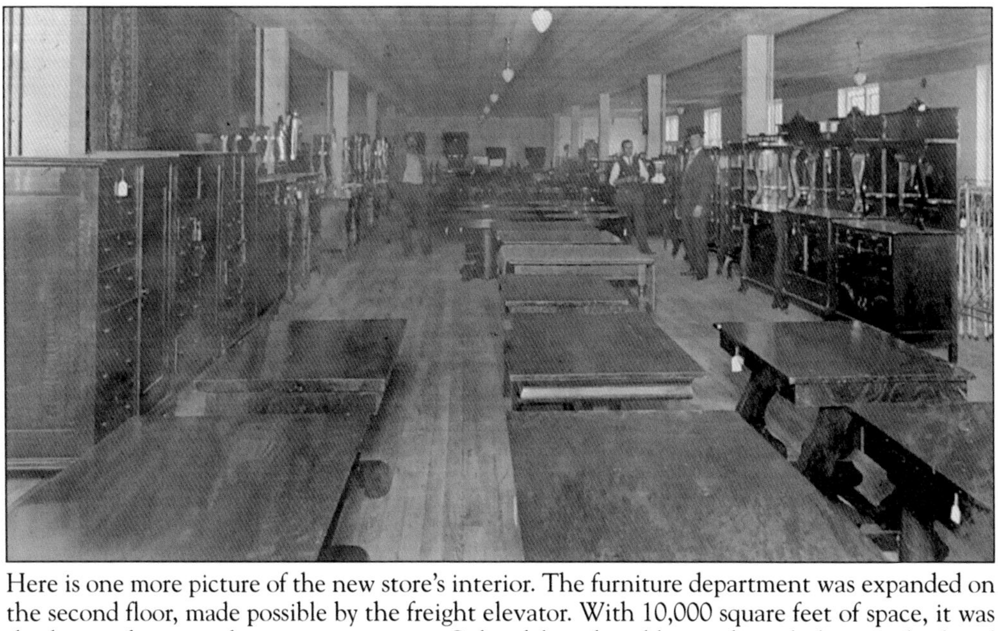

Here is one more picture of the new store's interior. The furniture department was expanded on the second floor, made possible by the freight elevator. With 10,000 square feet of space, it was the largest furniture department in town. Oak sideboards, tables, and wardrobes are displayed in this photo. Many family heirlooms in West Plains have "Aid Hardware Co." stamped on their bottom.

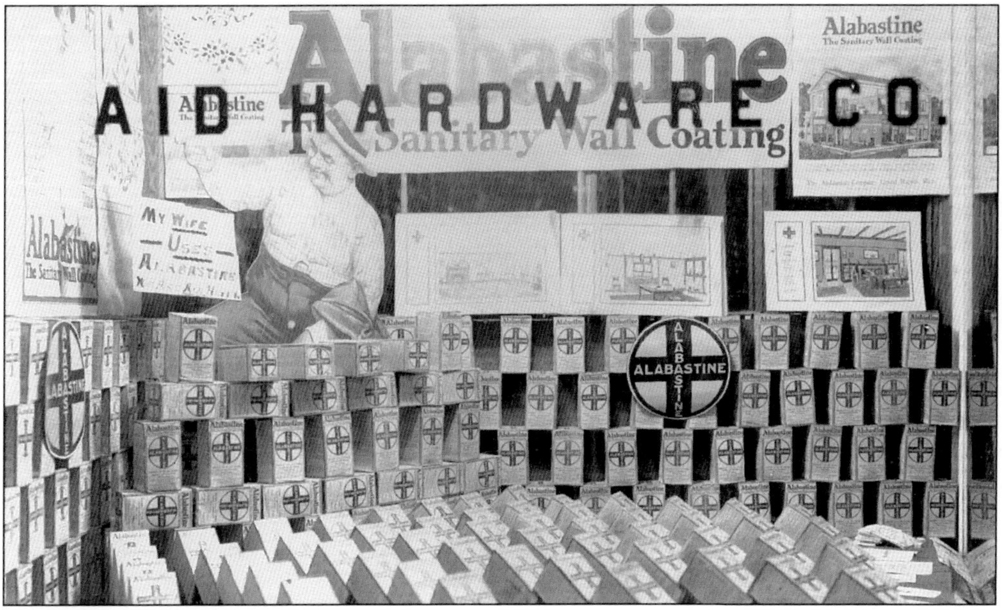

"Window dressing" reached its peak in the Roaring Twenties, before the Depression arrived. This display features Alabastine: "The sanitary wall coating." The new building had large show windows built across the front of the store. The windows had half-walls behind them to give displays a backdrop and to keep curious youngsters out.

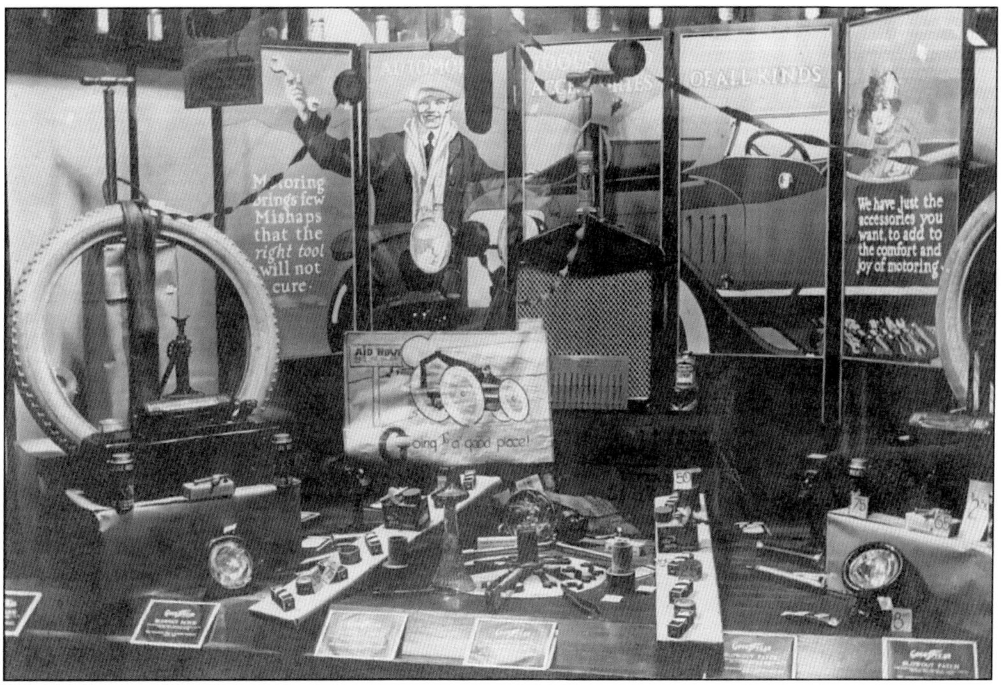

Don Watson created this window display. He was the son of the well-known St. Louis artist Dawson Dawson-Watson. Donald had friends in West Plains and created this display on one of his visits. This display shows that the store sold everything from sparkplugs to new tires for your automobile. "Motoring brings few mishaps that the right tool will not cure."

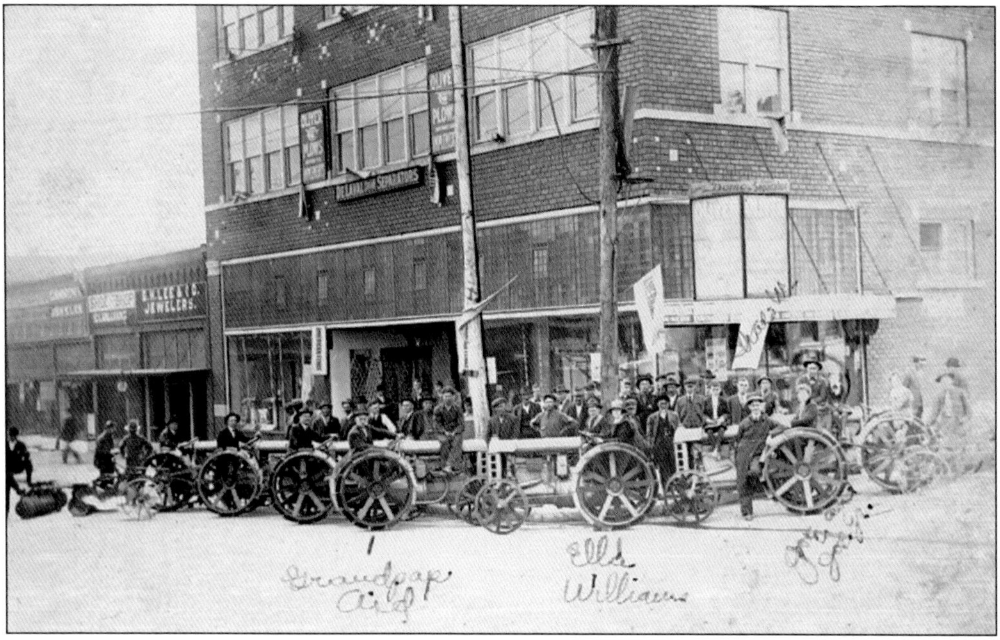

It was a short step from selling automobile parts and plows to becoming a tractor dealer. This group of Fordson Tractors *c.* 1920 shows that C.T. gave it a try, but it wasn't successful. For this photo he managed to get Ella Williams, one of the "Quill Sisters" to pose driving the tractor closest to the camera. C.T. is on the first tractor facing hers.

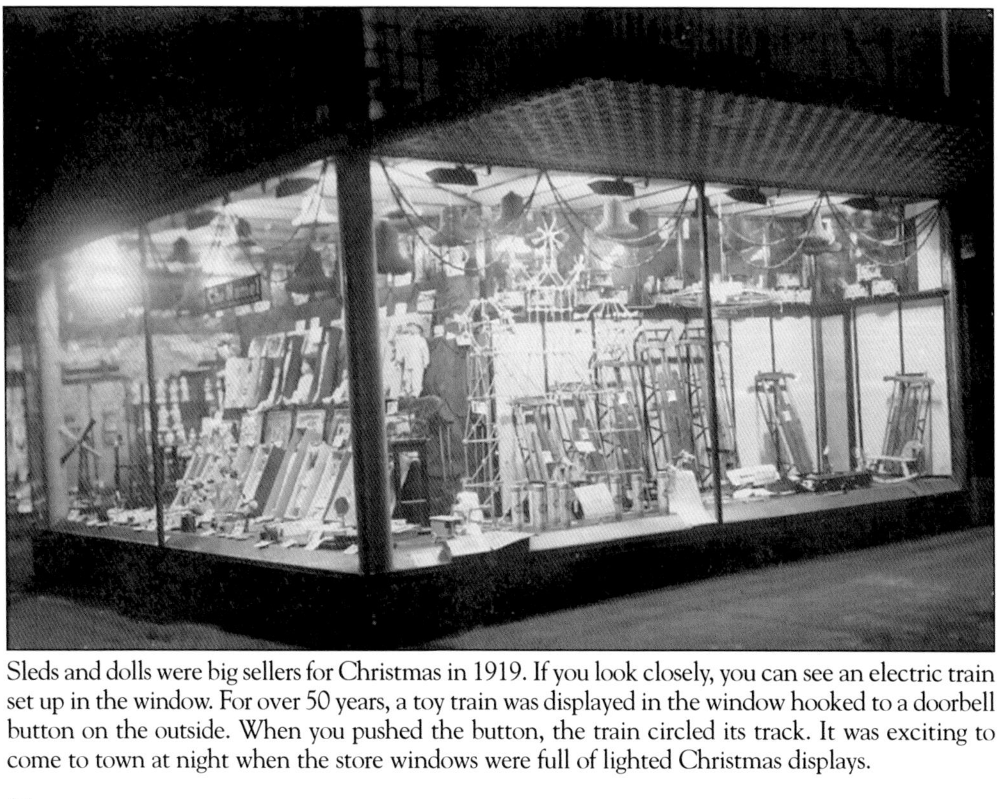

Sleds and dolls were big sellers for Christmas in 1919. If you look closely, you can see an electric train set up in the window. For over 50 years, a toy train was displayed in the window hooked to a doorbell button on the outside. When you pushed the button, the train circled its track. It was exciting to come to town at night when the store windows were full of lighted Christmas displays.

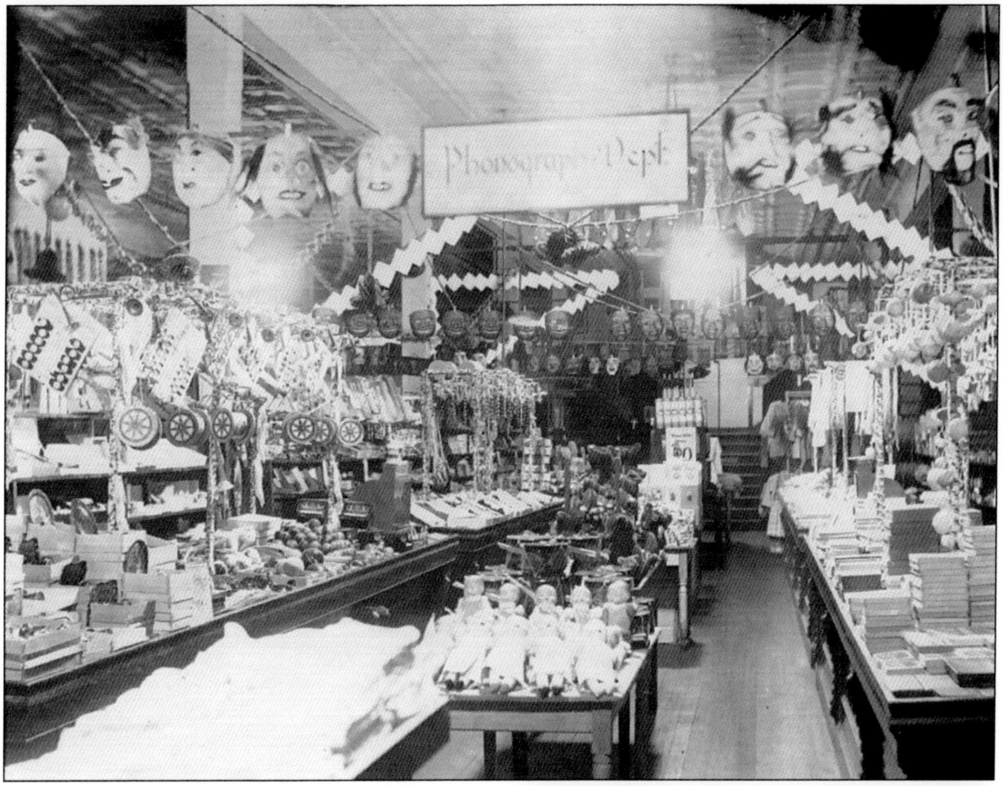

(*above*) Halloween was another time for special displays. Masks made of starched gauze and papier-mâché jack-o-lanterns filled the center aisle. A close look shows dolls, drums, and teddy bears, as Christmas was right around the corner. Upstairs on the balcony, there were lots of chairs for weary shoppers. On livestock sale days, while the men were at the stockyards, the balcony filled with women visiting and catching up on the news.

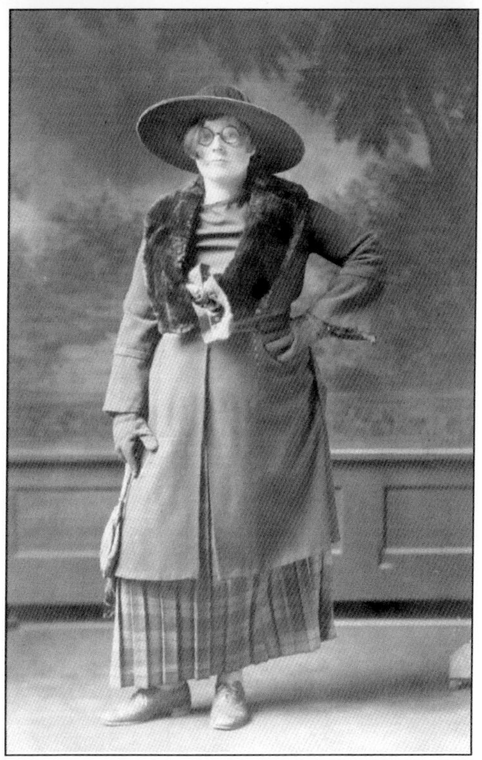

(*right*) May Milstead is show in a fashion show at the store. Milstead was in charge of the women's ready-to-wear department. Her specialty, for which she attended schools, was foundation garments. Around 1930 the balcony at Aid Hardware was expanded to add a larger ladies' clothing shop. May later opened her own business on the Square, Milstead's Ladies and Children's Wear.

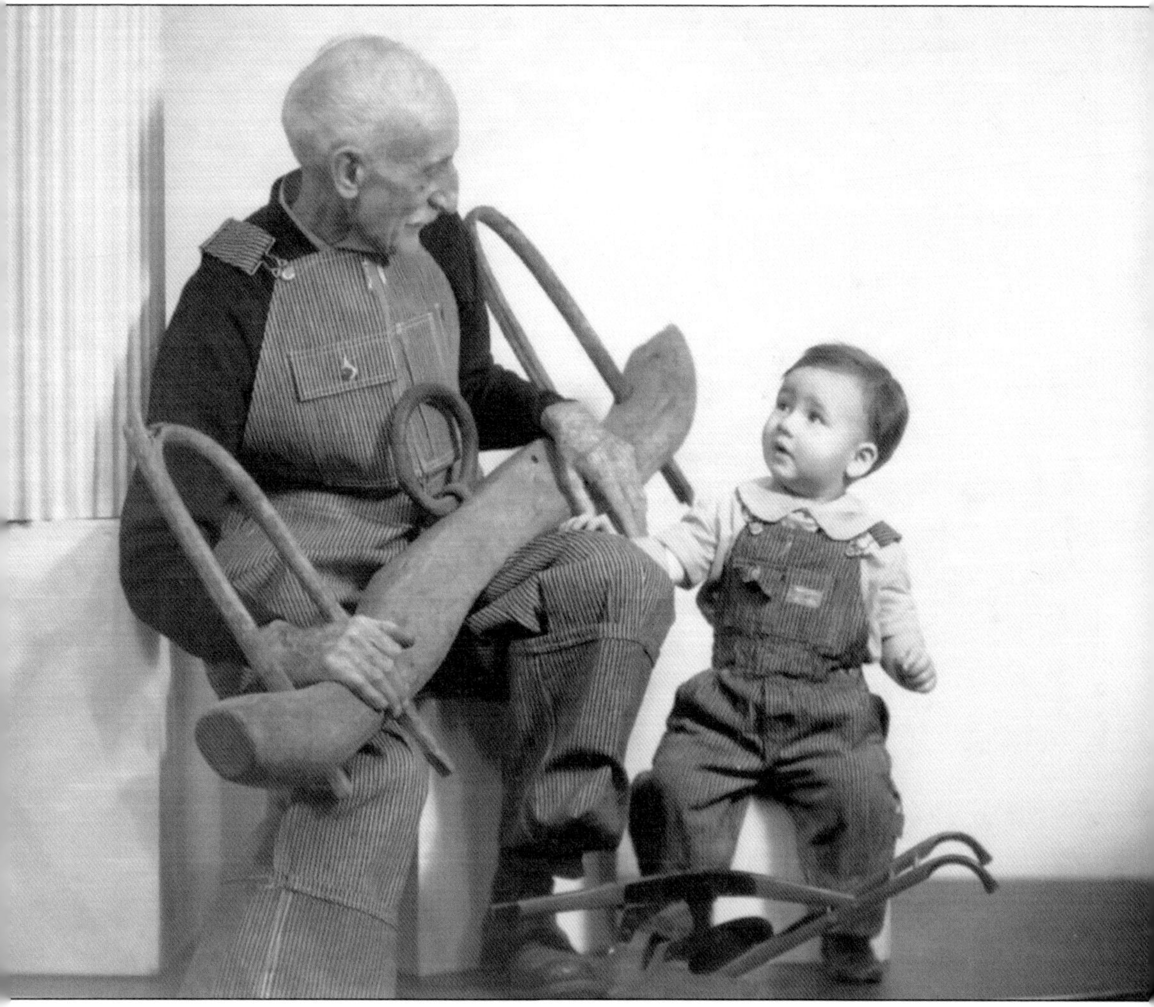

C.T. Aid had this portrait of himself and Joe Aid III, his grandson, taken in October of 1937 when he was 85 years old. Starting with his 75th birthday, C.T. had big birthday parties every five years to celebrate with the store's clerks and his friends. He even included the manufacturers of merchandise carried in his store by sending them an announcement of his new milestone. The store archives have hundreds of birthday cards he received in return from the management of these firms. At Joe's feet is a small salesman-sample Oliver Plow. C.T. holds an ox yoke. The plow and yoke hark back to the busy days of his career selling farm implements and promoting his big sales. C.T. died a year and a half after this picture was taken. His business survived another 50 years until 1990. Lawrence Champieux took this portrait.

Five

Disaster, War, Crime, and Other Big Events

This chapter examines some of the "Big" events that shaped the history of West Plains. The Dance Hall explosion was certainly one of these events. It occurred in 1928 and made headlines from coast to coast. People visiting town still ask where the dance hall was located. World War I was another event that changed life in the Ozarks. A generation of young men were called to arms. Many of them didn't return, many were maimed, and all of them came home with a new perspective on their world. Fires, plane crashes, murders, and politics were all things people talked about for years after they happened. They are all still great stories.

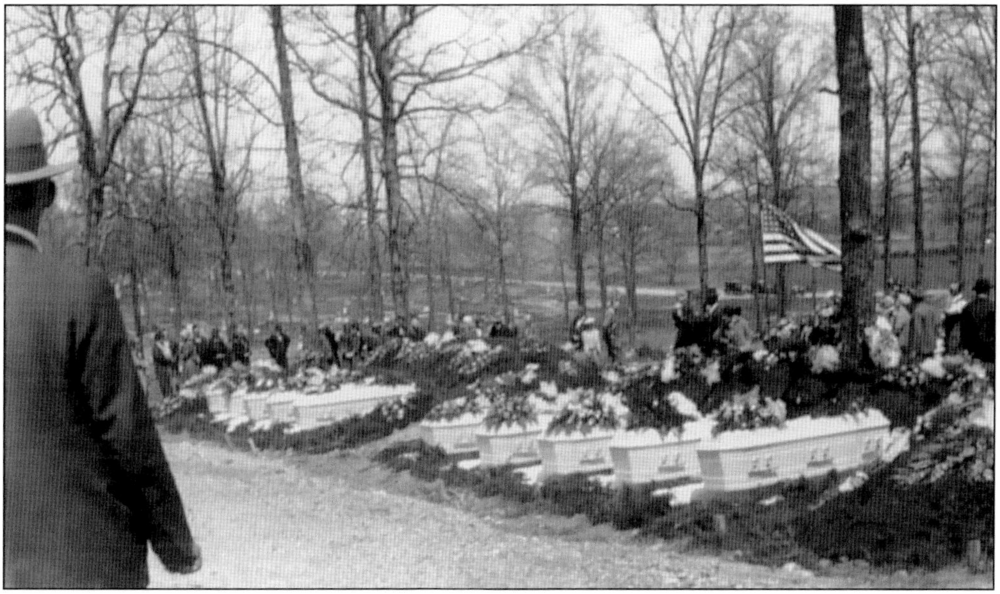

In the little town of West Plains, in old Missouri State,
'Twas in the month of April, they saw the hand of fate…
'Twas there the young folks gathered, one fatal Friday night,
And to the dance they wandered, with hearts so gay and bright…
The dance was nearly over, the evening nearly past,
When from the floor beneath them, there came an awful blast…

Vernon Dahlhart, "Ballad of West Plains Explosion," 1928 (excerpts).

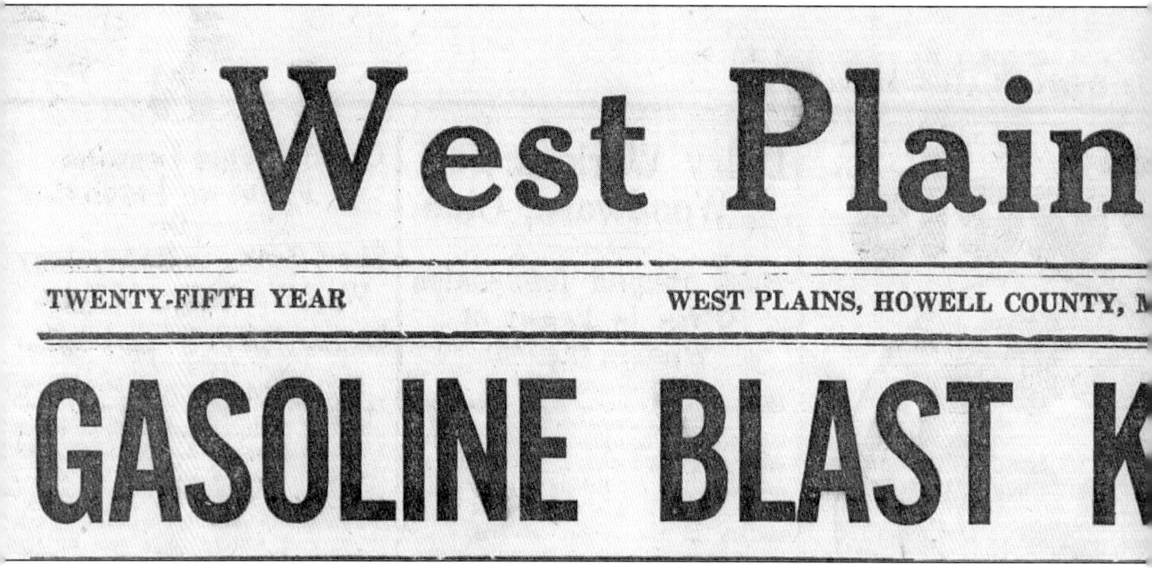
West Plain

TWENTY-FIFTH YEAR WEST PLAINS, HOWELL COUNTY, M

GASOLINE BLAST K

The dance took place on a pleasant April evening, Friday the 13th. The hall was on the second floor of the Bond Building on East Main Street. The Wiser Motor Company was on the first floor. Over 50 people were in the hall as the band prepared to take a break. Their last number, "At Sundown," was never completed. At 11:04 an explosion raised the dancers into the air, then collapsed the building trapping them in a raging fire. Thirty-seven of them died. The cause

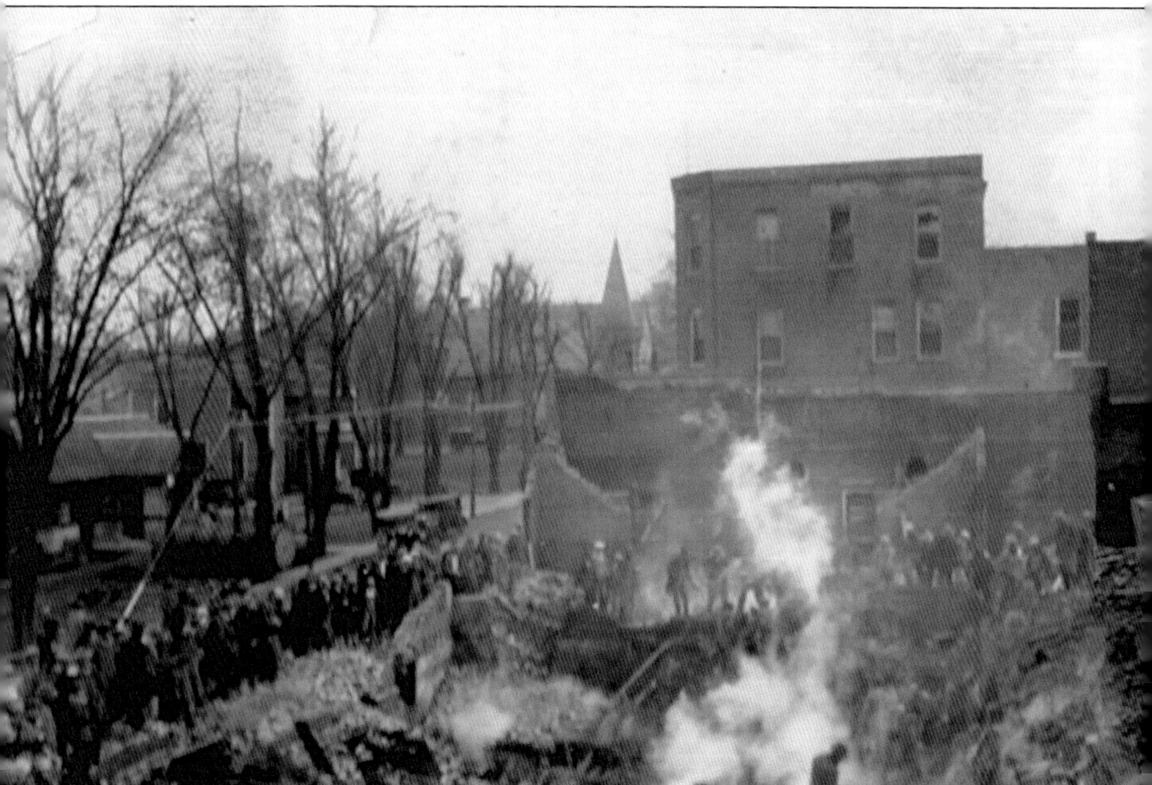

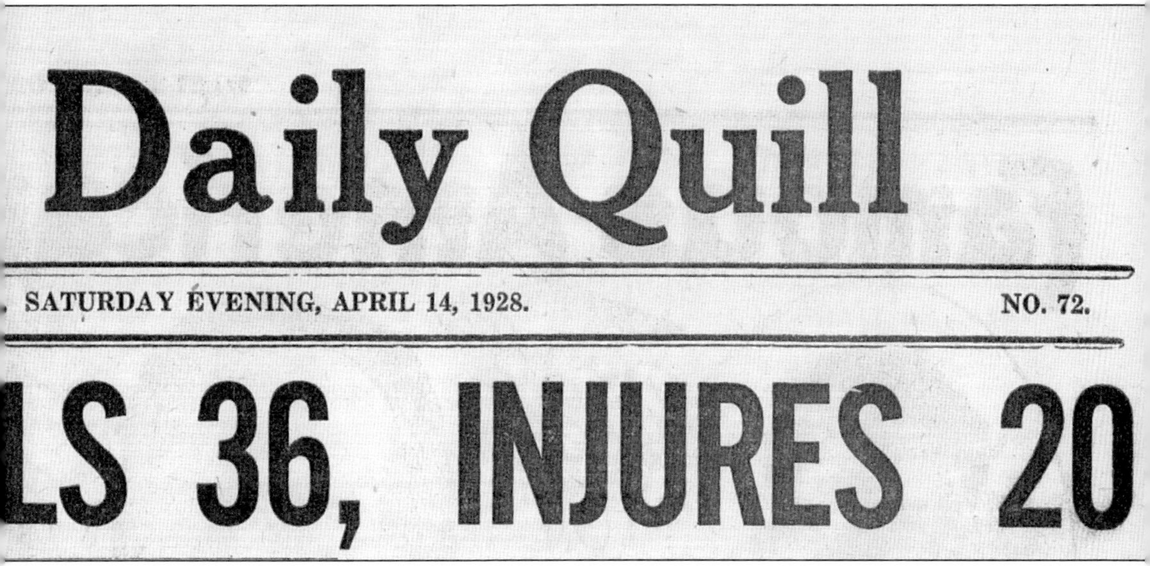

Daily Quill

SATURDAY EVENING, APRIL 14, 1928. NO. 72.

LS 36, INJURES 20

of the explosion was never discovered. The most common theory was that gasoline stored in the Motor Company caused it. The picture on page 87 shows the funeral for the 20 unidentified dead. Their graves are marked by one common monument in Oak Lawn Cemetery. Above is a composite of two photos taken the morning after the explosion by 15-year-old, Joe Aid Jr.

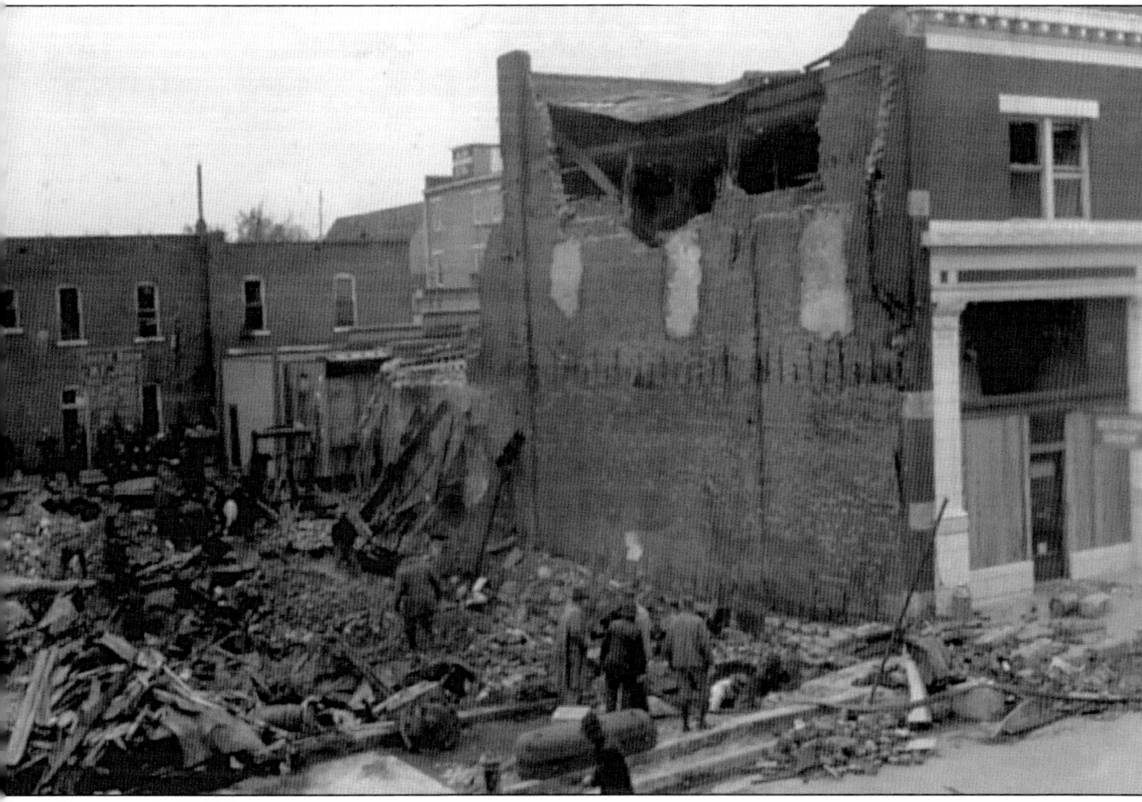

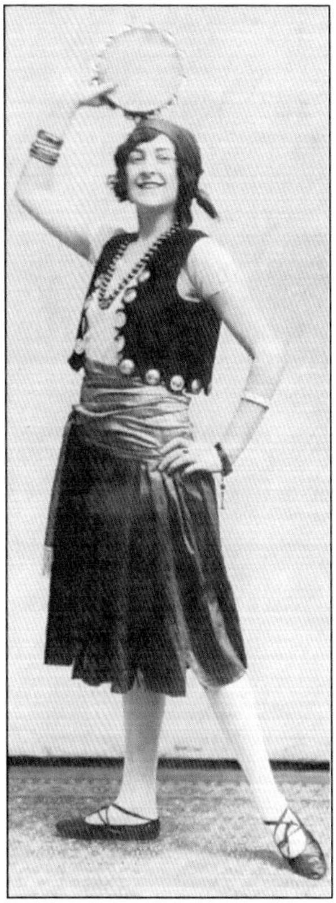

Frances "Billy" Drago, 22 years old, was one of the 20 unidentified victims of the explosion. Billy was the manager of the Western Union Office only two doors west of the dance hall. Her sister, Mrs. Susan Drago Rogers, was also killed in the fire. Billy took a telegraphy course from Western Union after high school graduation. She was the soprano soloist in the Episcopal Church's choir.

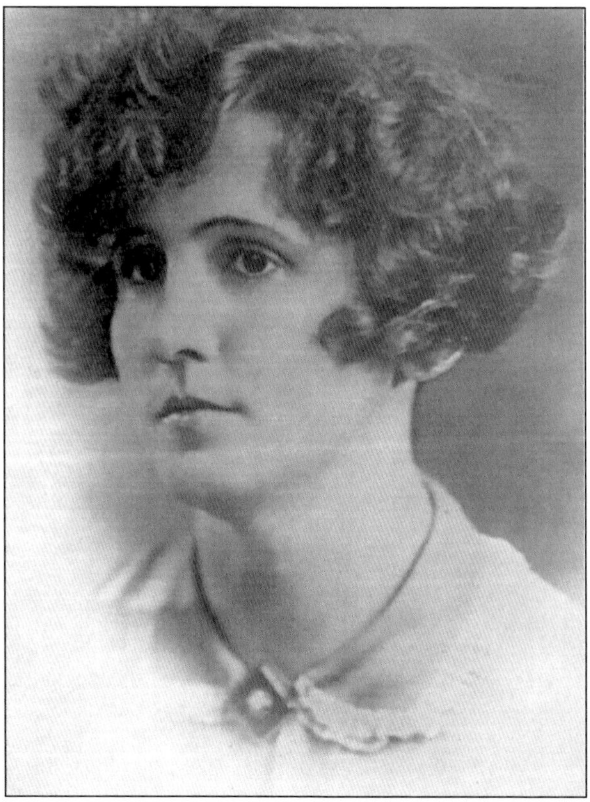

Kitty McFarland owned McFarland Undertaking Company, one block east of the dance hall. Her body was identified and a funeral held at her home on Grace Avenue. The *Quill* reported: "Few Women Escape. Only three women escaped alive while sixteen men escaped… due to the fact that the men were stronger." But, it could also be pointed out that more men died than women.

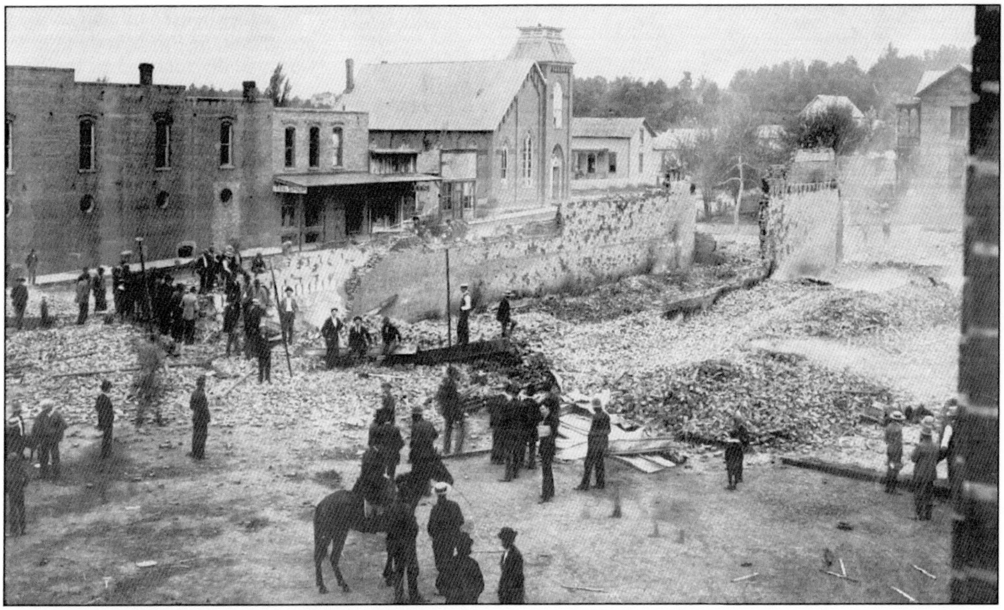

Fires could burn almost unchecked before the city installed its first water works in 1901. Even though the fire department had a pump wagon, wells and cisterns didn't hold enough water to fight a big fire. This fire on September 22, 1895 destroyed half of the southwest corner of the Square. The new Presbyterian Church can be seen in the background on South Street.

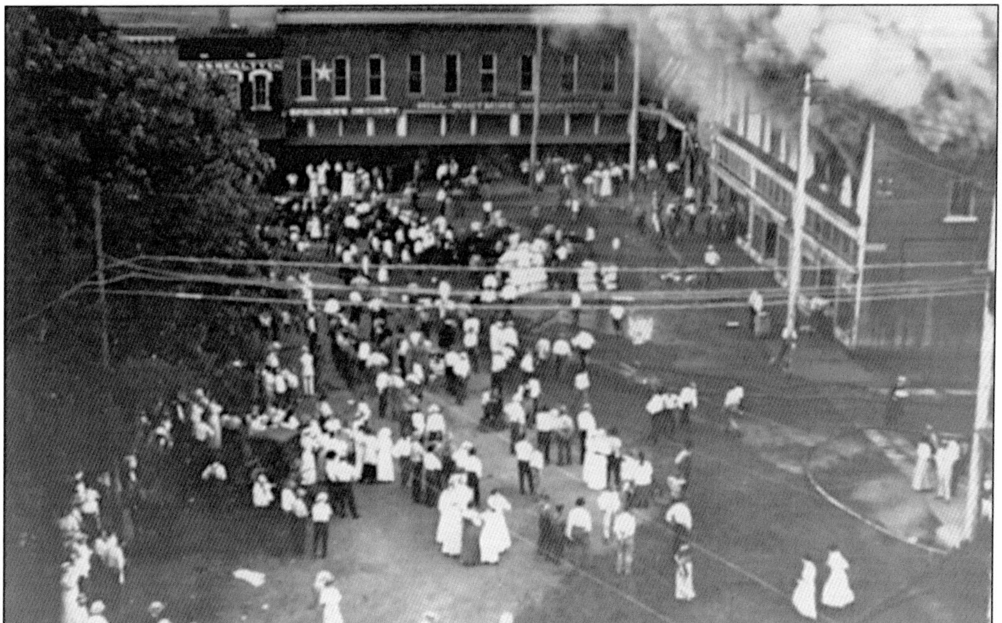

In 1914, 1915, and 1919, large commercial blocks on the Square were destroyed by fire. This photo shows Langston's burning in 1915. It was taken from the roof of the new Aid building, built after their fire the year before. In the center background is the Dixon Block, which burned in 1919. The fire department had a new motorized fire truck by 1919, but containment was still their goal.

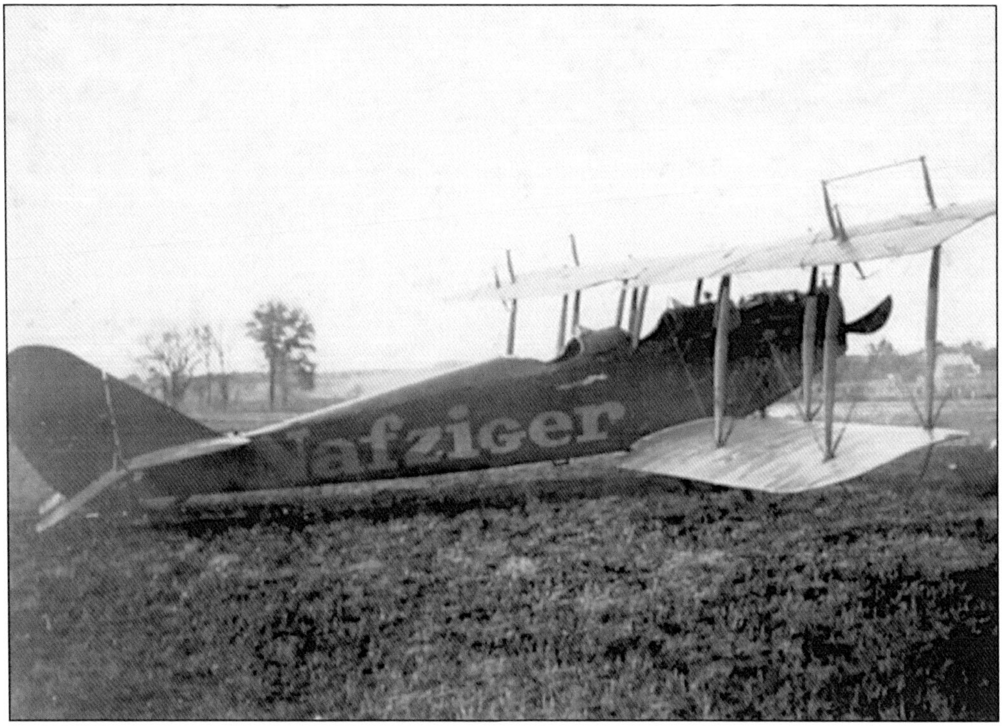

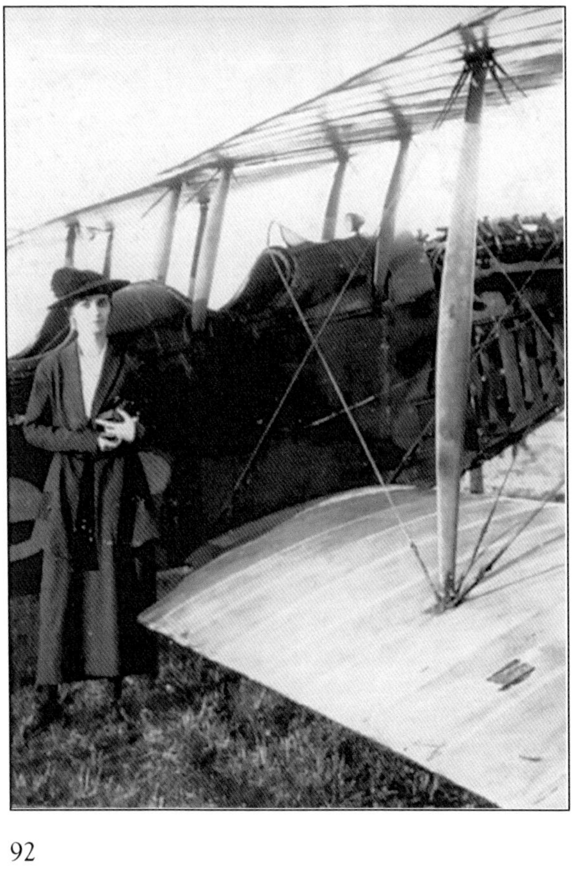

This is a barnstormer's biplane near West Plains in 1920. Here is the Quill's account of the first airplane to fly over town two years earlier, "Shortly after 10 o'clock this morning a huge plane passed over the city with flying flags and roaring motors... 30 minutes before it reached West Plains, telephone messages were received from Mammoth Spring, Ark., stating it was traveling this way. "The news that an aero plane was headed toward West Plains spread over the city, seemingly on magic wings. The roaring of the machine was heard as it came up Howell Valley, the streets were lined with people with eager upturned faces. Following the Frisco tracks, the plane swept like a huge, roaring bird up the valley into WP." At left, Olive Kingsbury waits for her first airplane ride."

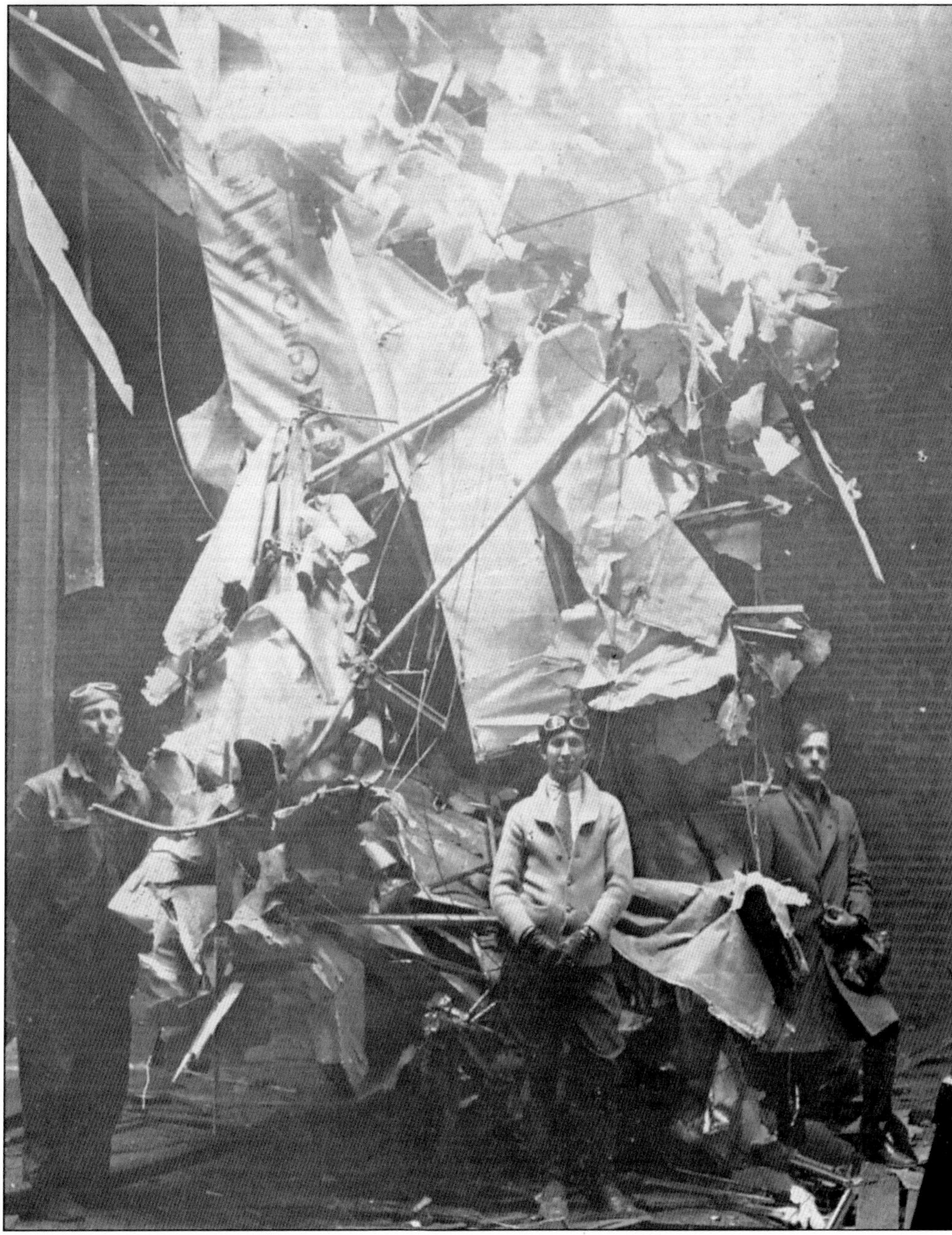

Two barnstorming pilots from Kansas were performing in West Plains when Frank Rosser, a local man, talked Captain H. R. Heimer into giving him a ride. As Heimer preformed a stunt 700 feet over town the Curtis biplane's rudder cable snapped and sent it into a nosedive. The large crowd watching the plane feared both men were dead. The plane fell nose first straight into the southern half of the Bond Building (Butler Furniture) on Washington Avenue. Amazingly the plane slammed through the roof then hung in the rafters. That is where employees of the West Plains Transfer Company, on the first floor, found both men in their safety harnesses strapped into their seats with only minor injuries. Heimer and his partner "Dare Devil" Davis were in town as part of an advertising promotion. They had to take the train back to Kansas.

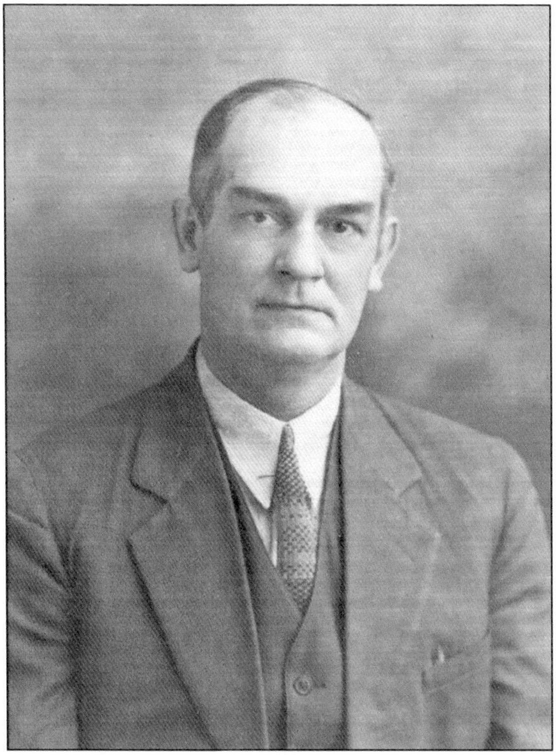

C. Roy Kelly, Howell County Sheriff, was shot and killed by members of the "Ma" Barker Gang on December 19, 1931. Two nights before, McCallon's Men Wear, on the west side of the Square, had been robbed. The robbers took their time, picking the sizes and colors they wanted from the best clothes in the store. A young couple reported seeing a blue DeSoto near the scene.

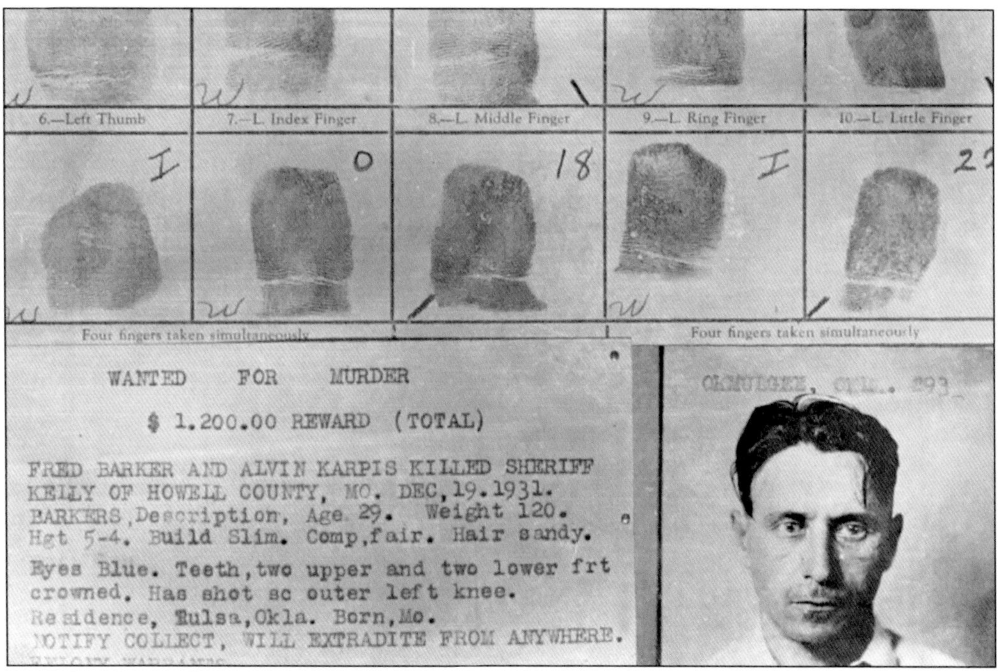

6.—Left Thumb | 7.—L. Index Finger | 8.—L. Middle Finger | 9.—L. Ring Finger | 10.—L. Little Finger

Four fingers taken simultaneously

Four fingers taken simultaneously

WANTED FOR MURDER

$ 1.200.00 REWARD (TOTAL)

FRED BARKER AND ALVIN KARPIS KILLED SHERIFF KELLY OF HOWELL COUNTY, MO. DEC,19.1931.
BARKERS,Description, Age 29. Weight 120.
Hgt 5-4. Build Slim. Comp,fair. Hair sandy.
Eyes Blue. Teeth,two upper and two lower frt crowned. Has shot sc outer left knee.
Residence, Tulsa,Okla. Born,Mo.
NOTIFY COLLECT, WILL EXTRADITE FROM ANYWHERE.

Two days later, Sheriff Kelly was coming out of the post office on East Main when "Crick" Davidson crossed the street to tell him three suspicious men in a Blue DeSoto were at his garage. Kelly went to investigate. As he approached the car one of the occupants shot Kelly four times. The men quickly fled the area. Later they were identified as Fred Barker and Alvin Karpis.

Alice Cary Risley served as a volunteer nurse in New Orleans during the Civil War. Because Alice's father was a federal soldier, she and her mother, Phoebe Farmer, fled their rural Louisiana home to find protection with Federal Troops in New Orleans. Only 15 years old, she nursed many wounded soldiers there. Those boys didn't forget Alice. Many wrote her poems and letters after they recovered, and one, Sam Risley, married her.

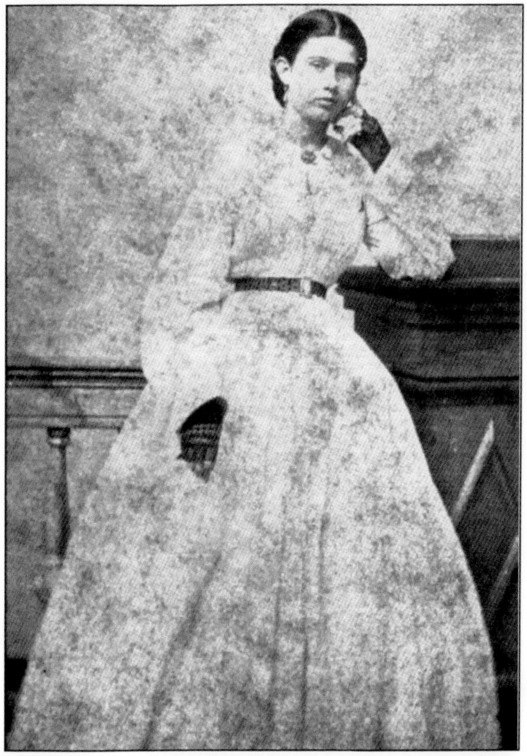

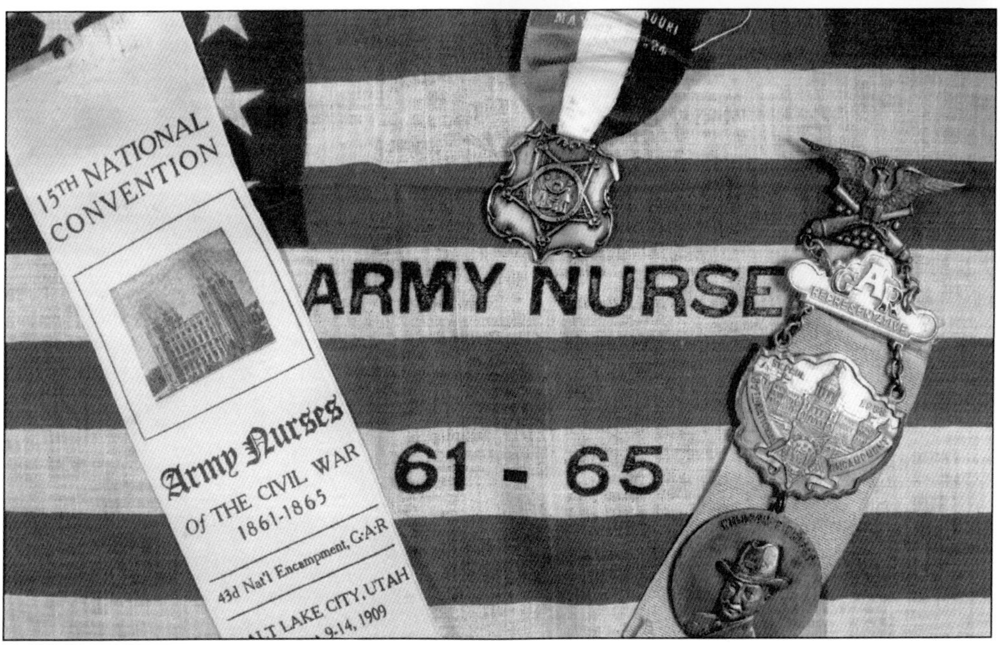

Alice and Sam moved to West Plains in the 1870s. Sam ran the *South Missouri Journal*. Later he was mayor and postmaster, and in his absence Alice was also postmaster. Still, it was her service as a Civil War nurse that gained Alice fame. Here are ribbons and decorations she wore at war reunions. She was the last surviving member of the National Association of Civil War Nurses on her death in 1939.

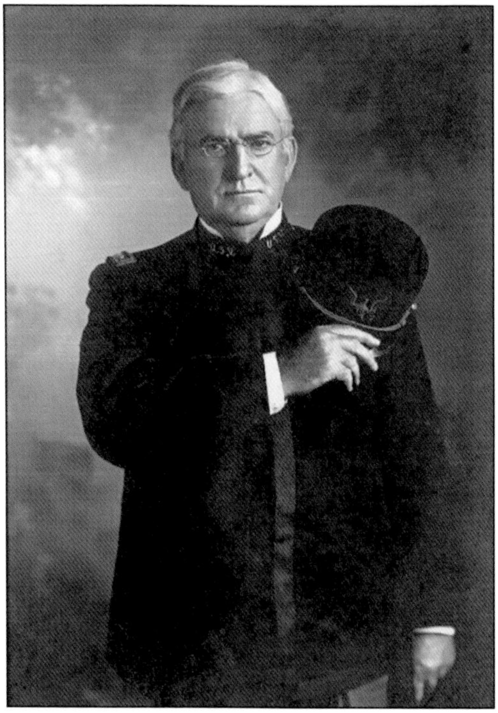

Colonel Jay Lynn Torrey was born in Illinois in 1852. During the Spanish American War he organized the Second U.S. Volunteer Calvary, "Torrey's Rough Riders." After the war he was an influential lobbyist in Washington, D.C. and proposed a federal bankruptcy bill that is still in use today. In 1906 he bought 10,000 acres of land 14 miles southeast of West Plains and established the community of Fruitville.

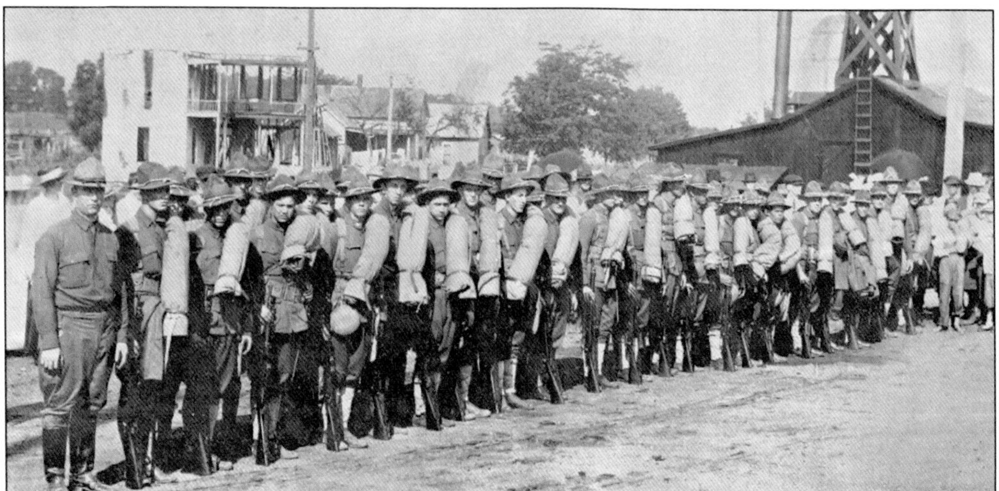

Company D of the Missouri National Guard prepares to leave for France during WWI. Captain Mark Springer (at right) was its commander. At the battlefront it became part of the 130th Machine Gun Battalion and fought at Verdun. Captain Springer and several of his men were injured there by mustard gas. Thirty-four men from Howell County died in the war, over half from the flu epidemic.

On April 21, 1919, a special train arrived in town carrying a battle tank. World War I was over, and it was time to celebrate with a parade. The tank lead, followed by 50 veterans of the recent war in Europe. Then came the Victory Girls dressed in white, singing patriotic songs. Floats carrying Civil War and Spanish American War veterans, Boy Scouts, and school groups followed them.

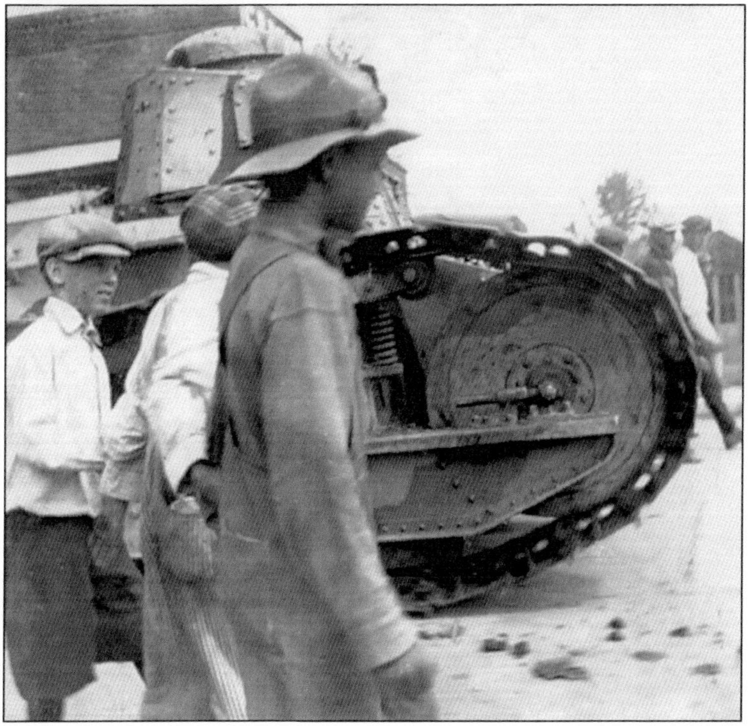

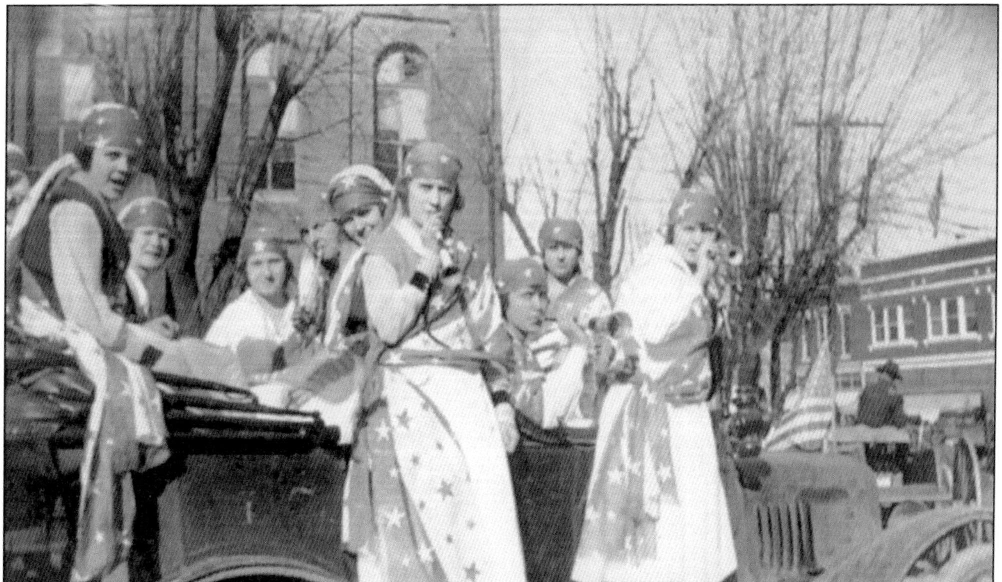

The Victory Girls were a group of young women who helped promote the sale of War Bonds during World War I. With all the young men drafted in the war effort, they joined together to travel over Howell County giving patriotic skits and singing songs. Here, wearing their red, white, and blue costumes, they blow horns celebrating the end of the war.

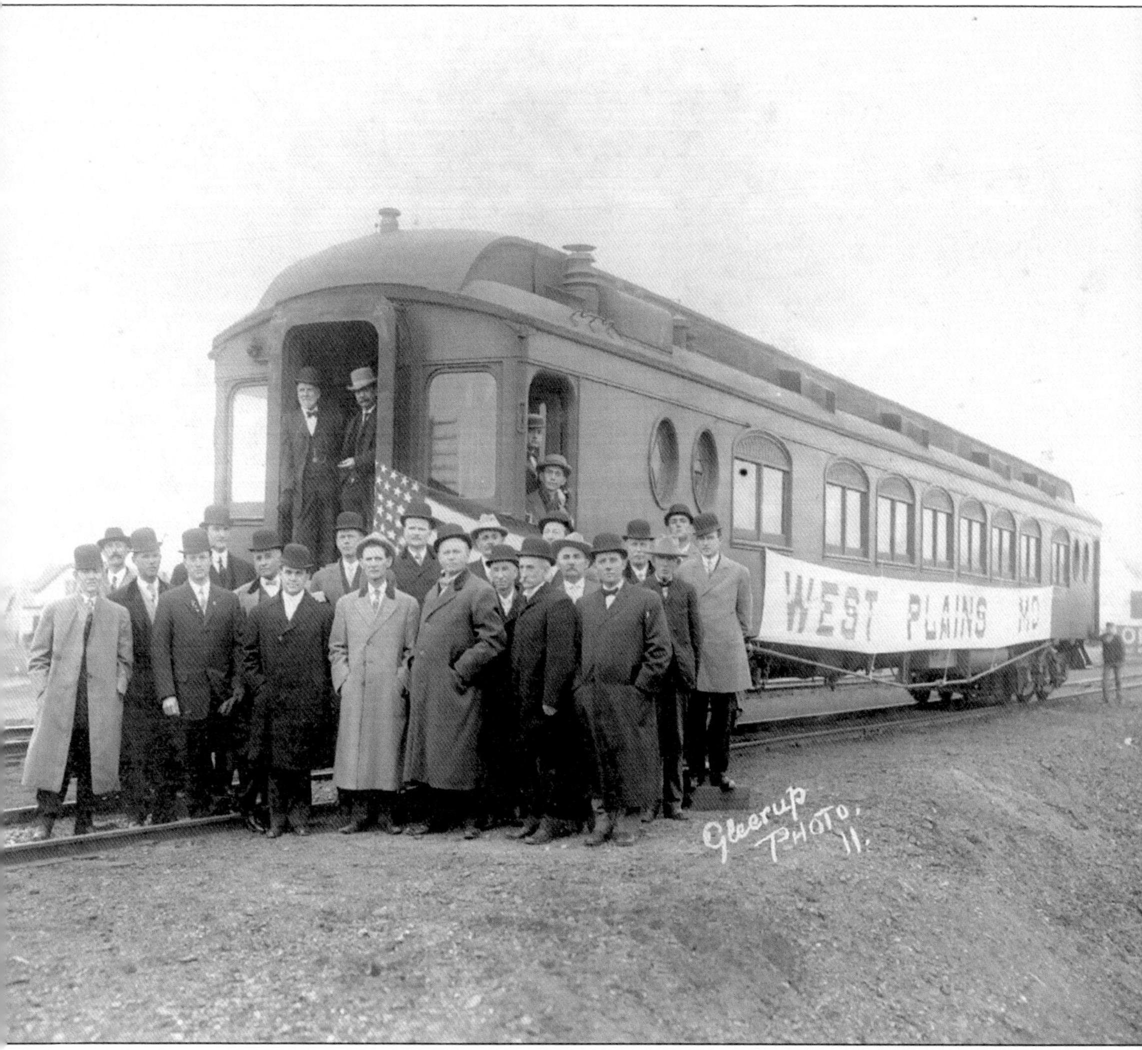

The Commercial Club, founded July 10, 1900, was the first Chamber of Commerce in the State of Missouri. Here, in March of 1911, the club gets ready to board the Pullman car "Agra" to tour the state boosting the West Plains area and Colonel Torrey's goal of moving the state capitol to Howell County. They left West Plains on Sunday and toured in St. Louis on Monday, calling on the city's newspapers promoting their plans. On Tuesday they were in Jefferson City where they visited the penitentiary. C.E. Kimberlin, an ex-Howell County sheriff and treasurer of the club, led the tour. At the warden's office they were treated to a visit with Ben Richardson who had murdered the West Plains jailer, Alf Henry, during a jailbreak earlier that year. Wednesday was spent in St. Joseph and Kansas City, and Thursday they returned home. Gleerup took this photo east of the passenger depot.

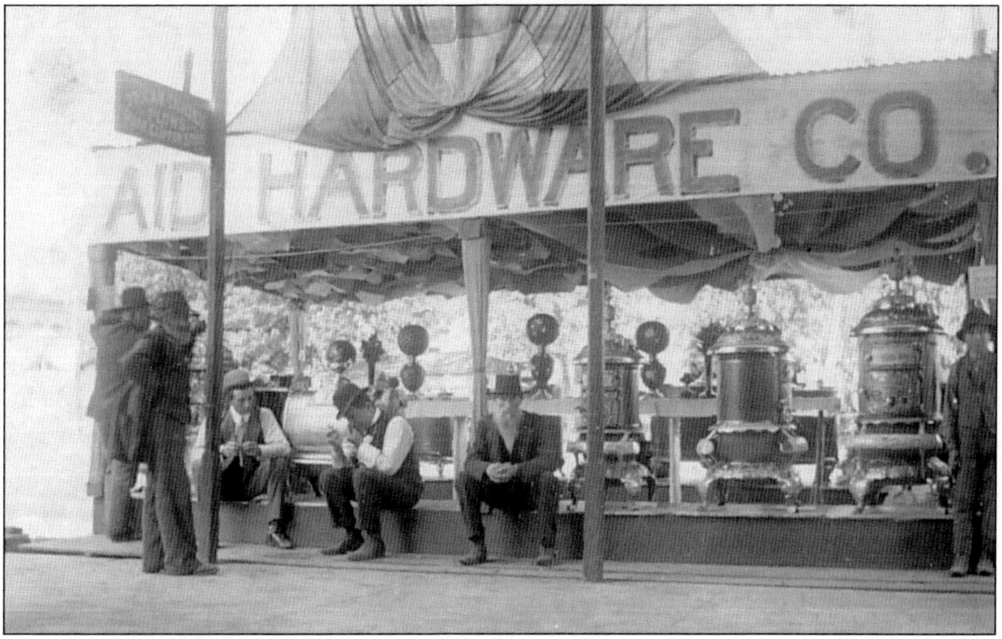

The first project of the Commercial Club was to sponsor a "street fair." It was their version of a local trade show with booths set up around the downtown area. The Aid Hardware booth featured the latest in stoves, kerosene banquet lamps, and miniature lamps. Other projects for the club in 1900 were an attempt to establish a pearl button factory and a zinc ore reduction plant in West Plains.

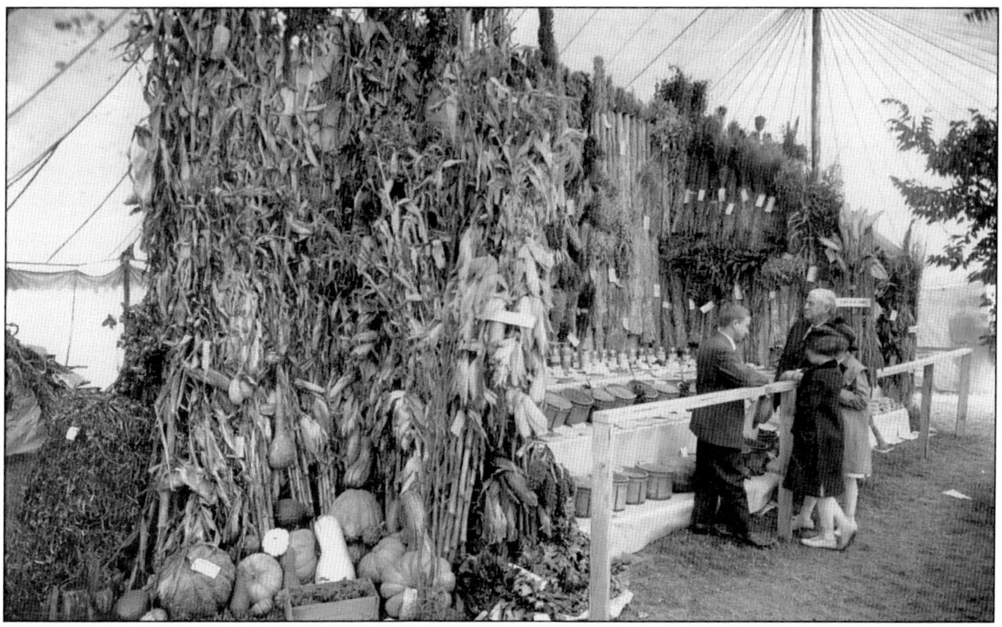

The Commercial Club helped sponsor the Howell County booth at the 1912 State Fair in Sedalia. Here Colonel Torrey is shown in front of a display of agricultural products produced in the area. The corn is indeed "as high as an elephant's eye." Canned fruit, nuts, pumpkins, squash, and even leaves from oak tress are part of the impressive display.

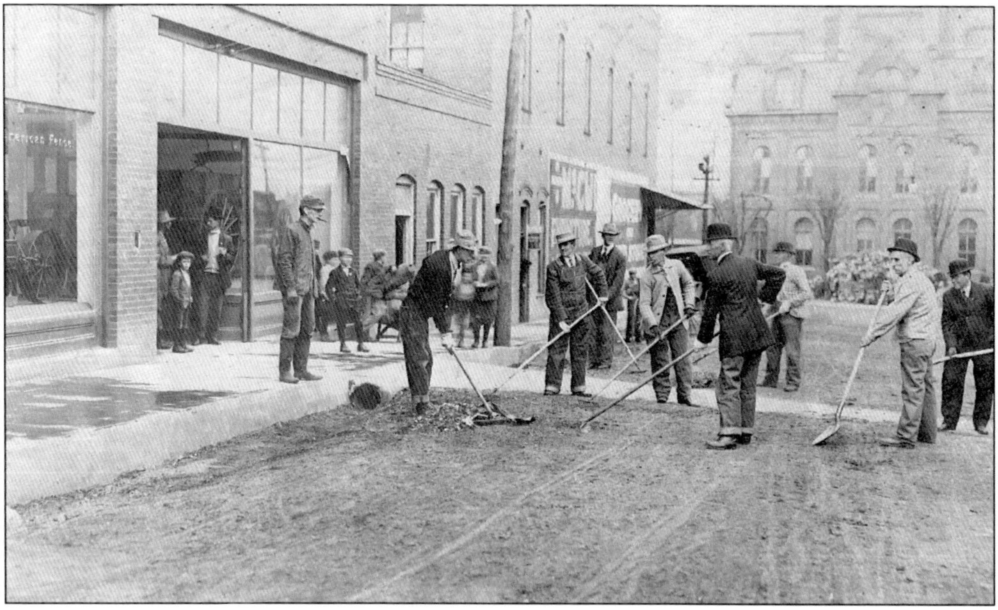

Mayor James P. Harlin declared Arbor Day, April 7, 1911, as city Clean-Up Day. The Commercial Club formed the "Order of the Overalls" and pitched in to help. From the left are Hal Woodside (with cigar), Hence Cobb, Elmer Kellett, Arch Hollenbeck, Will McBride, Mayor Harlin, C.E. Kimberlin, C.T. Aid, and unidentified. Note the huge pile of cans and bottles in the background by the Courthouse.

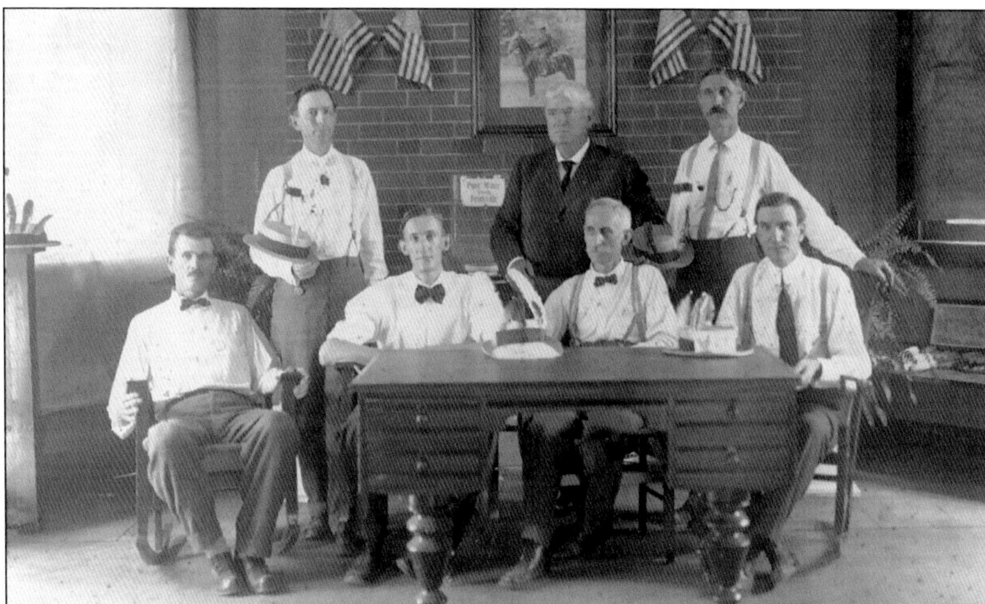

The reception committee for the Farmers' Poultry Picnic in West Plains on September 3, 1913, gathered at "Little Fruitville" before the event (note the chicken feathers in their hats). From left to right are: (front row) G.H. Cobb, E.M. Herring, C.T. Aid (mayor), and Arch T. Hollenbeck; (back row) Dr. A.H. Thornburgh (man with camera on this book's cover), Col. Jay L. Torrey, and C P. Harper.

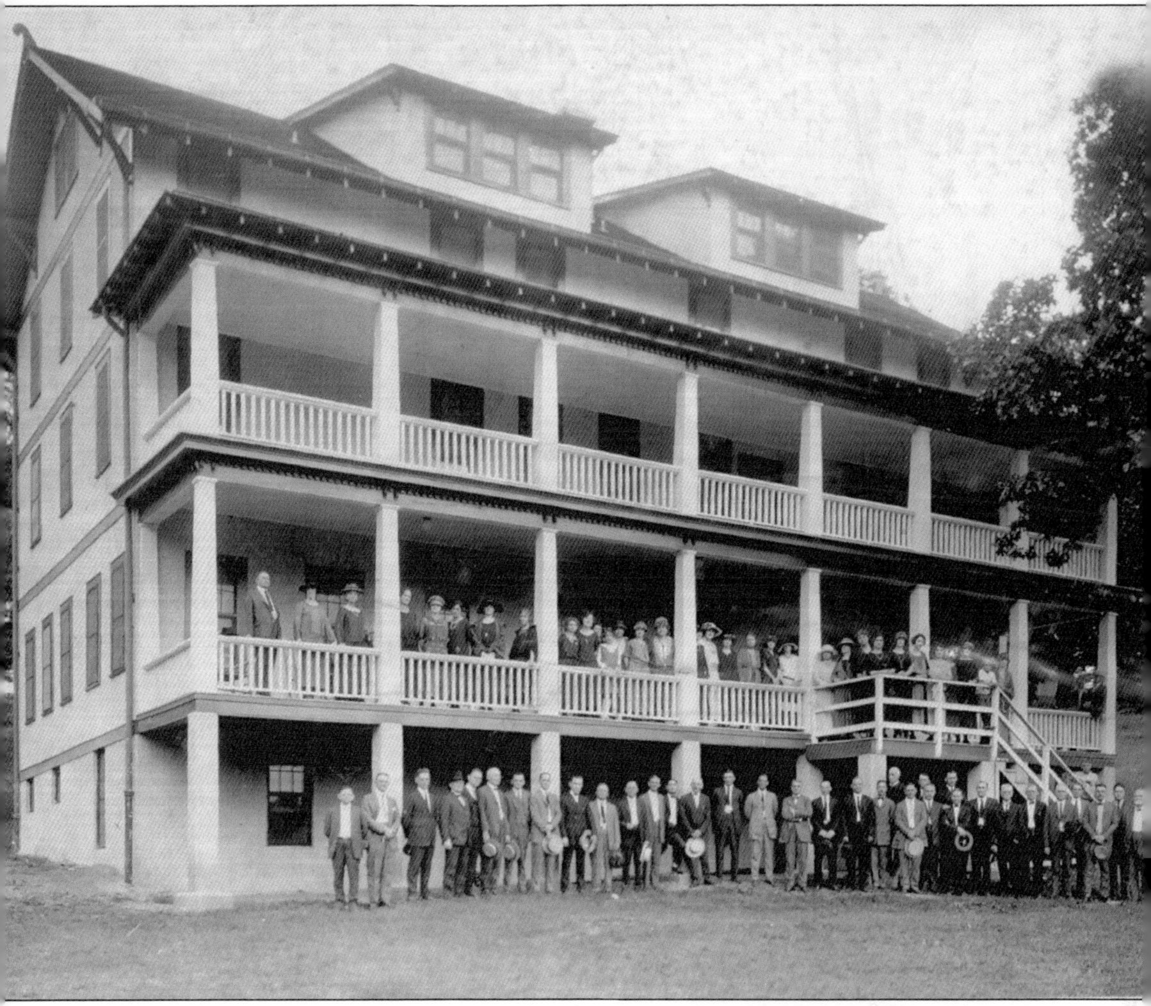

The Commercial Club visited the new Pinebrook Inn at Siloam Springs on September 15, 1921. The Inn was a health resort featuring the waters of 10 different mineral springs. N.O. Tate of Miami, Florida, built it on 287 acres of land 15 miles from West Plains. A bus made two trips daily from the train depot in West Plains to Pinebrook carrying the health seekers. The lobby featured a gravity fed dispenser that allowed customers to choose waters to drink from each of the 10 springs. Baths were in the basement. The four-story Inn had a total of 48 rooms for guests, a swimming pool, and a nine-hole golf course. A mason from Italy stuccoed the exterior of the lodge using a mixture of granite, quartz, and seashells. His work remains in excellent condition. Today, the Eckhart family runs it as a bed and breakfast.

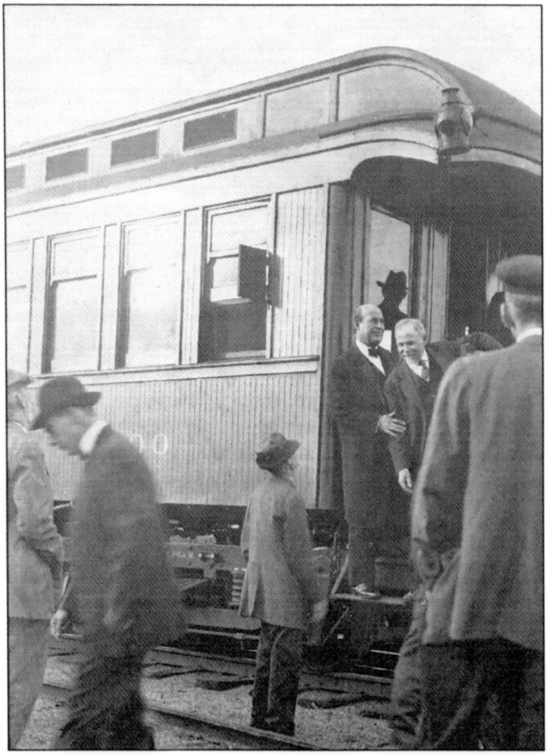

The biggest crowd ever drawn by a politician visiting West Plains was by William Jennings Bryan on October 18, 1914. Bryan had run unsuccessfully for president three times as a Democratic candidate. But he still drew large crowds everywhere he went. In 1912 President Wilson had appointed him secretary of state and he held that high office on this visit to West Plains. Bryan is on the steps at left in this photo.

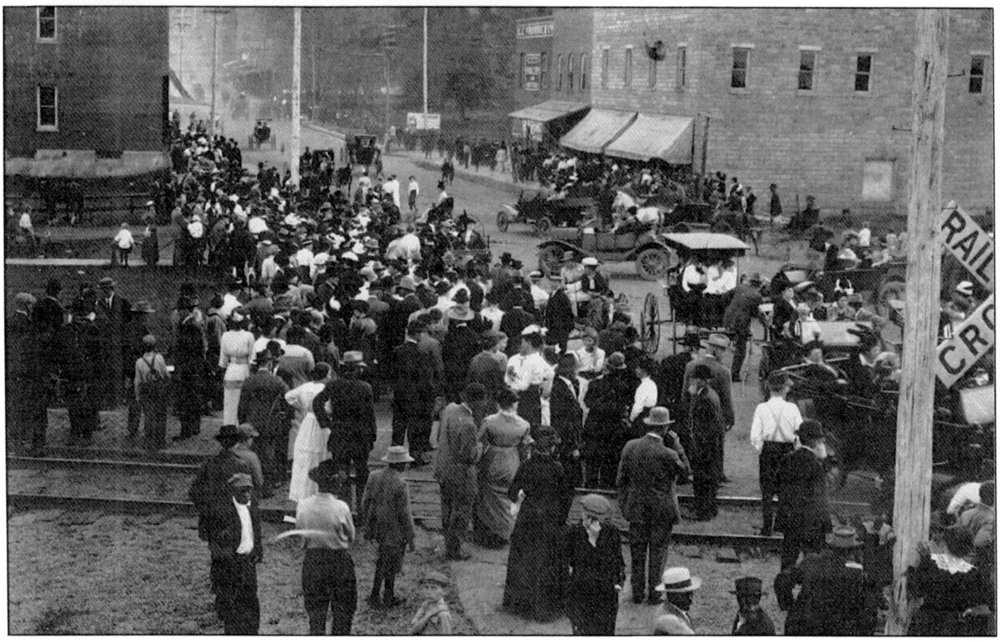

Bryan was famous as an orator, able to speak to over 30,000 people outside with no microphone. Everywhere he appeared, huge crowds came, and they were not disappointed by the performances he gave. Ten years later he participated in the famous Scopes Monkey Trial. Here the crowd in West Plains disperses to the south up Washington Avenue after his speech from the train's platform.

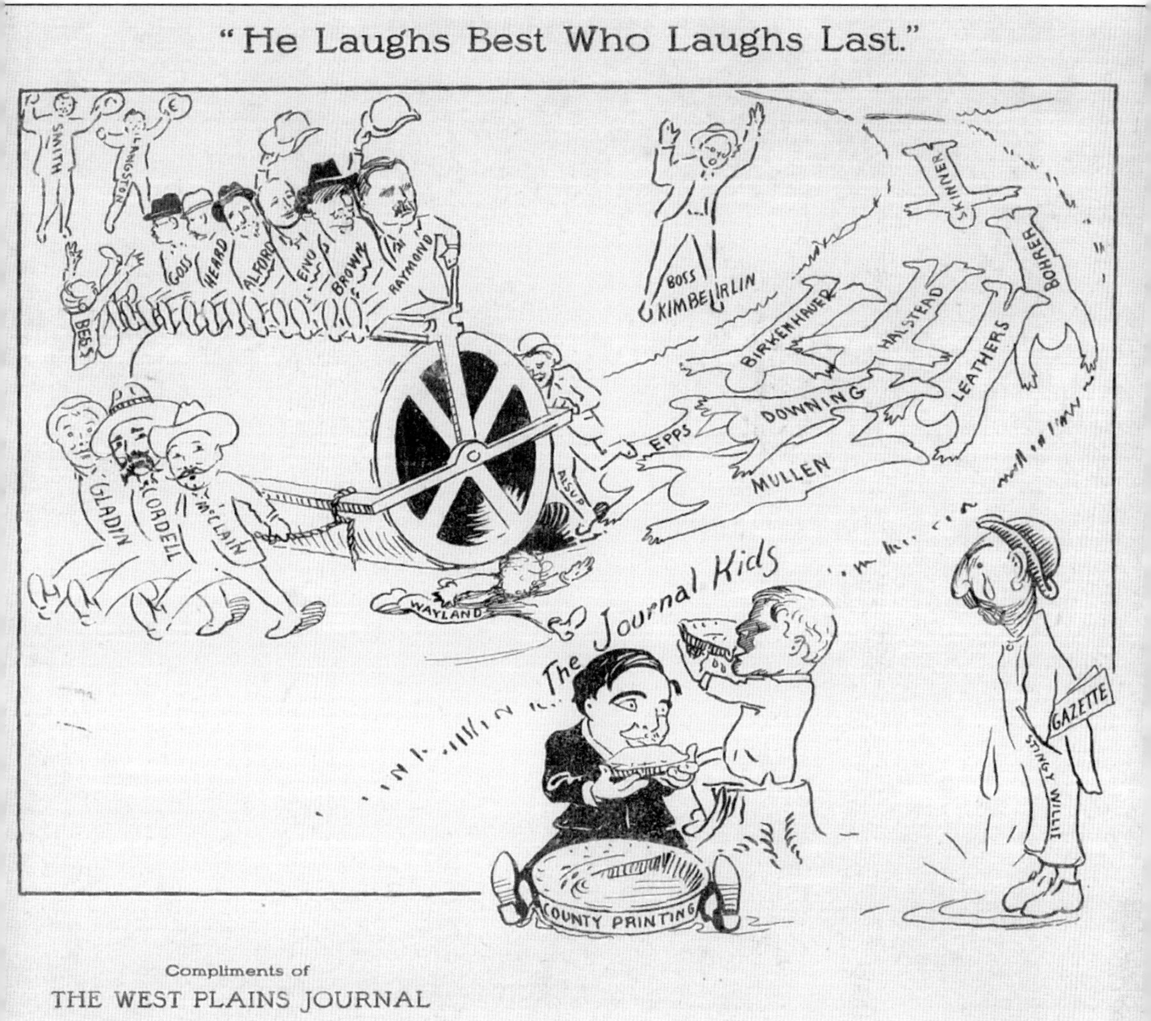

In the November 8, 1906, Republicans candidates swept all but two offices in the county election. This political cartoon, published by the Republican editors of the *West Plains Journal*, shows the result of that election. "Boss" Kimberlin and his crew are steamrolling the Democrats. Will Zorn, lower right, Democratic editor of the *Gazette* cries as the Journal gets all the "pie," the county's printing business.

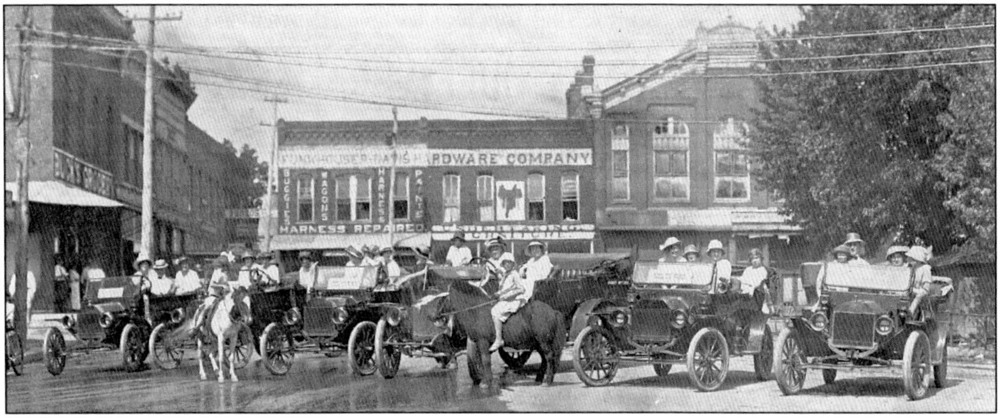

The women of West Plains joined their sisters in larger cities in demonstrating for women's suffrage and the passage of the 19th amendment. This parade on the Square features local suffragettes young and old including the Williams sisters. Their signs declare, "Votes for Women." The amendment won ratification in 1920. Alice Cary Risley as president of the Civil War Nurses Association was active in the movement.

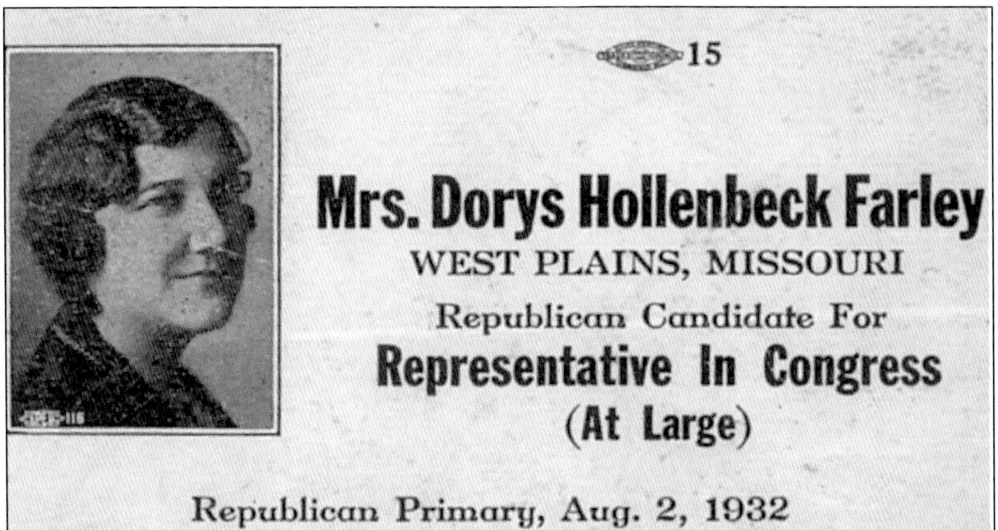

Arch T. Hollenbeck was involved in state and national politics all his life. It was only natural that his daughter Dorys should be too. Both Arch and Dorys were delegates to National Republican Conventions. This card is from Dorys' unsuccessful run for the House of Representatives. Dorys was born in 1895 and studied journalism at Oklahoma University.

Six

From Grace Avenue to Illinois Town Neighborhoods, Churches, and Schools

From the row of grand Victorian homes along Grace Avenue to the tarpaper shanties of Illinois Town, West Plains had many neighborhoods. Most of the town's churches and schools were located in these residential areas, away from the business district. This chapter shows where the generations that succeeded the first settlers grew up, learned the three R's, and received their religious training. Just as the business district boomed with the arrival of the railroad, so did these neighborhoods. Between 1880 and 1914, seven new school buildings were built in West Plains. At the same time seven churches were constructed and many homes.

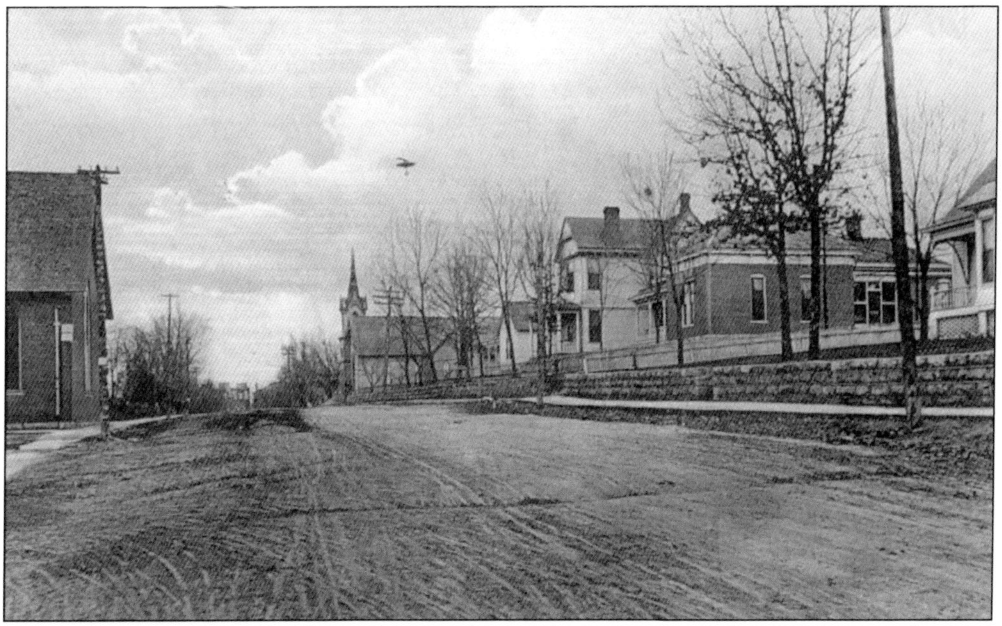

This post card, by the West Plains photographer William Theodore Gleerup, was part of a series he produced around 1910. It was taken at the corner of Missouri Avenue and West Main facing east. Gleerup was also a fine portrait photographer. He moved to West Plains in 1902 and built a studio lighted by natural light in the Catron Arcade. He left for St. Louis in 1912.

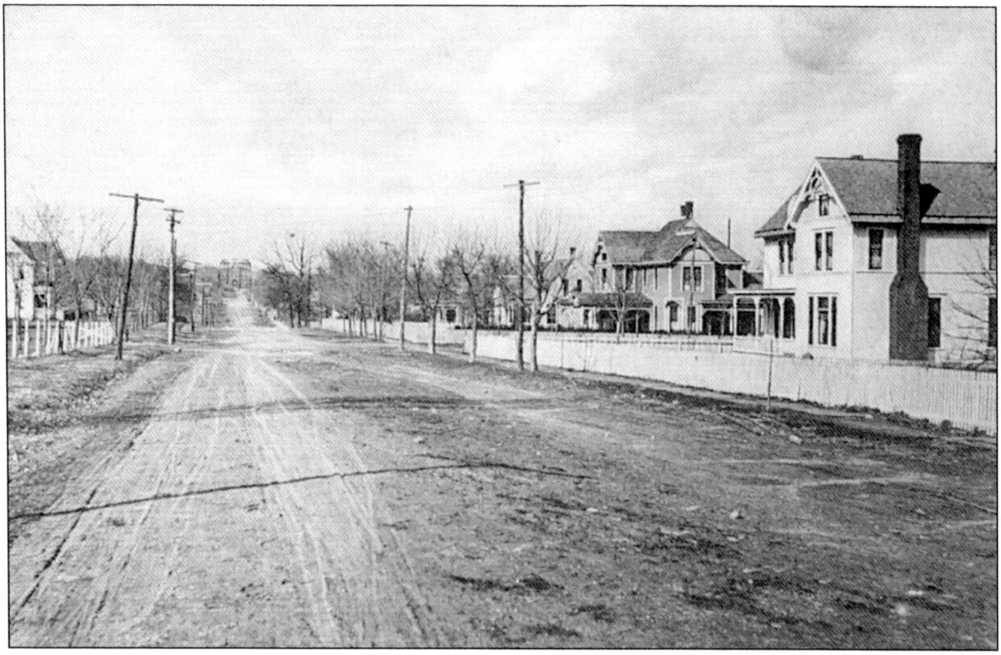

This is another card from the same series produced by Gleerup. It is on East Main in front of the West Plains Academy, near College Street, looking west. The houses that lined both East and West Main were very comfortable homes for the time, reflecting the affluence West Plains was experiencing. Although the streets are not paved in this photo or the one before, there are cement sidewalks beside them.

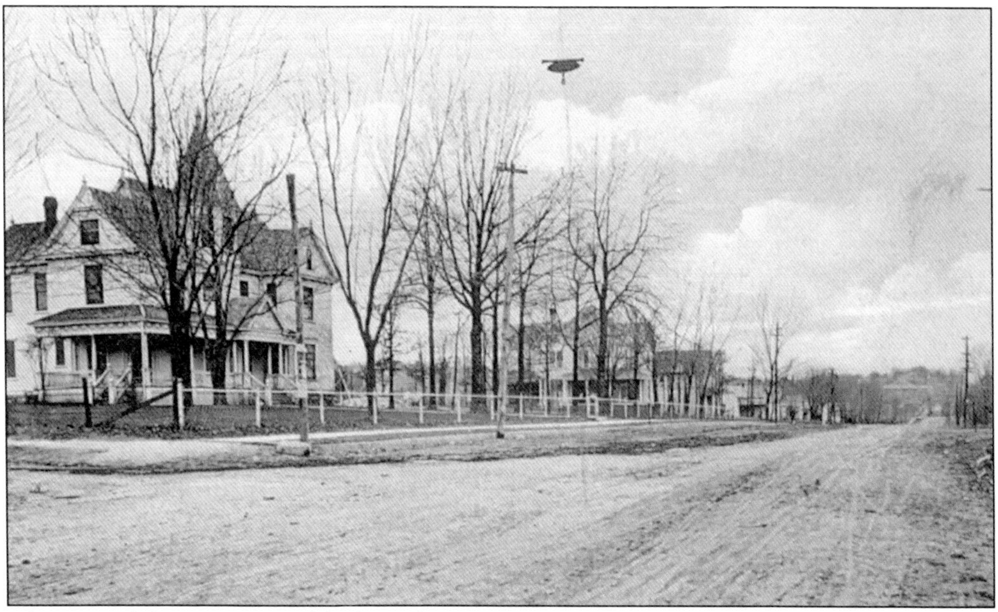

Gleerup took his camera one block south to snap this shot on Grace Avenue. In the foreground is the Knoerle House, one of the most impressive Victorian homes in West Plains. Joe Knoerle, a real estate investor, built it in the 1890s. It was and is West Plains' largest and finest Victorian house. The Hogan and Hilburn families are among those who have lived in this home.

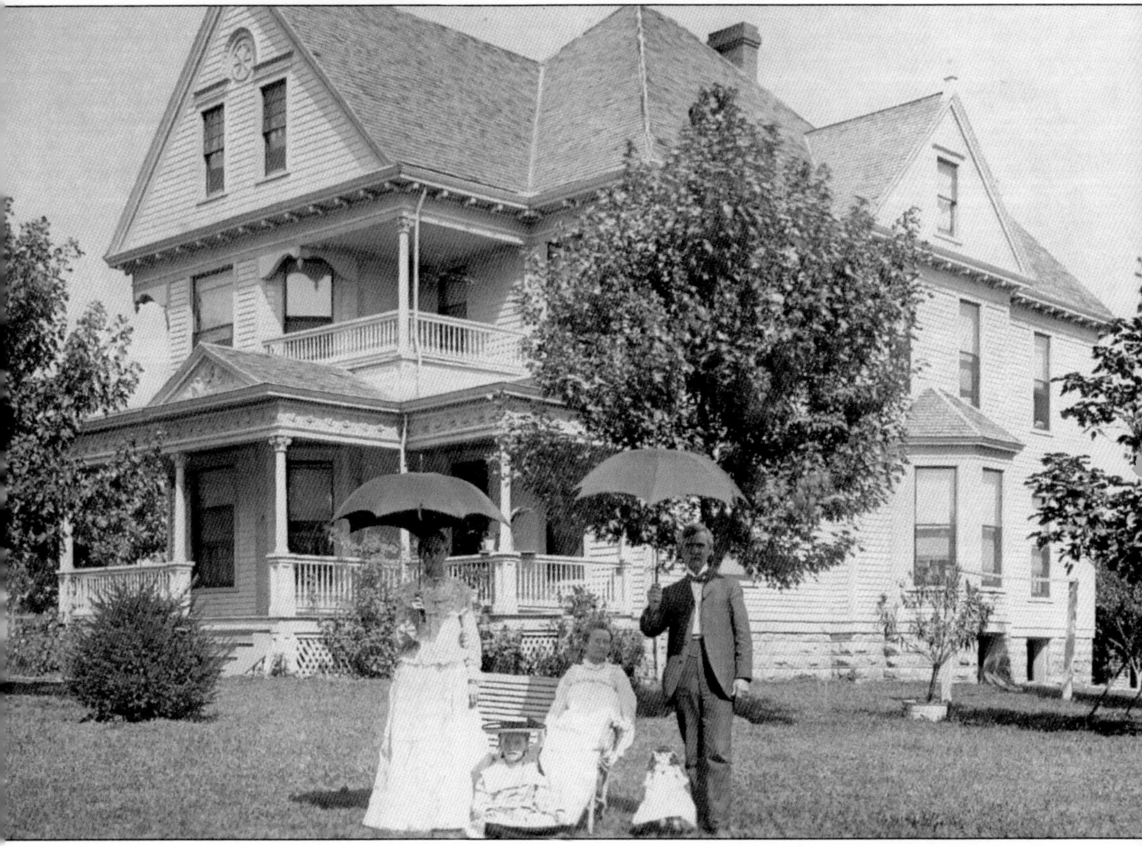

The Langston family is seen in a Gleerup portrait taken in front of their home around 1905. Jeff Langston built this three-story, 12-room Victorian home in 1896 on the corner of West Main and Arkansas. At the time, that was the far western edge of town. Jeff and his brother Sam owned Langston's Department Store. This home reflects the successful business they ran. He purchased 18 acres to build it on from Mrs. J.E. Porter. As the house rose from its hand hewn stone foundation, the construction site became a popular destination for Sunday afternoon sightseers. Shown here, from left to right, are Jeff's sister Margaret Durham, his daughter Clara, Sally his wife, and Jeff. This house can be seen in the background of the Hinckey-Dinckey baseball game on page 54.

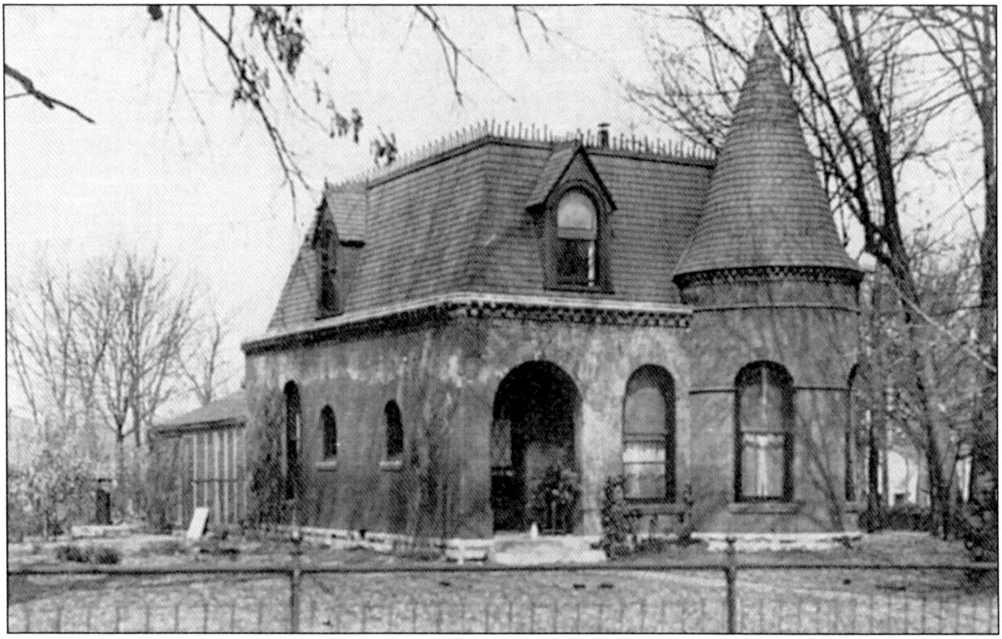

Ed Toler built this wonderful, small Victorian house around the turn of the century on Garfield Street. It featured a rounded turret at one end of the living room. Its yard was surrounded by cast iron fence and featured a garden with a goldfish pond. Photos from around 1920 show the entire house covered in ivy. It was torn down in 1965 in order to build a new post office.

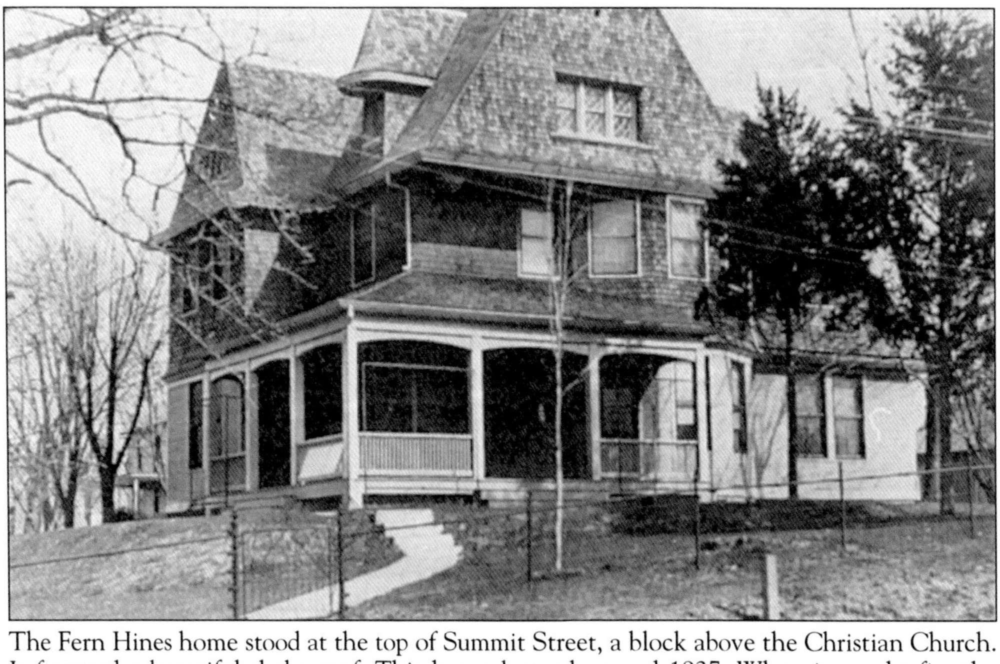

The Fern Hines home stood at the top of Summit Street, a block above the Christian Church. It featured a beautiful shake roof. This house burned around 1927. When it caught fire the students at Central School ran two blocks up the hill and formed a bucket brigade, but the house was lost. Mayor J.P. Harlin lived immediately east of this house in "Shadow-Lawn." It is now the Harlin Museum.

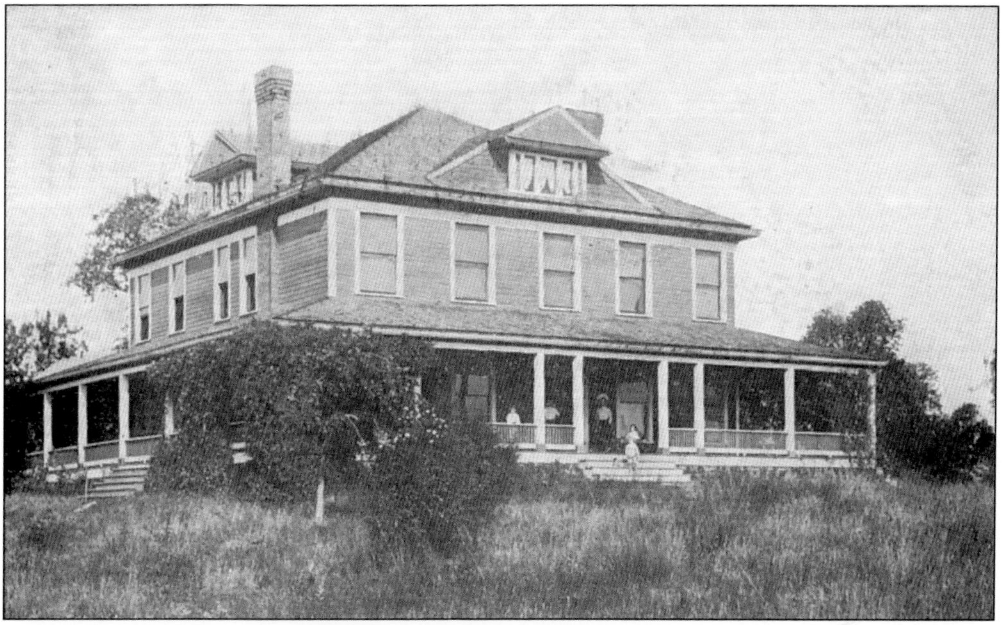

Colonel E.C. Markham built Fairview in 1894. Markham came here from Chicago to invest money in B.F. Olden's West Plains Fruit Company. In 1905 he sold the house to Thomas Walton, a partner in the West Plains Telephone Company. Walton sold Fairview to Dr. R.A. Sparks in 1910. Dr. Sparks and his family lived there for many years. Today it is the Victoria Gardens Bed and Breakfast.

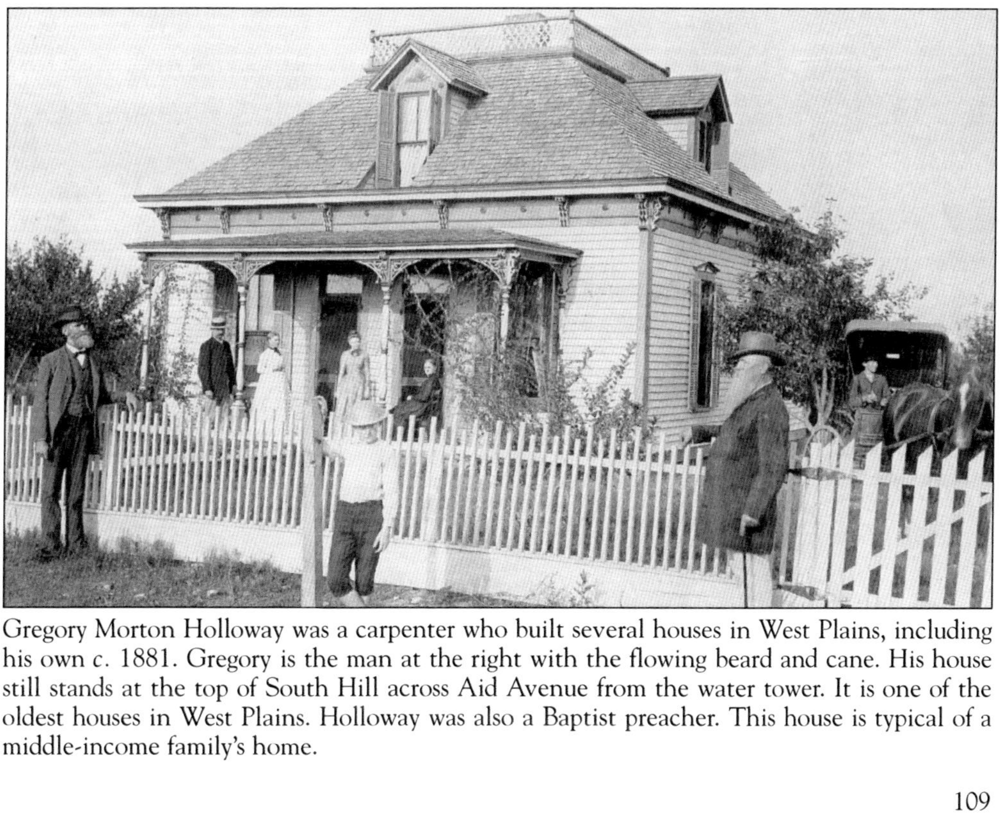

Gregory Morton Holloway was a carpenter who built several houses in West Plains, including his own *c.* 1881. Gregory is the man at the right with the flowing beard and cane. His house still stands at the top of South Hill across Aid Avenue from the water tower. It is one of the oldest houses in West Plains. Holloway was also a Baptist preacher. This house is typical of a middle-income family's home.

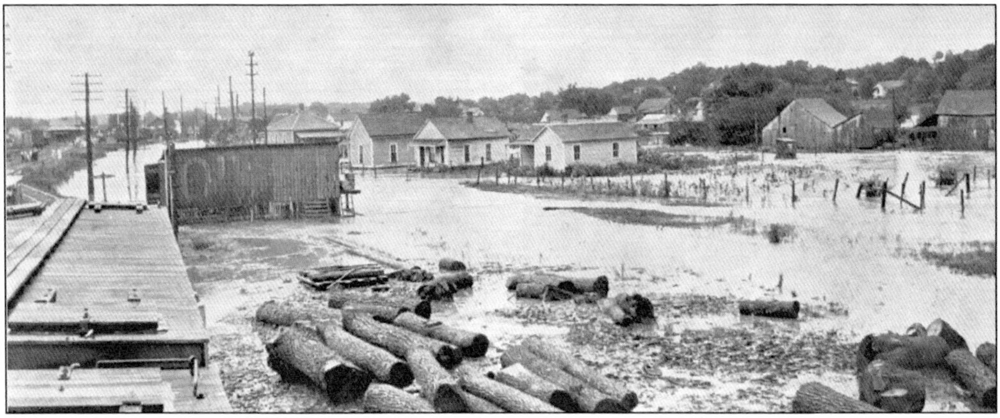

This neighborhood of small houses lay north of the railroad tracks, east of the depot. Howell Creek often flooded and inundated them. This scene is from the 1915 flood. These low laying homes along the railroad were lower income housing. It wasn't until the 1960s and the establishment of a Land Clearance Authority that the flood plain was cleared of houses.

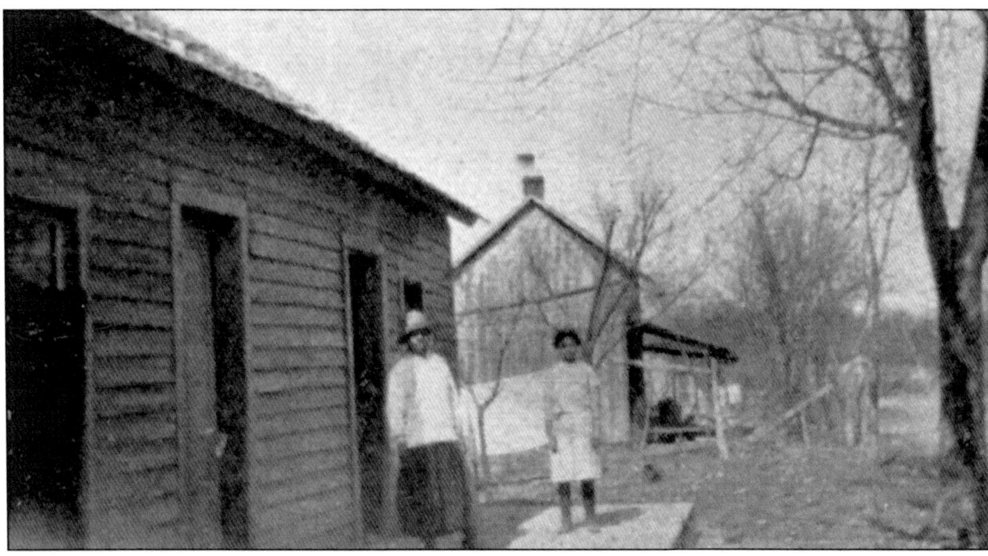

Farther from the railroad, on the hill in northern West Plains was "Illinois Town." It was the neighborhood where black families lived. Partially it grew up around the house of B. F. Olden who brought many black families here from around Oxford Mississippi to work on his fruit farms. Several families of these black workers also lived south of Olden on the railroad near the Highway 14 junction.

The Presbyterian Church was completed in 1887 at a cost of $4,000. It is the oldest church building in West Plains. During the first year of worship, the Presbyterian congregation shared their building with the First Baptist congregation. J.E. Leyda was the first permanent Presbyterian pastor, serving until 1894. A three-story addition was built on the rear of the church in 1910.

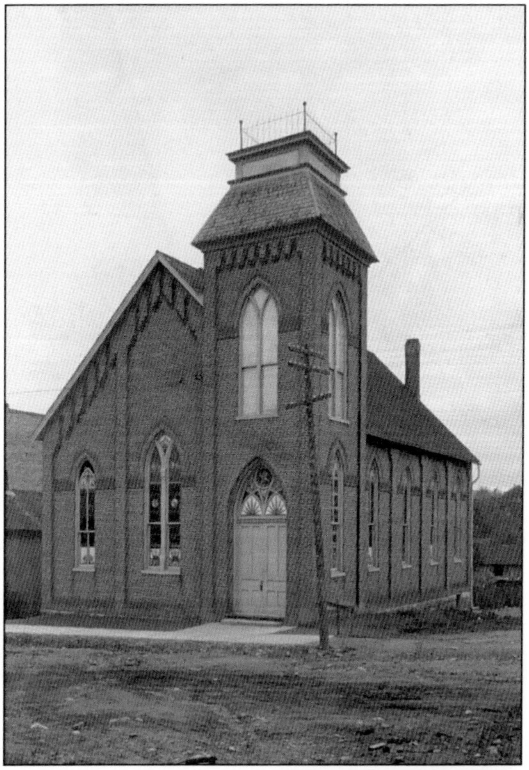

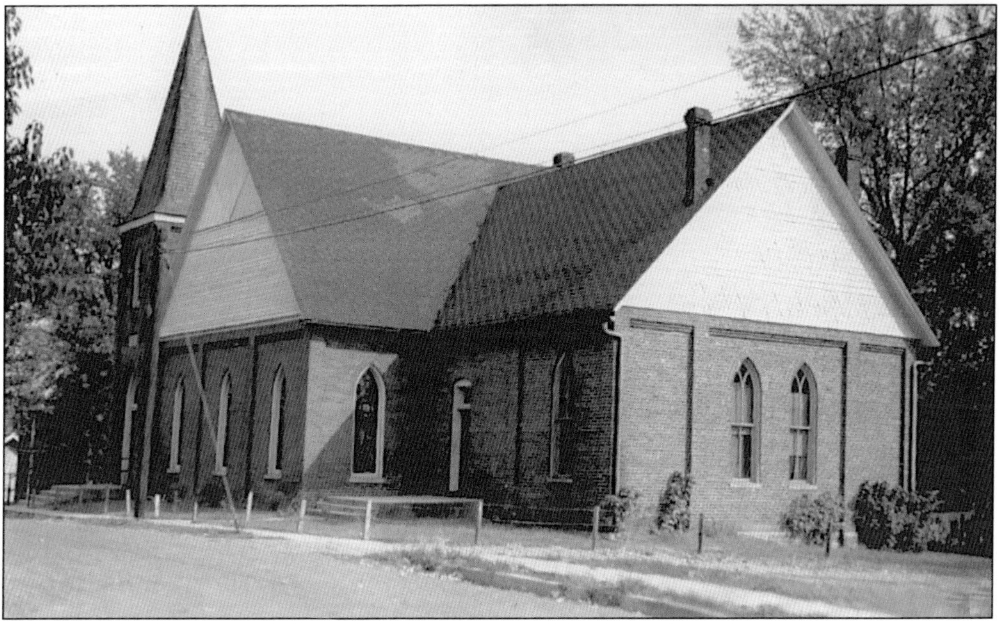

The First Baptist Church was officially formed on August 4, 1884. This building was begun in 1888 and the first service held in it in October of 1889. The tower and steeple were added in 1900 and stained glass windows in 1904. The south wing was added in 1904 when a mission church was moved there and attached for a parlor. Ever since, the Baptists have been making additions to their church.

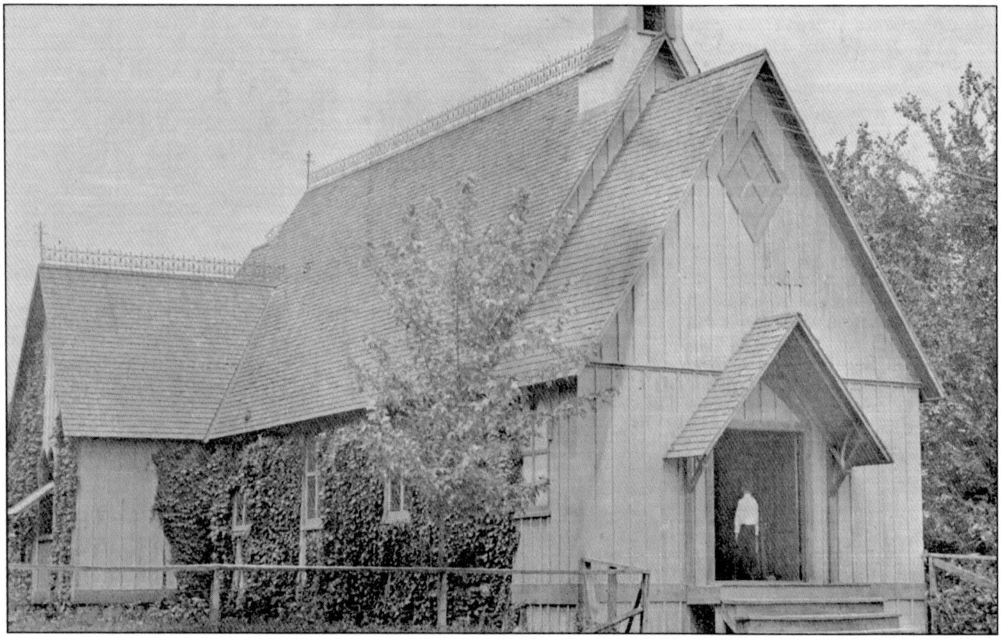

In 1888 the city disinterred the bodies in their old cemetery and moved them several blocks east to a more spacious site named Oak Lawn. Joseph Lyle Thomas and his wife Elizabeth bought the empty cemetery on Curry Street and built this Episcopal Church. Its corner stone was laid in September of 1888. As the church's founder, Thomas named it All Saints for his favorite celebration of the church year.

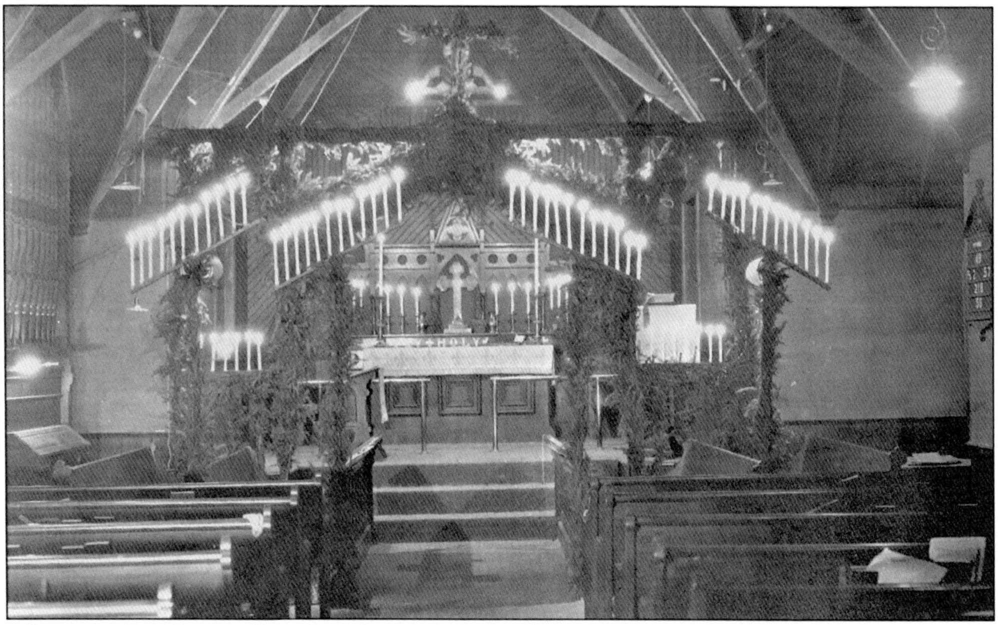

All Saints' building and its furnishings were purchased as a kit that arrived on the railroad. Today, 115 years later, the interior remains practically unchanged. To the left in this photo is the Hook and Hastings "tracker" type organ installed *c.* 1890. The organ had a pump behind it that small boys operated when it was played. It is still in service today, but with an electric pump.

The first building occupied by the First Christian Church was built in 1883. It stood on the same site as the current church (1925) on West Main at Summit. Adam Wright organized the congregation in the home of Col. William Monks in June 1878. Before the building was completed the congregation met in the Court House. C.T. Aid had this photo of the church made for a postcard around 1910.

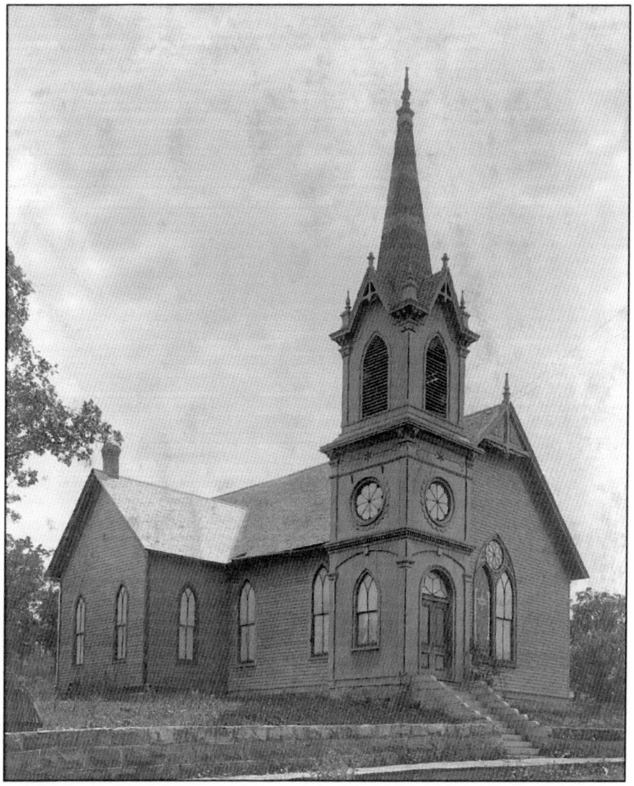

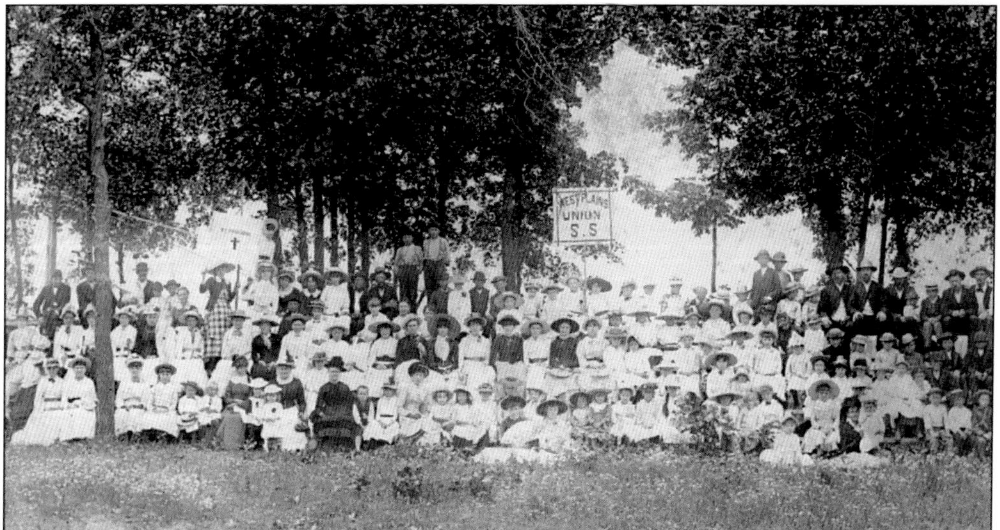

The West Plains Union Sunday School posed for this portrait around 1890. Early churches in town often shared their buildings with other denominations that didn't have a building of their own. The schools and the Courthouse were always available for religious services too. In the same spirit of cooperation, once a year the churches combined their Sunday Schools to hold classes, parade downtown, and have picnics.

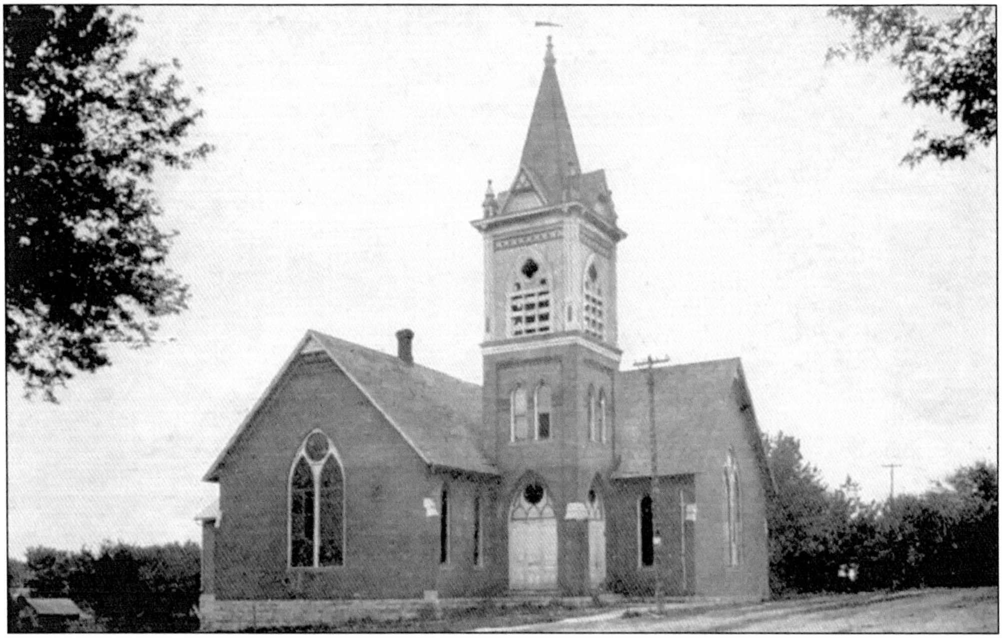

The M.E. Church South was constructed in 1889–1891 on the corner of Missouri and West Main. An earlier building constructed in 1883 had stood two blocks northwest. This photo was taken looking south on Missouri Avenue. In 1927 the M.E. South and North in West Plains united their congregations. In 1930 they built a large new church at this location.

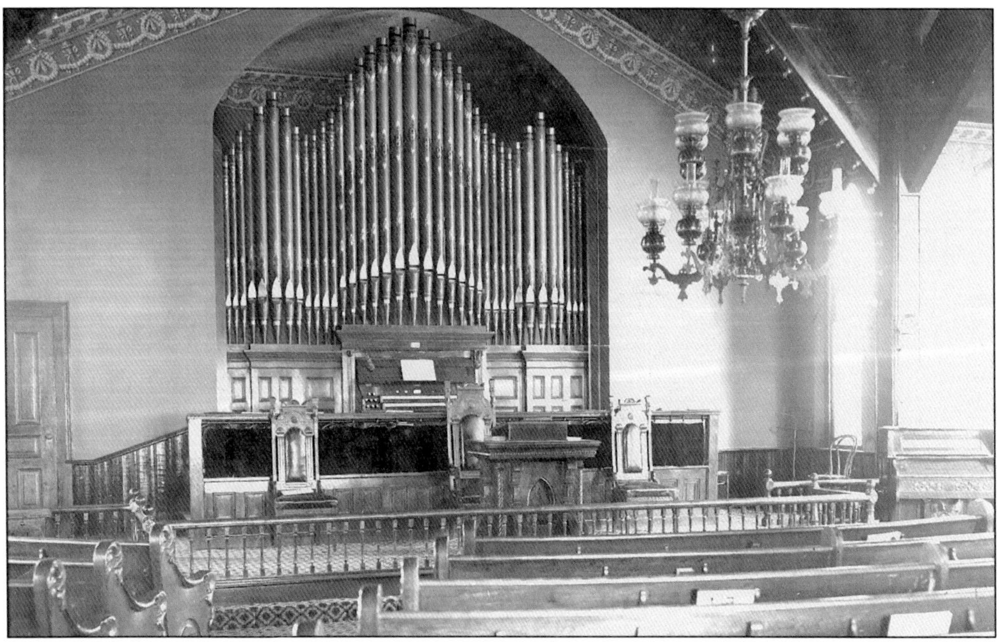

This is the interior of the 1890 M.E. Church South. A beautiful kerosene chandelier adorned that early church. Behind the chandelier we see its more convenient replacement, a row of bare electric light bulbs on a ceiling beam. A new Wicks Organ replaced the pipe organ in this photo when the new church was built in 1930. Gleerup took this photo c. 1910.

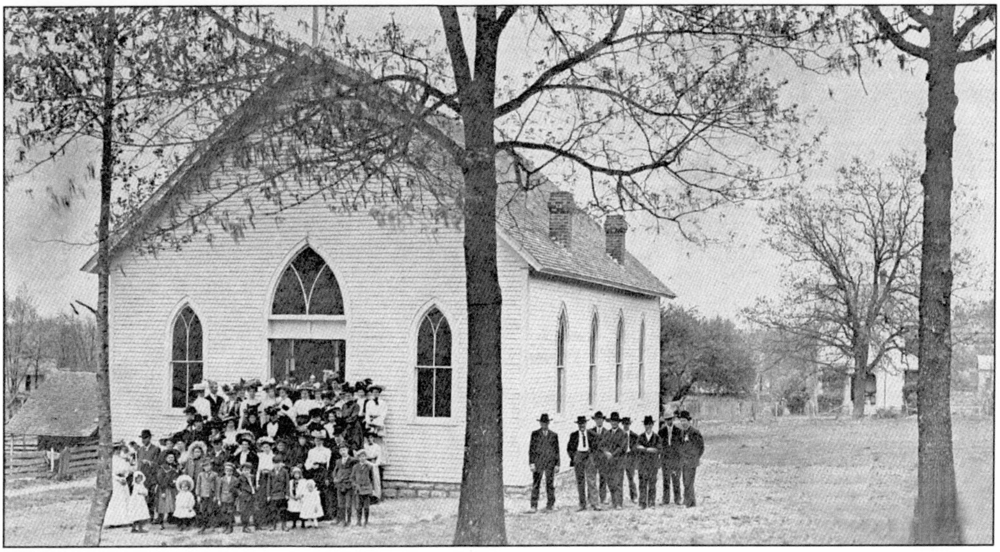

St. Mary's Catholic Church was built on South Hill Street in 1908–1909. Earlier services had been held over Mike Fitzgerald's plumbing store on the south end of Washington Avenue. This 40 by 60 foot church served 52 families in 1910. Around 1920 a parish hall was added to the rear on the south side. The house at the right rear was later used as a rectory.

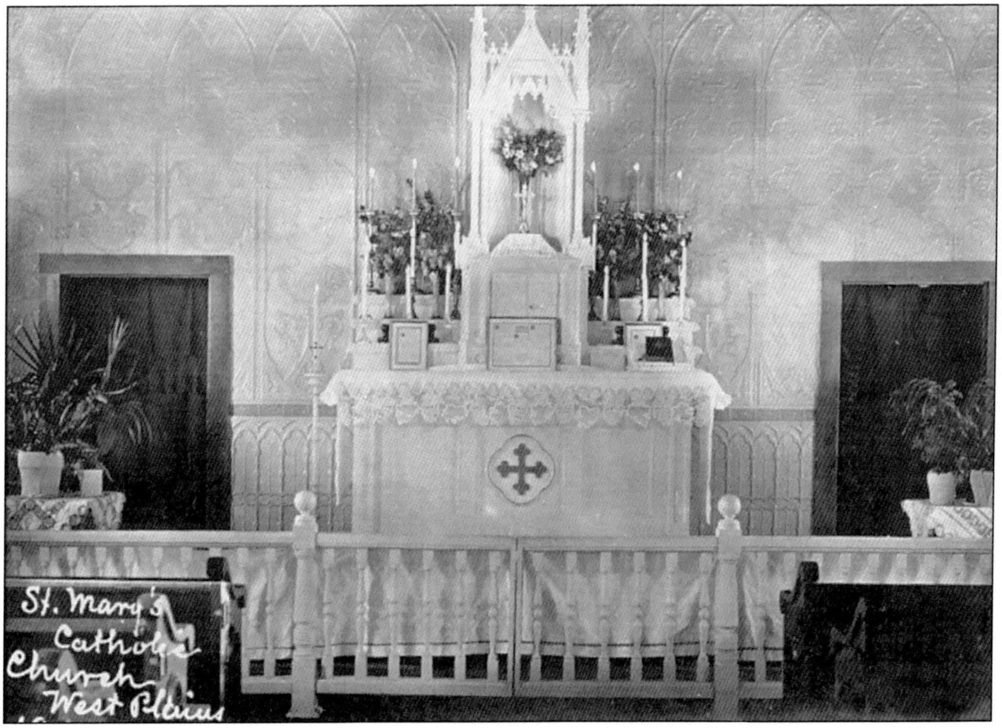

Saint Mary's altar is seen in this Gleerup photo taken in 1909. The early center of Catholic activity in this area was St. Joseph's Church at White Church. Priests from that church served the mission in West Plains. In 1948 St. Mary's became a parish and received its own priest. Father Francis Donovan became the first pastor.

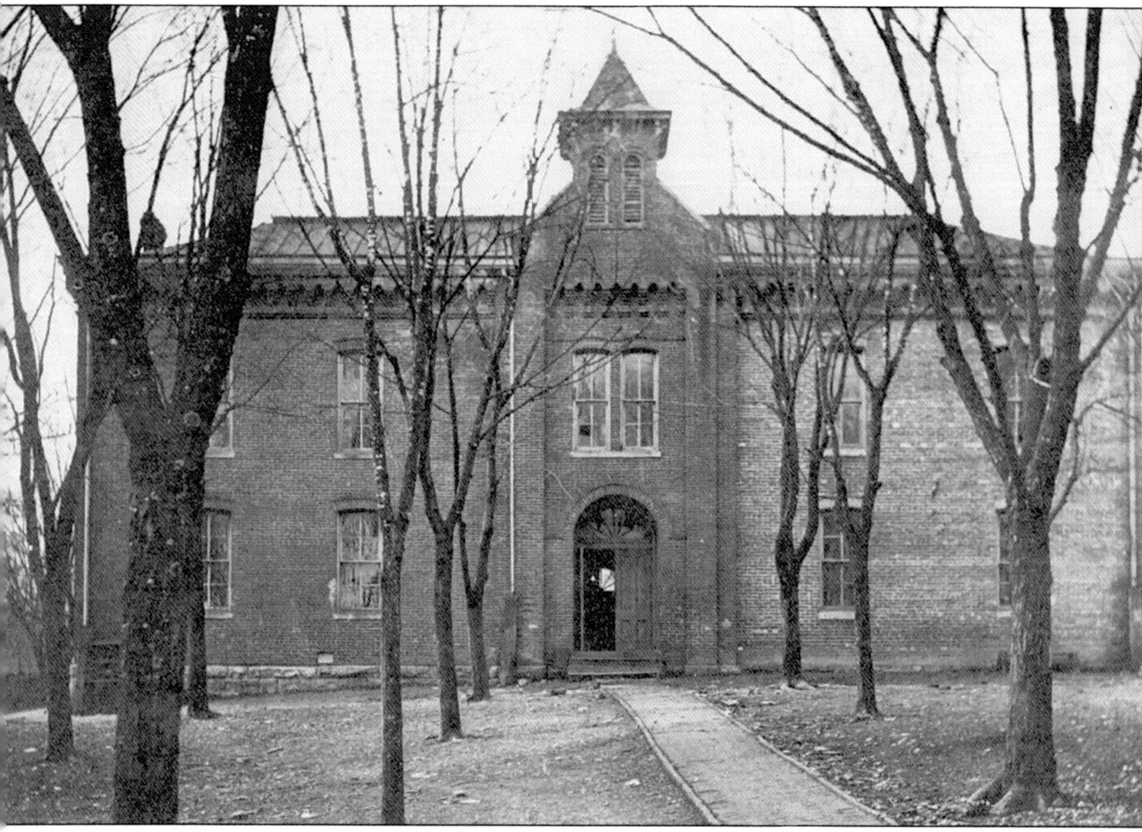

Old Central School was built in 1880, the first brick building in West Plains. It faced Cleveland along the west edge of Langston Street. Four classrooms were on the first floor and a large hall upstairs. It was torn down in 1914 when a new building was built on Garfield, one block west. The following excerpt, from the 1910 WPHS Annual, is a short of history of local schools before Central was built: "The first school taught in Howell County after the Civil War was in West Plains, near where the West Plains College now stands. The building was a little log house, so worthless that it had escaped the 'fire-bug' of war days, and for a time was the only church and school house available in this section; the first teacher, as nearly as can be learned, being Mrs. Lydia J. Hines. This building was shortly abandoned and one secured near the present site of the Cumberland Presbyterian Church (Aid Avenue and Worcester); and here taught S.D. Foster, Samuel Padon, and a Mrs. Tucker."

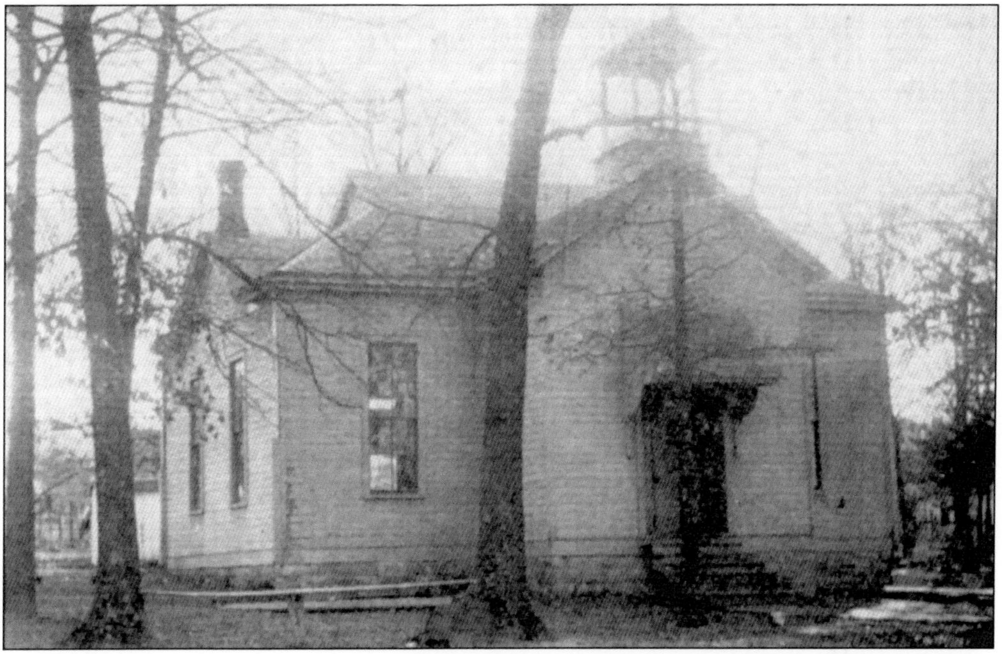

T.B. Carmical was Superintendent of Schools when Central was built. Only first through the eighth grades were offered until 1886 when high school classes were added. In May 1891 the first senior class graduated. Central became so crowded by 1888 that two buildings were built for the lower grades, the East and North Ward schools. This picture is of the East Ward on Locust just off Grace Avenue.

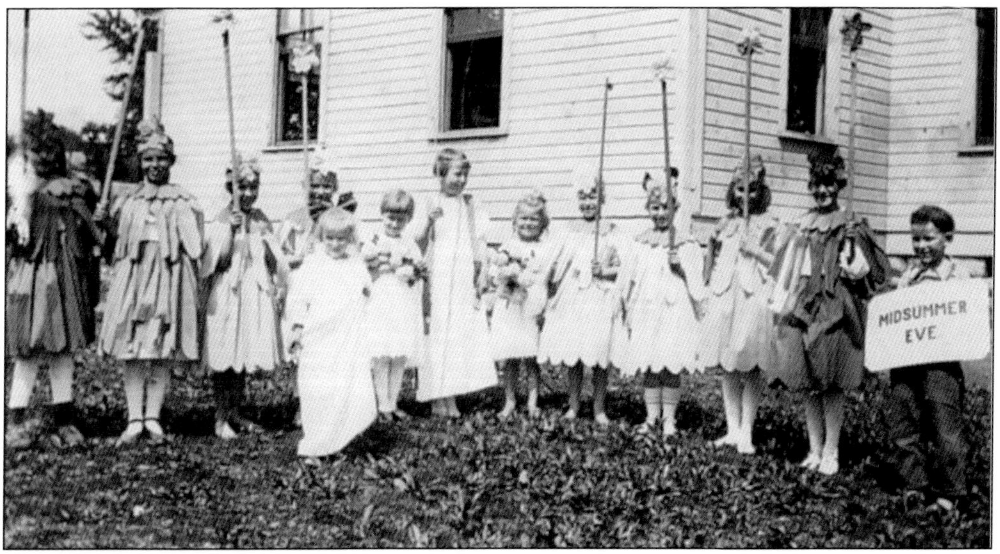

These students are performing "Midsummer Eve" at the North Ward School in the 1920s. To accommodate the crowd of parents, the play was held outside. Mayree Davis was their teacher. The North Ward School was where Foster School stands now. Even though it was located on the edge of Illinois town it was segregated. Black students went to the Lincoln School further north.

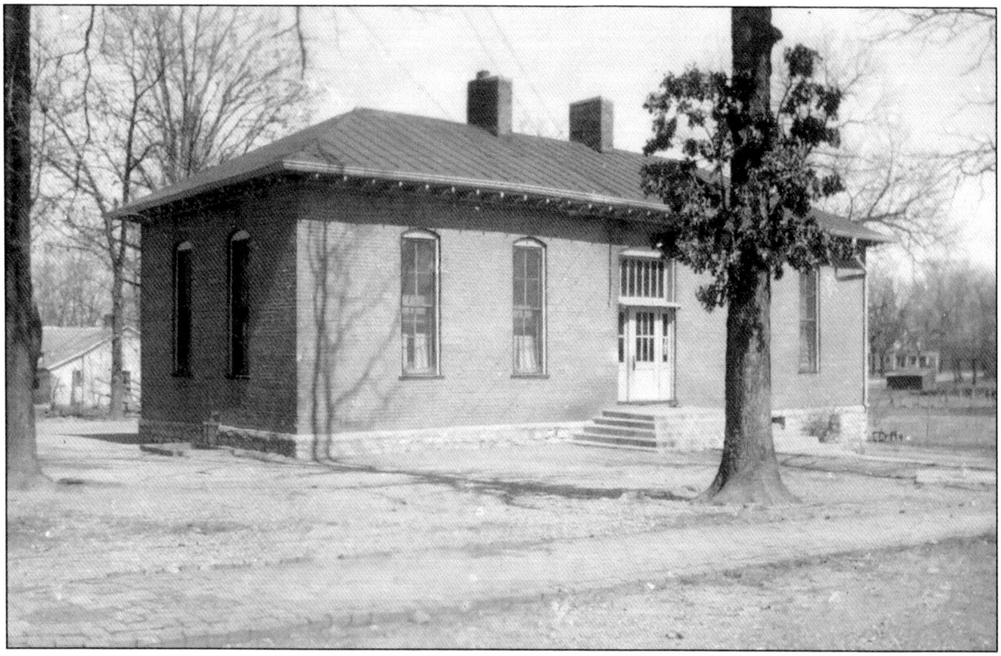

In 1890 the three school buildings in West Plains accommodated nine teachers and 576 students, or 64 students per room! To relieve this pressure the West Ward School was built at Pennsylvania and Cass in 1892. This photo shows that building *c.* 1930. In the 1930s the WPA built three, large elementary schools to replace the old Ward buildings.

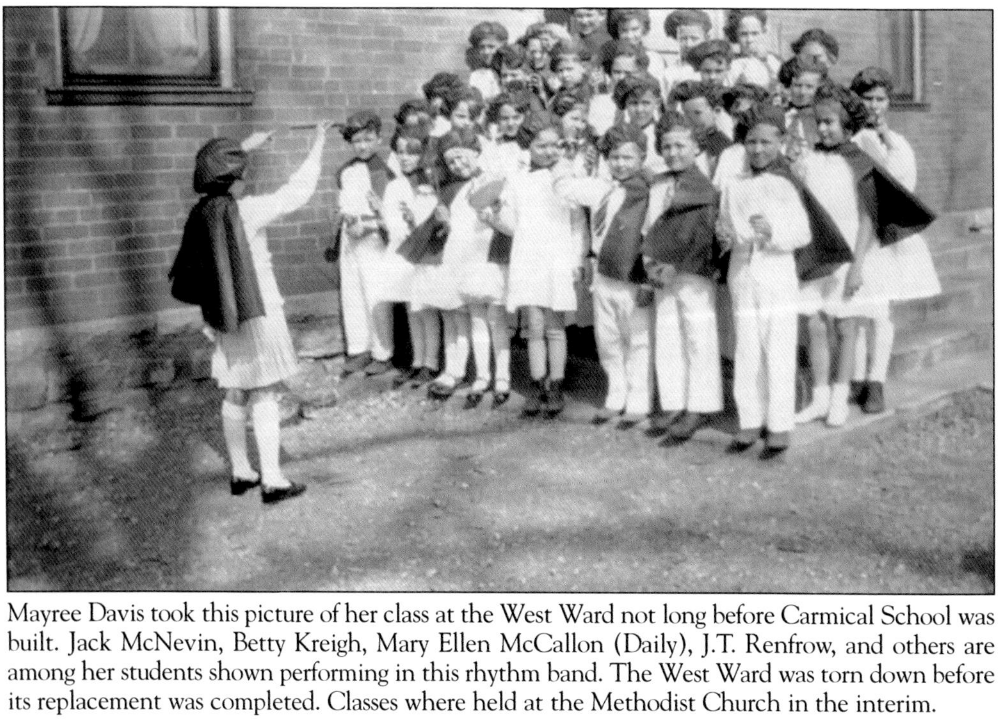

Mayree Davis took this picture of her class at the West Ward not long before Carmical School was built. Jack McNevin, Betty Kreigh, Mary Ellen McCallon (Daily), J.T. Renfrow, and others are among her students shown performing in this rhythm band. The West Ward was torn down before its replacement was completed. Classes where held at the Methodist Church in the interim.

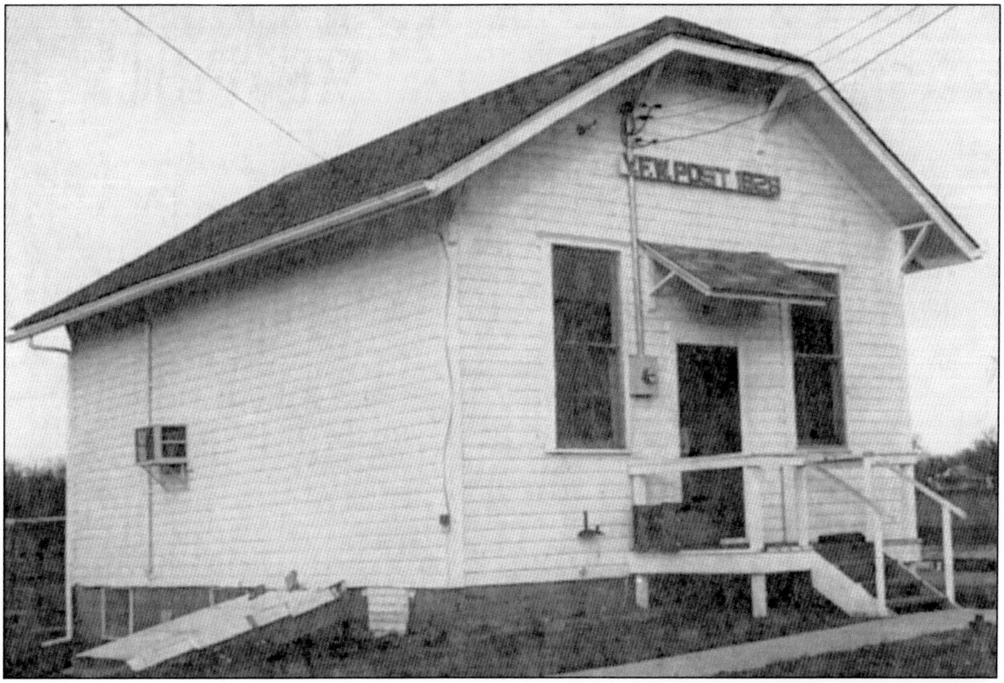

The first school for blacks was at Gum Springs, northeast of town, in 1892. Lincoln School (shown here) was built around 1900 for primary to the eighth grade. Its books and equipment were much poorer than the Ward Schools. The 1916 WPHS Annual has an article about a class trip to Lincoln School. Monk Oaks was the first black to graduate from WPHS in 1957.

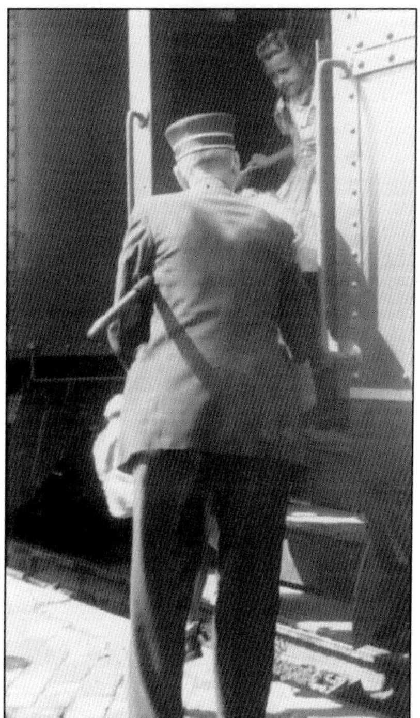

The big annual event for second graders in West Plains for over 30 years was their free ride on the passenger train. The last week of school they would meet the train at the depot and ride to Thayer or Mammoth Springs. There they would have a picnic, then return to West Plains by bus. This picture shows Bertie Sue Amyx (Judd) being helped off the train by the conductor.

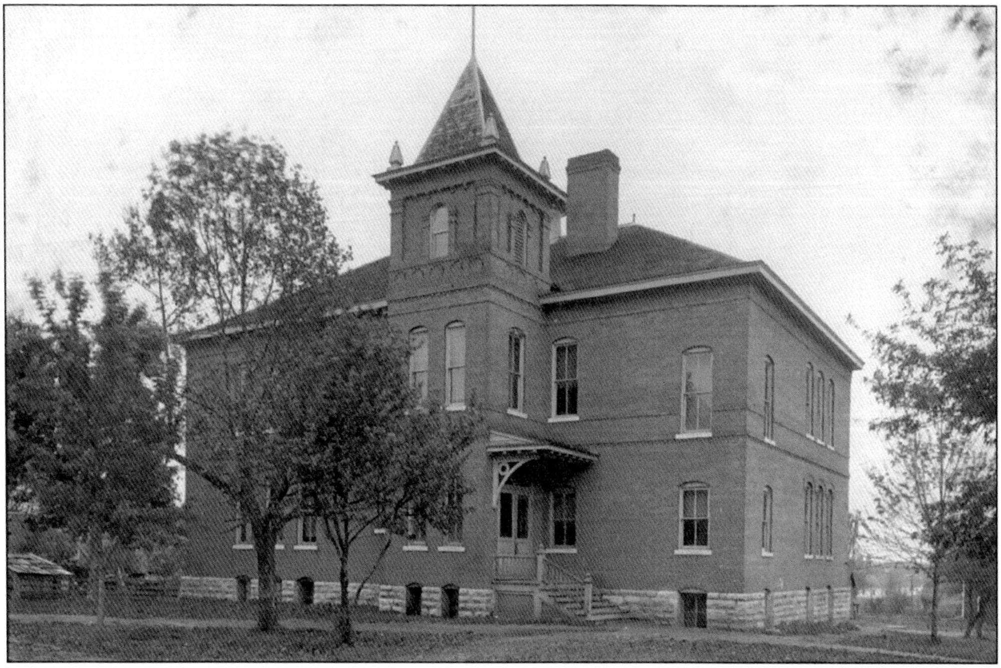

Construction began on D.W. Reese High School in August of 1904 on Walnut Street, south of the Baptist Church. It was 48 by 63 and two stories tall. There were six rooms with a large vestibule and broad halls. It cost $6,647 to build. It was also one of three schools called "Central" at various times. In 1905 the high school moved here and the middle grades occupied "Old" Central on Cleveland.

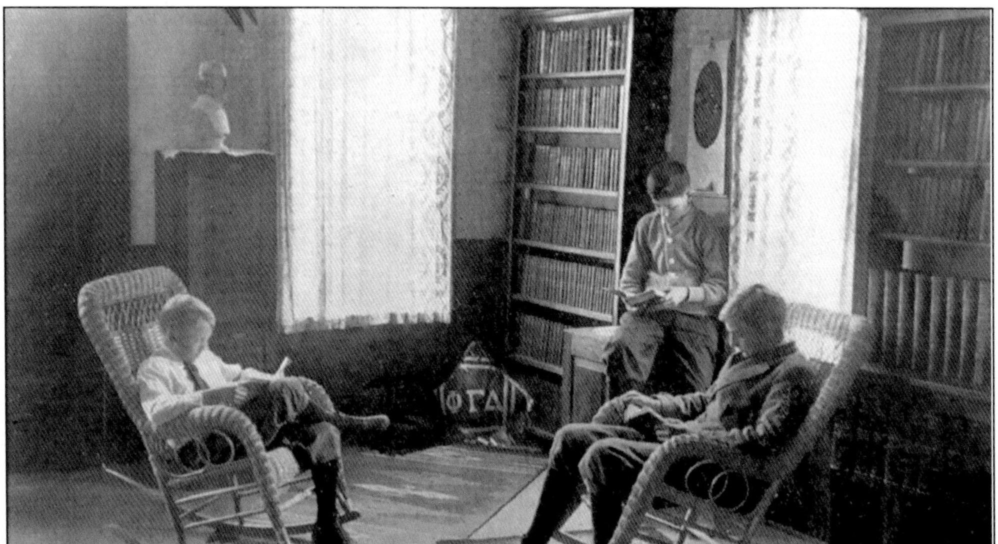

This photo from the 1910 Zizzer annual shows the school library. It had 5,300 volumes and Margaret E. Thomas was the librarian. Three years earlier in 1907 the first school yearbook was published. When the seniors presented the 16-page book to Miss Phoebe Davidson, their advisor, she exclaimed, "Oh, what a Zizzer!" That is how WPHS yearbooks and athletic teams received their name.

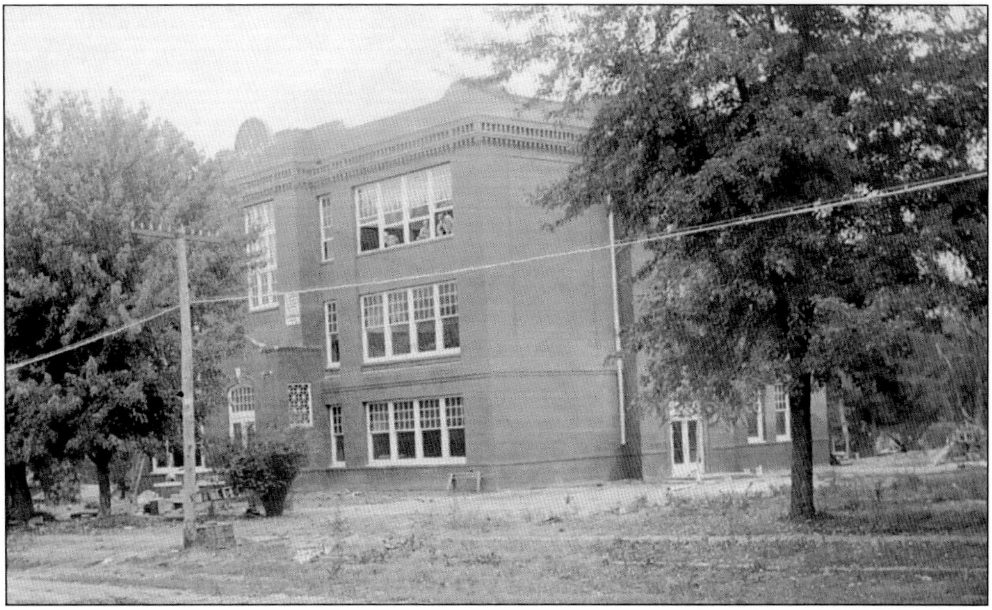

In 1912 a bond issue raised $33,000 for a new high school. It was built west of "Old" Central, on Garfield. Construction began in January of 1914, and at the same time "Old" Central was dismantled. Classes were held in storerooms and churches as work progressed. Grades seven thru twelve moved into the new Central the next year. Intermediate grades went to the old high school on Walnut Street.

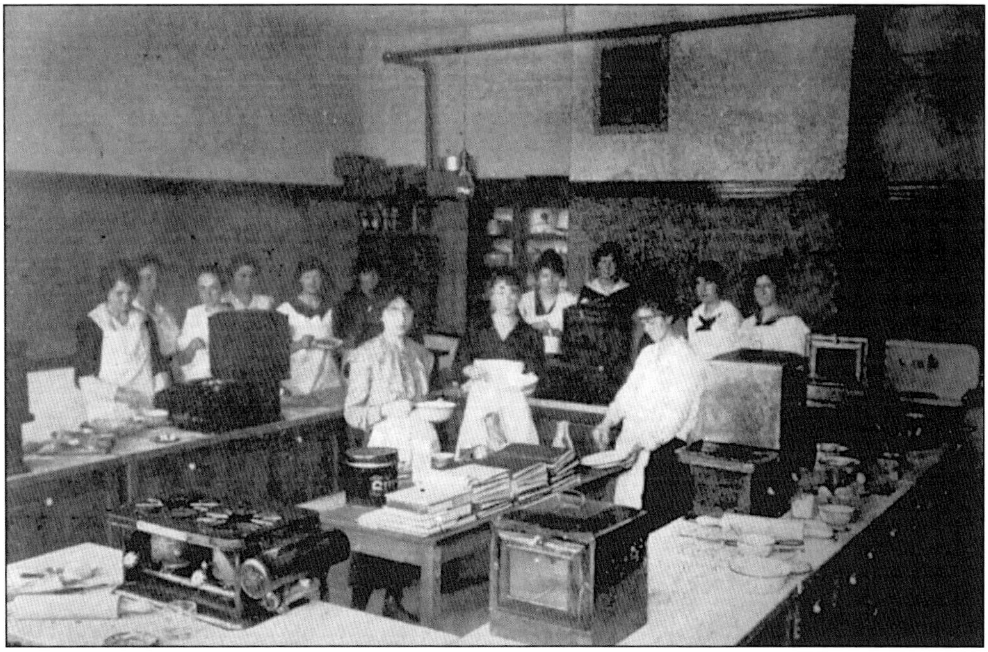

The new high school had three laboratories, a lecture room, and a library on its lower floor. Harriet Haskell, at left center, taught domestic science in one of the laboratories. There was also a manual training lab directed by William Schauer with $2,200 worth of new machinery. On the third floor was an auditorium that held 300 persons and could also be used as a study hall.

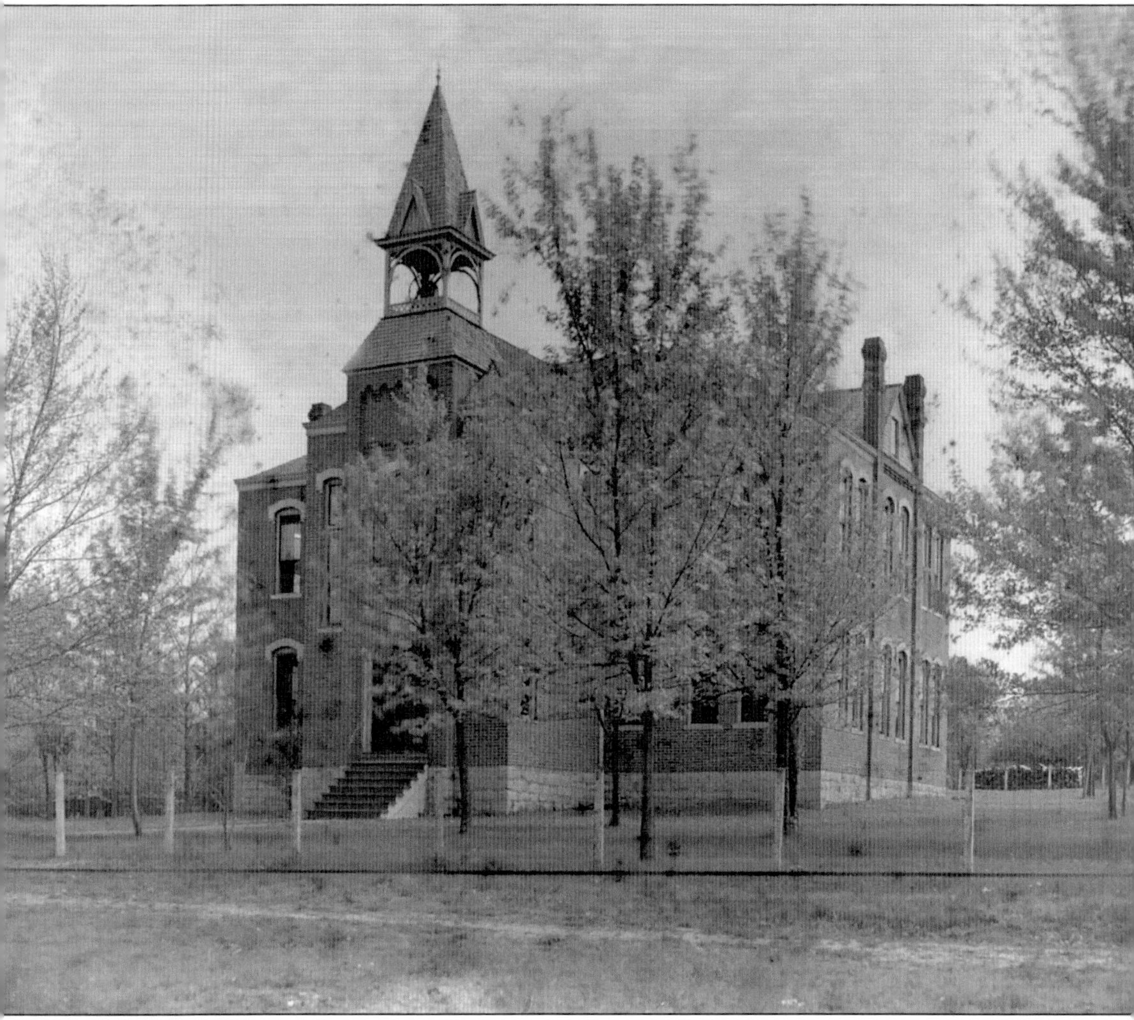

The West Plains College opened on January 5, 1891. Professor Leyda was in charge of its 19 students. Soon attendance reached 40, and Professor Emeric was also named to its faculty. In 1913 the Sisters of Charity purchased the college and opened a boarding and day school for girls. In 1920 Dr. R.S. Hogan opened West Plain's first hospital in the old college building. It was named Christa Hogan for his daughter.

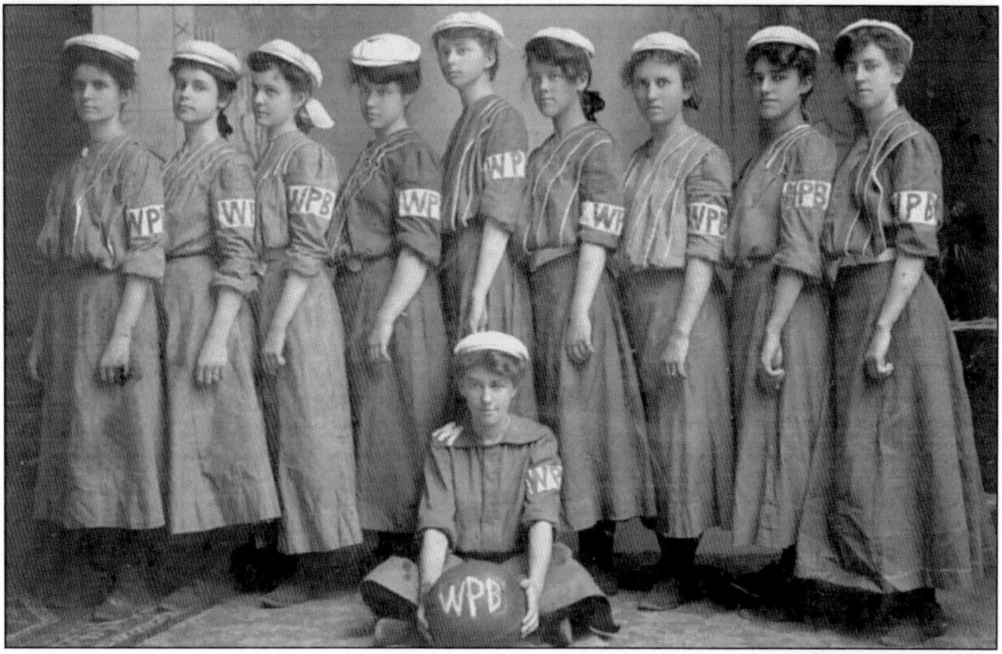

High school sports began in the 1890s. Girls as well as boys competed in basketball and tennis. This Gleerup photograph is of the Girls B Team, *c.* 1902. The players are, from left to right, Estelle Green, Pearl Mumford, Cecil Carter, Ella Orchard, Lillian Thompson, Ada Pitts, Nora Moore, Margaret Thomas, May Farmer, and Gertrude Farmer. This is a good illustration of proper attire for girl basketball players.

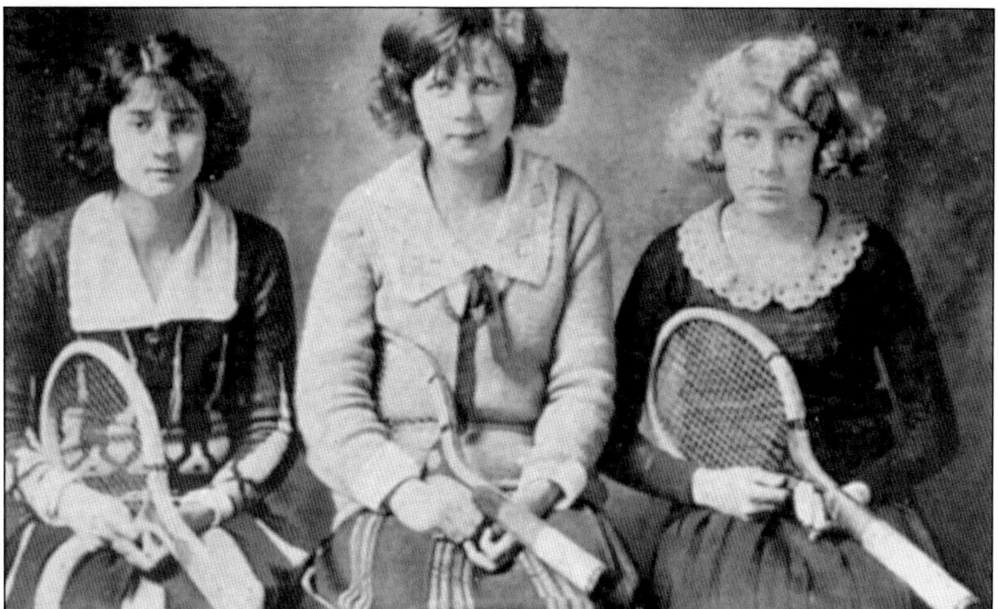

Tennis was a sport in which girls competed against other schools. In 1923 Maxine Langston (center) defeated Juanita Ferrell of Mountain View for the singles title. Kathleen Sullivan (right), and Gail Williams took third in doubles play.

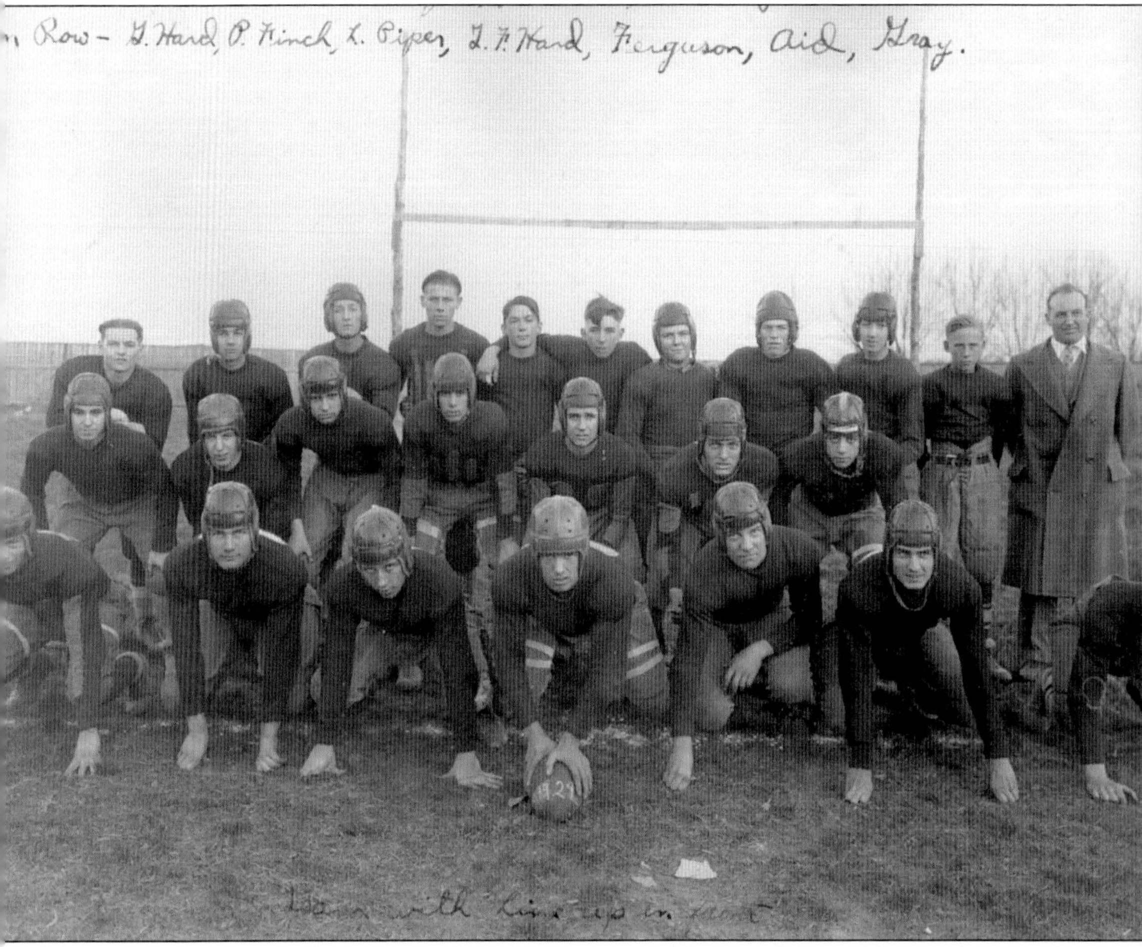

The 1929 Zizzer football team under coach Piper posed for this photo. Although the town had a football team earlier, the first school team mentioned in a high school yearbook was in 1911. The hardest part of football in the teens was finding another team to play against. In 1914, the school team sent challenges to every town from Memphis to Springfield seeking an opponent. It looked like the only game they would get to play was against a local alumni team, but late in the season Springfield accepted the challenge. The team took the train to Springfield the night before the game, but proved no match for the bigger players there, losing 52–0. In 1915 they played against the alums and Mountain Grove. In 1916 they played Mountain Grove twice, but lost both games beginning a long time rivalry between the two schools. In the 1920s the tradition of a Thanksgiving football game against a team from Willow Springs began. That rivalry grew over the years and became an event anticipated in both towns.

Basketball games were easier to organize than football. A team only took five players. All Saints Episcopal Church had its own team *c.* 1906. Churches, businesses and schools all formed teams to play each other before a school conference was formed in 1919. Pictured here in the front row from left to right are ? Presley, Jake Ellis, and Joe Aid. In the back row are Ben Cook, Leo Harper, and Ralph Ward.

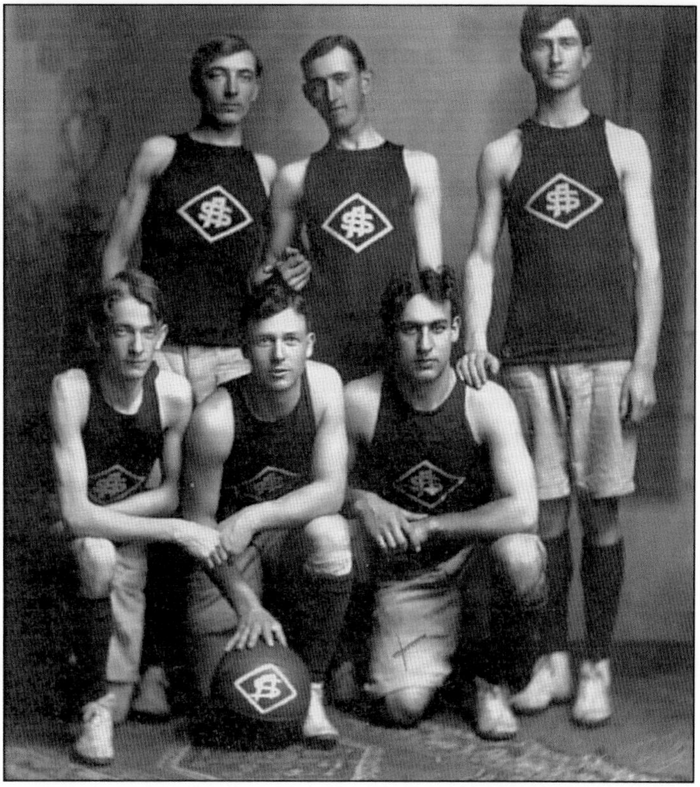

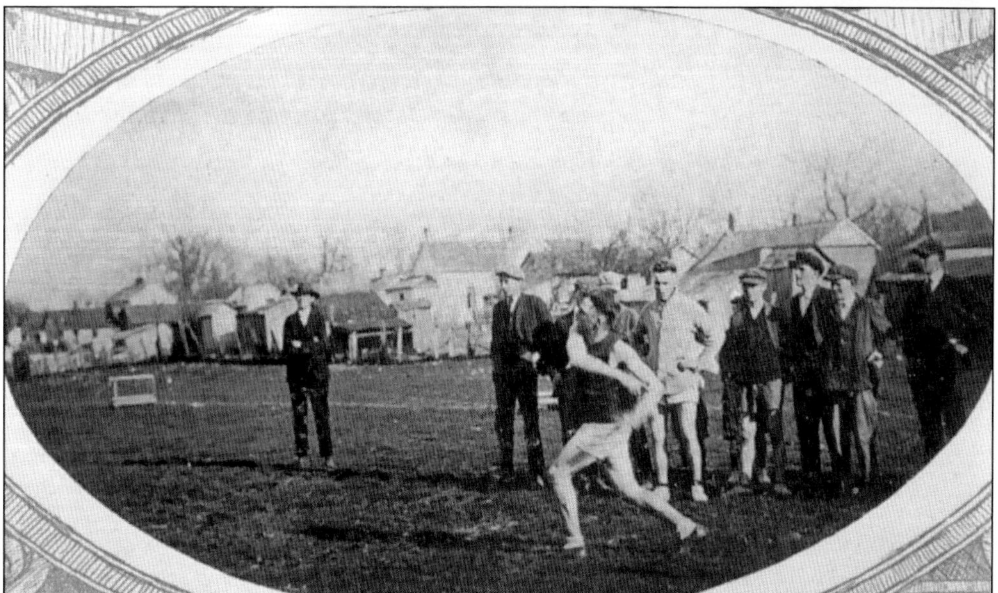

The first South Central Association inter-scholastic track and field meet was held in West Plains in 1915. Houston, Mountain Grove, Willow Springs, and West Plains fielded teams. Houston won the meet. This photo is of ? King of West Plains in the "discus hurl" at the 1917 meet in Willow Springs. Houston won again, defeating West Plains in the final event, the mile relay, to take first place.

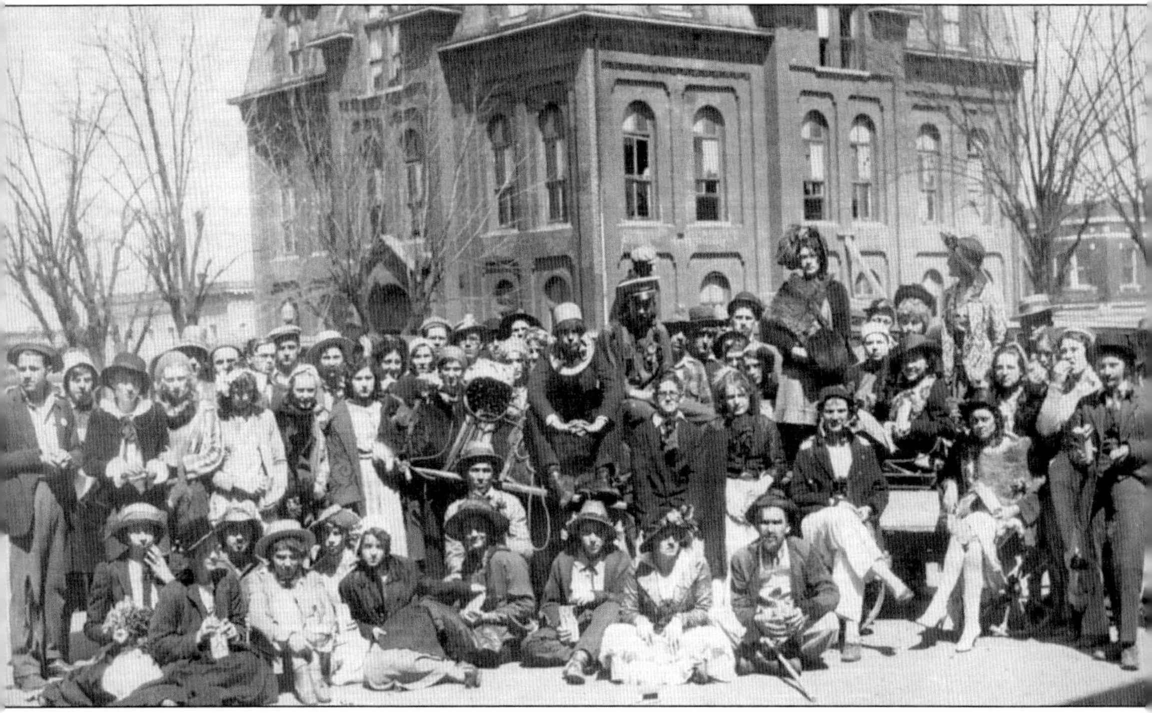

The Senior Class looked forward to the annual Hobo Day. On that day all the seniors would dress as "hobos" and parade downtown to have their picture taken. The class of 1931 is in this photo. Note the old Courthouse in the background with the walls braced and the windows broken. It was abandoned in 1928 after the dance hall explosion weakened its structure.

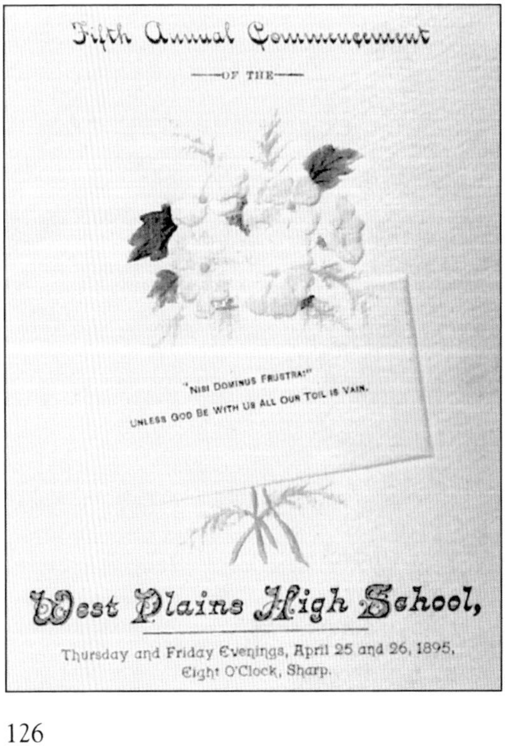

Fifth Annual Commencement

—OF THE—

"Nisi Dominus Frustra!"

Unless God Be With Us All Our Toil Is Vain.

West Plains High School,

Thursday and Friday Evenings, April 25 and 26, 1895.

Eight O'Clock, Sharp.

This is the cover for the "Fifth Annual Commencement" on April 25 and 26, 1895. Early graduation exercises lasted two nights. The first night the Junior Class would perform a play poking fun at the seniors. Other students would perform music and recitations. The formal graduation ceremony was held the second night. The 1895 ceremonies were held at the Opera House.

INDEX